HEBREW
FOR LIFE

Though I am growne aged, yet I haue had a longing
desire, to see with my owne eyes, somthing of that most
ancient language, and holy tongue, in which the Law,
and oracles of god were write; and in which god,
and angels spake to the holy patriarks, of old
time; and what names were giuen to things,
from the creation. And though I cañot
attaine to much herein, yet I am refresh=
ed, to haue seen some glimpse hereof;
(as Moyses saw the land of ca=
nan a farr of) my aime and
desire is to see how the woyds,
and phrases lye in the
holy texte; and to
discerne somewhat
of the same,
for my owne
Contente.

3

שֶׁם פָּחֲדוּ פָחַד לֹא הָיָה פָחַד	חֶסֶד יְהֹוָה מָלְאָה הָאָרֶץ
Ther they feared a fear, wher no fear was	The earth is full of y mercie of yehouah
הוֹן יוֹסִיף רֵעִים רַבִּים	וַיַּרְא אֱלֹהִים כִּי טוֹב
Riches gather many friends	And god saw that it was good
רַע רַע יֹאמַר הַקֹּנֶה	לֹא טוֹב הֱיוֹת הָאָדָם לְבַדּוֹ
It is naught, it is naught, saith the buyer	It is not good that man should be alone
מָצָא אִשָּׁה מָצָא טוֹב	כַּבֵּד אֶת אָבִיךָ וְאֶת אִמֶּךָ
he that findeth a wife findeth good	honour thy father, and thy mother
וַאֲנִי בְּרֹב חַסְדְּךָ אָבוֹא בֵיתֶךָ	וּשְׂמַח מֵאֵשֶׁת נְעוּרֶיךָ
But I in multitude of thy mercies, will come into thy house	And rejoyce with the wife of thy youth
וְהָיָה כְּעֵץ שָׁתוּל עַל פַּלְגֵי מָיִם	זְנוּת וְיַיִן וְתִירוֹשׁ יִקַּח לֵב
And he shall be as a tree planted by the brooks of waters	whordome, and wine, a new wine take away the harte
חָכְמוֹת נָשִׁים בָּנְתָה בֵיתָהּ	קוֹל דְּמֵי אָחִיךָ צֹעֲקִים אֵלָי
A wise woman buildeth her house	The voyce of thy brothers blood crieth unto me
נְקִי כַפַּיִם וּבַר לֵבָב	דַּן דִּין עָנִי
Innocente in hands e pure in harte	... Iudge the ...

Page from William Bradford, *Of Plimoth Plantation*. Archived at the State Library of Massachusetts.

HEBREW FOR LIFE

Strategies for
Learning, Retaining, and Reviving
Biblical Hebrew

Adam J. Howell, Benjamin L. Merkle,
and Robert L. Plummer

Foreword by Miles V. Van Pelt

B
Baker Academic
a division of Baker Publishing Group
Grand Rapids, Michigan

Published by Baker Academic
a division of Baker Publishing Group
PO Box 6287, Grand Rapids, MI 49516-6287
www.bakeracademic.com

Printed in the United States of America

Library of Congress Cataloging-in-Publication Data
Names: Howell, Adam J., 1980– author. | Merkle, Benjamin L., 1971– author. |
    Plummer, Robert L. (Robert Lewis), 1971– author.
Title: Hebrew for life : strategies for learning, retaining, and reviving biblical
    Hebrew / Adam J. Howell, Benjamin L. Merkle, and Robert L. Plummer ;
    foreword by Miles V. Van Pelt.
Description: Grand Rapids : Baker Academic, a division of Baker Publishing
    Group, 2020. | Includes bibliographical references and index.
Identifiers: LCCN 2019031834 | ISBN 9781540961464 (paperback)
Subjects: LCSH: Hebrew language—Textbooks. | Hebrew language—Grammar.
Classification: LCC PJ4567.3 .H69 2020 | DDC 492.4/5—dc23
LC record available at https://lccn.loc.gov/2019031834

ISBN 978-1-5409-6275-1 (casebound)

In keeping with biblical principles of
creation stewardship, Baker Publishing Group advocates the responsible
use of our natural resources. As a
member of the Green Press Initiative, our company uses recycled
paper when possible. The text paper
of this book is composed in part of
post-consumer waste.

20   21   22   23   24   25   26   7   6   5   4   3   2   1

CONTENTS

FOREWORD

Like the authors of this book, I love to teach the biblical languages. It is one of the great joys of my life. Each year I am reinvigorated as I watch students emerge from the flood waters of paradigms and vocabulary memorization to experience God's word in a completely new way. But let's be honest, teaching and learning these languages is really the easy part of the process. We set aside time together in class, we have introductory resources shaped to our various levels and needs, and we are invested with the excitement of being able to read our first verse without recourse to a grammar or lexicon.

No doubt, learning the basics requires hard work, but the real challenge lies beyond the basics, in the land of life and ministry after we have completed our education. The classroom is behind us, our classmates have dispersed, and the demands of life and ministry begin to reshape our priorities and commitments. This is the moment of decision, the edge of the cliff. Sadly, it is at this point that the hard-fought treasures of the biblical languages are regularly jettisoned over the cliffs of pragmatism and lost forever.

In the twenty-first century, however, it appears that winds of providence are blowing in our favor. There is what seems to be a healthy and exciting resurgence of the appreciation, study, and use of the biblical languages both in the United States and in other parts of the world. This is exactly why we need a book like *Hebrew for Life*. Why? Because Hebrew is life! Over 75 percent of the Christian Bible was originally written in Hebrew, and this portion of God's word is both living (Heb. 4:12) and life-giving (Ps. 119:50, 93). The word of God in the Old Testament restores the soul, makes wise the simple, gladdens the heart, brings light to the eyes, endures forever (Ps. 19:8–10), and, most importantly, bears witness to the person and work of Jesus Christ (Luke 24:44; John 5:39–40, 46).

I wonder how many of us who serve as ministers of the word of God reflect the true value of God's word in our time and study as we give ourselves to maintaining and improving skill in the biblical languages? We are fortunate to live in a day of unprecedented print and electronic resources to aid us in our study of the languages. We are without excuse, and so we ought to follow this scriptural admonition: "Do your best to present yourself to God as one approved, a worker who has no need to be ashamed, rightly handling the word of truth" (2 Tim. 2:15 ESV).

Miles V. Van Pelt
Professor of Old Testament and Biblical Languages and
Director of the Summer Institute for Biblical Languages,
Reformed Theological Seminary, Jackson, Mississippi;
coauthor of *Basics of Biblical Hebrew* and
author of *Basics of Biblical Aramaic*

PREFACE

We want you to love the God of the Hebrew Bible. Therefore, we want you to read, study, and enjoy the Hebrew Bible for the duration of your ministry. We want you to look back at the end of your life and say, "I was faithful with the knowledge and training the Lord gave me."

The authors of this book have been teaching Greek and Hebrew for many years. During that time, we have seen many students begin to use the biblical languages effectively, only to watch their skills slowly erode after graduation from college or seminary. This book is one of our efforts to arrest such linguistic apostasy before it takes place.

This book has several potential readers:

1. If you are a *seminary or college student*, we hope to inspire you with many quotes and devotionals throughout this book, as well as equip you with the best study skills and lifetime habits to make reading the Hebrew Bible a regular part of your life.

2. If you are a *teacher of Hebrew*, we hope this book provides ideas to incorporate into your classes. Perhaps you will consider using this book as a supplementary textbook for your Hebrew courses.

3. If you are a *pastor or Christian leader who is using Hebrew* in ministry, we want this book to encourage and sharpen you.

4. If you are among the *Hebrew exiles* wandering amidst a
   nation whose language you do not know (Jer. 5:15), we are
   looking for you! If you are reading this sentence, we are calling you out of exile to the joys of the language of Canaan
   (שְׂפַת כְּנַעַן)! After reading this preface, you might consider
   turning directly to chapter 9, "Getting Back in Shape." It is
   never too late to return to the Hebrew Bible, or even to venture there for the first time.

Regardless of your background, this book includes elements to both
instruct and inspire you. In each chapter, you will find sidebars with
inspiring quotes about studying Hebrew or devotional insights from
the Hebrew Bible. Just as a chef-in-training is encouraged to keep
laboring in the kitchen after tasting the delicacies produced by chefs
who have completed their training, we hope these insights will nour-
ish your mind and spirit.

Below is a brief description of each chapter. Adam extensively
revised *Greek for Life* to prepare it for an audience of Hebrew students. Ben originally wrote chapters 1, 3, 4, and 6, and Rob originally composed chapters 2, 5, 7, and 9. But in this volume, Adam
has now put his personal Semitic touch on those materials. Chapter
8, "Hebrew's Close Cousin—Aramaic," has been added by Adam.
In each chapter, the first-person references are from Adam unless
otherwise noted.

- Chapter 1: "The Goal of the Harvest." This chapter shows
  students why knowing Hebrew matters in the life and ministry of a future leader in the church. If a student's primary
  goal is to be a better interpreter and preacher of God's word,
  then the intermediate goal should be to have a working
  knowledge of Hebrew.
- Chapter 2: "Weighed in the Balances and Found Wanting."
  This chapter grounds the student in the proper study habits
  in order to start learning Hebrew on a firm footing.
- Chapter 3: "Review the Fundamentals Often." This chapter
  stresses the value and importance of reviewing vocabulary
  and paradigms. It will give the student the proper strategy for

how to most effectively build vocabulary and retain memory paradigms.

- Chapter 4: "Develop a Next-Level Memory." This chapter emphasizes the need to use as many senses as possible to learn Hebrew, including reading, writing, listening to, and singing Hebrew.
- Chapter 5: "Strategically Leverage Your Breaks." This chapter provides specific texts that students can read over the summer (or any other extended break), along with exercises to work through to maintain their Hebrew.
- Chapter 6: "Read, Read, Read." This chapter highlights the value (and necessity) of reading Hebrew daily. We suggest ways to use Hebrew in personal devotions and in Scripture memorization as a method for both knowing the Bible better and knowing Hebrew better.
- Chapter 7: "The Wisdom of Resources." This chapter provides an overview of resources (including software) that can aid one's use of the Hebrew language as well as strategies to best utilize them.
- Chapter 8: "Hebrew's Close Cousin—Aramaic." This chapter gives some practical advice on learning the Aramaic of the Old Testament.
- Chapter 9: "Getting Back in Shape." This chapter offers practical ways to reenter the arena of Hebrew if it has been neglected for some time.

At the end of each chapter, you will find a devotional reflection from the Hebrew Bible. We hope these brief meditations whet your appetite for a devotional life spent in the Hebrew text. We also want to keep before you the ultimate goal of your Hebrew study: *to know and love the Triune God and to love people who are made in his image.*

This book would not exist without the input of many people besides the three authors whose names appear on the cover. First, we give thanks to the Triune God, who graciously saved three sinners and then gave us the privilege of serving him. Second, we thank our teachers, colleagues, and students. The best ideas in this book are the fruit of communal learning and reflection. Third, we thank Jim Kinney, Bryan Dyer, and others at Baker who believed in this book and helped bring it to fruition. Fourth, we thank various friends and publishers who allowed their work to be quoted or featured within: Miles Van Pelt, Peter Gentry, Bruce Steventon, Daniel Wilson, Michael Austin, Rob Starner, Andrew Yates, Jodi Hiser, Nancy Ruth, Will Ross, Steve Hallam, Tom Blanchard, Rusty Osborne, Dominick Hernández, Greg Wolff, Baylor University Press, Crossway, Hendrickson, and all others who have contributed to the joy of this project. Fifth, gratitude is in order for various friends, research assistants, and secretaries who shared historical quotes, searched for citations, and carefully proofread the manuscript.

Last of all, we dedicate this book to our families, who lighten the burdens of life and keep us grounded in the most important matter of loving God and loving others.

ABBREVIATIONS

General and Bibliographic

BDB   Francis Brown, S. R. Driver, Charles A. Briggs, James Strong, and Wilhelm Gesenius. *The Brown-Driver-Briggs Hebrew and English Lexicon: With an Appendix Containing the Biblical Aramaic: Coded with the Numbering System from Strong's Exhaustive Concordance of the Bible*. Peabody, MA: Hendrickson, 1996.

BHHB   Baylor Handbook on the Hebrew Bible

BHS   Rudolf Kittel, Karl Elliger, Wilhelm Rudolph, Rüger Hans Peter, G. E. Weil, and Adrian Schenker. *Biblia Hebraica Stuttgartensia*. Stuttgart: Deutsche Bibelgesellschaft, 1997.

DCH   David J. A. Clines. *Dictionary of Classical Hebrew*. Sheffield: Sheffield Phoenix, 2011.

ESV   English Standard Version

GKC   Wilhelm Gesenius. *Gesenius' Hebrew Grammar*. Edited and enlarged by E. Kautzsch. Translated by A. E. Cowley. Mineola, NY: Dover, 2006.

HALOT   Ludwig Kohler, Walter Baumgartner, M. E. J. Richardson, Johann Jakob Stamm, and Benedikt Hartmann. *The Hebrew and Aramaic Lexicon of the Old Testament*. Leiden: Brill, 2001.

HCSB   Holman Christian Standard Bible

Joüon   Paul Joüon. *A Grammar of Biblical Hebrew*. 2nd ed. Translated and revised by T. Muraoka. Rome: Biblical Institute Press, 2006.

JSOT   *Journal for the Study of the Old Testament*

LSJ   Henry George Liddell, Robert Scott, and Henry Stuart Jones. *A Greek-English Lexicon*. 9th ed. with revised supplement. Oxford: Clarendon, 1996.

MT   Masoretic Text

NASB   New American Standard Bible
NCBC   New Cambridge Bible Commentary
NICOT   New International Commentary on the Old Testament
NIDOTTE   Willem A. VanGemeren, ed. *New International Dictionary of Old Testament Theology and Exegesis.* Grand Rapids: Zondervan, 2012.
NIV   New International Version
NKJV   New King James Version
NRSV   New Revised Standard Version
SBJT   *Southern Baptist Journal of Theology*

Old Testament

Gen.	Genesis	Neh.	Nehemiah	Obad.	Obadiah
Exod.	Exodus	Esther	Esther	Jon.	Jonah
Lev.	Leviticus	Job	Job	Mic.	Micah
Num.	Numbers	Ps(s).	Psalm(s)	Nah.	Nahum
Deut.	Deuteronomy	Prov.	Proverbs	Hab.	Habakkuk
Josh.	Joshua	Eccles.	Ecclesiastes	Zeph.	Zephaniah
Judg.	Judges	Song	Song of Songs	Hag.	Haggai
Ruth	Ruth	Isa.	Isaiah	Zech.	Zechariah
1 Sam.	1 Samuel	Jer.	Jeremiah	Mal.	Malachi
2 Sam.	2 Samuel	Lam.	Lamentations		
1 Kings	1 Kings	Ezek.	Ezekiel		
2 Kings	2 Kings	Dan.	Daniel		
1 Chron.	1 Chronicles	Hosea	Hosea		
2 Chron.	2 Chronicles	Joel	Joel		
Ezra	Ezra	Amos	Amos		

New Testament

Matt.	Matthew	Eph.	Ephesians	Heb.	Hebrews
Mark	Mark	Phil.	Philippians	James	James
Luke	Luke	Col.	Colossians	1 Pet.	1 Peter
John	John	1 Thess.	1 Thessalonians	2 Pet.	2 Peter
Acts	Acts	2 Thess.	2 Thessalonians	1 John	1 John
Rom.	Romans	1 Tim.	1 Timothy	2 John	2 John
1 Cor.	1 Corinthians	2 Tim.	2 Timothy	3 John	3 John
2 Cor.	2 Corinthians	Titus	Titus	Jude	Jude
Gal.	Galatians	Philem.	Philemon	Rev.	Revelation

The Goal of the Harvest

Since the Bible is written in part in Hebrew and in part in Greek,
. . . we drink from the stream of both—we must learn these
languages, unless we want to be "silent persons" as theologians. Once we understand the significance and the weight of
the words, the true meaning of Scripture will light up for us as
the midday sun. Only if we have clearly understood the language
will we clearly understand the content. . . . If we put our minds
to the [Greek and Hebrew] sources, we will begin to understand
Christ rightly.

—Melanchthon (1497–1560)[1]

In 2007 my wife and I celebrated the birth of our first son. Thus we
began the journey of parenting. Before our son was born, it seemed
like parenting might be doable. Give some direction here, a little
correction there, hold regular family devotional times, and voilà,
a God-honoring offspring. It only took one night—*one night*—for

1. Melanchthon's inaugural address on "The Reform of the Education of Youth"
(1518), quoted in Hans J. Hillerbrand, ed., *The Reformation: A Narrative History
Related by Contemporary Observers and Participants*, new ed. (Grand Rapids: Baker,
1987), 59–60.

us to realize it wasn't that easy. The first morning after our son was born, my wife and I found ourselves begging my parents to watch our son while we slept for a few hours. They agreed, and when we got to our bedroom, we sat on the bed, looked into each other's eyes, and began to cry.

We knew vaguely what we signed up for and the journey we just began, but we were overrun with emotion because in that moment, the end goal of parenting was not clear to us. Sure, we knew the intended outcome we wanted from our parenting. We wanted to raise children who love the Lord and who desire to honor him by living for his kingdom. But in that precise moment on our bed, this vision wasn't driving our emotions.

Several years later, my wife was at a class for wives of students at our seminary, and she heard about "the law of the harvest." It was presented as a way to persevere in parenting, knowing that there is a goal in the end—namely, the "harvest" of children who love the Lord. She learned that the journey to that harvest would be hard work. It would be dirty labor in muddy fields. It would involve hard soil that requires regular tilling and care. But all of this tedious labor is worthwhile because it leads to an intentional, tangible, and desirable goal. The task of parenting (for us) is more joyful or less joyful to the degree that we keep that goal of the harvest at the front of our minds. There are setbacks and difficulties for sure, but the small progress we see toward the harvest keeps us pressing on. Parenting is not the end goal, but it is the pathway to the end goal.

Likewise, the study of Hebrew is not an end in itself. The end goal of studying Hebrew is to know the God who has revealed himself through his word. God chose to use the Hebrew language to convey his will for his people through the Law, Prophets, and Writings. The goal of learning Hebrew (or Greek) is not to parade one's knowledge before others, seeking to impress a congregation or friend. Rather, the goal is first and foremost to behold unhindered the grandest sight—God himself revealed through his inspired word. Therefore, the journey of learning Biblical Hebrew has as its goal the most important thing in all of life: the knowledge of God as revealed in the Scriptures. Although we don't need to read the Bible in the original languages to learn about God, some things are lost in translation.

In addition, for those who are planning to preach or teach God's word on a regular basis, the need for reading the Bible in its original languages is of utmost importance.

Many students ask me if the acquisition of Biblical Hebrew is difficult. The acquisition of any language involves hard work and requires constant attention, but Hebrew seems to need more nurture and care along the way. When we get wrapped up in the jots and tittles of the text, we may feel discouraged or tempted to cast Hebrew aside. However, one of the joys I find in Hebrew is the richness it adds to the "flavor" of the Old Testament. The words I use in classes to describe Hebrew are *thick* and *robust*. It is as if Hebrew is rich molasses, so that when it hits the tongue, it provides full-bodied flavor to the text you're enjoying. This thick joy of seeing God's character revealed in the Old Testament is worth every minute that you invest in learning and retaining your Hebrew. If we don't keep that end in sight, we will certainly lose motivation and consider abandoning the path. We don't need to wait a semester or year to experience the delight of Hebrew. There is joy in the journey! But we also must remember that a solid knowledge of Hebrew will produce a lifetime of benefits both to us and to those we can influence.

The remainder of this chapter consists of three sections. First, we will offer four reasons why the study of biblical languages (focusing on Hebrew) is needed. Second, we will answer three common objections to studying biblical languages. Finally, we will encourage readers to take the responsibility and privilege of studying the original languages seriously. Throughout the chapter we will bring in the testimony of others who likewise see the importance of knowing the languages that God chose to use to convey his word to the world.

Why Study Hebrew?

Hebrew Is the Language of the Old Testament

In the New Testament, God chose to reveal his word (and thus his will) to his people in the Greek language. But the Old Testament was written in Hebrew and Aramaic. Although we have dozens of good English translations of the Bible, all translations are interpretations.

This is because no two languages are the same. There are lengthy conversations about why translation committees choose to trans-late certain words, phrases, and verses the way they do. Most (if not all) of these ex-planations are influenced by theological pre-suppositions and grammatical restrictions of the target language, leading to the translation chosen. Something is inevitably lost when one language is translated into another.

"Reading the Bible in translation is like kissing your new bride through a veil."

—Jewish poet Haim Nach-man Bialik (1873–1934)[a]

Translations are good and helpful, but they are God's word only insofar as they accurately reflect the Hebrew and Greek originals. John Owen (1616–1683) says, "Translations contain the word of God, and are the word of God, perfectly or im-perfectly, according as they express the words, sense, and meaning of [the] originals."[2] Bruce K. Waltke expresses the importance of this: "Shortly after I began the study of Hebrew, . . . I became motivated to comprehend the biblical languages when I realized that most of my knowledge of God was derived from Holy Scripture, and the ac-curacy of that knowledge was contingent upon the correctness with which I handled its lan-guages. . . . The logic of this Christian theology, that God revealed himself through the Scripture, inescapably led me to the conclusion that the authenticity of that knowledge rested on a pre-cise understanding of the biblical languages."[3]

"To be sure we have good translations, but as the Italian proverb goes, 'Traduttore tra-dittore,' 'translations are treacherous.'"

—Bruce K. Waltke[b]

In a very real way, then, the biblical languages are the means by which the gospel message is preserved throughout the canon. The great Reformer Martin Luther (1483–1546) testified to this reality:

> We will not long preserve the gospel without the languages. The lan-guages are the sheath in which this sword of the Spirit [Eph. 6:17] is

2. John Owen, "The Hebrew and Greek Text of the Scripture," in *The Works of John Owen*, ed. William H. Goold, (1678; repr., Carlisle, PA: Banner of Truth Trust, 1968), 16:357.

3. Bruce K. Waltke, "How I Changed My Mind about Teaching Hebrew (or Re-tained It)," *Crux* 29, no. 4 (1993): 10–11.

contained; they are the casket in which this jewel is enshrined; they are the vessel in which this wine is held; they are the larder in which this food is stored; and . . . they are the baskets in which are kept these loaves and fishes and fragments. If through our neglect we let the languages go (which God forbid!), we shall . . . lose the gospel.[4]

Luther later added, "It is inevitable that unless the languages remain, the gospel must finally perish."[5] For Luther, it was while reading the original language of the Greek New Testament that his eyes were opened to the reality of God's righteousness being revealed in the gospel. Because we believe in the inspiration of all sixty-six books of the Bible, Luther refers to a gospel that can be seen throughout the canon. For our purposes, then, to put aside the Hebrew language is to put aside our surest guide to the truth of the gospel from the Old Testament.

> "As we value the gospel, let us zealously hold to the languages."
> —Martin Luther[c]

Hebrew Helps Us to Rightly Interpret the Bible

Although knowledge of Hebrew increases our ability to rightly interpret the Bible, we don't mean that knowledge of Hebrew guarantees that we will come to a correct interpretation. Knowing Hebrew does not solve all the interpretive questions. It does, however, help us to eliminate certain interpretations and allow us to see for ourselves what are the strengths and weaknesses of various possible positions. Jason DeRouchie rightly notes, "Knowing the original languages helps one observe more accurately and thoroughly, understand more clearly, evaluate more fairly, and interpret more confidently the inspired details of the biblical text."[6] The goal of the exegete is to be able to carefully evaluate the text by using all the tools at one's disposal. Likewise, the goal of the pastor is to be able to deliver

4. Martin Luther, "To the Councilmen of All Cities in Germany That They Establish and Maintain Christian Schools," in *The Christian in Society II*, ed. Walther I. Brandt, trans. Albert T. W. Steinhaeuser and Walther I. Brandt, Luther's Works 45 (Philadelphia: Muhlenberg, 1962), 360.

5. Luther, "To the Councilmen," 360.

6. Jason S. DeRouchie, "The Profit of Employing the Biblical Languages: Scriptural and Historical Reflections," *Themelios* 37, no. 1 (2012): 36.

that careful evaluation of the inspired text to parishioners via the preaching of God's word. John Piper argues that translations tend to discourage pastors from careful analysis of the text. If a pastor doesn't refer to the original languages in preparation, "the preacher often contents himself with the general focus or flavor of the text, and his exposition lacks the precision and clarity which excites a congregation with the word of God. Boring generalities are a curse in many pulpits."[7] Scott Hafemann convincingly states that studying the Bible in the original languages

> provides a window through which we can see for ourselves just what decisions have been made by others and why. Instead of being a second-hander, who can only take someone else's word for it, a knowledge of the text allows us to evaluate, rather than simply regurgitate. . . . [Consequently] we will be able to explain to ourselves and to others why people disagree, what the real issues are, and what are the strengths of our own considered conclusions. It will allow us to have reasons for what we believe and preach, without having to resort to the papacy of scholarship or the papacy of personal experience.[8]

Those without knowledge of the original language are necessarily limited and must rely on others for the interpretation of various texts. Thus, they become "second-handers." A. T. Robertson explains, "The only alternative is to take what other scholars say without the power of forming an individual judgment."[9] Our goal is to be able to evaluate and thus come to a studied and reasoned opinion regarding the meaning of a text. But neither the gift of the Holy Spirit nor personal piety assures a correct interpretation. We must work hard to learn the languages of the Bible so that we can know for ourselves what the inspired text says. We still hold our conclusions

> "Secondhand food will not sustain and deepen our people's faith and holiness."
> —John Piper[d]

---

7. John Piper, *Brothers, We Are Not Professionals: A Plea to Pastors for Radical Ministry*, updated and expanded ed. (Nashville: B&H, 2013), 100.

8. Scott Hafemann, as part of "The *SBJT* Forum: Profiles in Expository Preaching," *SBJT* 3, no. 2 (1999): 87–88.

9. A. T. Robertson, *The Minister and His Greek New Testament* (1923; repr., Birmingham, AL: Solid Ground Christian Books, 2008), 81.

with an open hand, but with the languages, we are able to hold our conclusions with conviction. We study Hebrew so that we can better interpret God's holy and infallible word.

Of course, the end goal is not merely to interpret the Bible correctly but to better know the God who revealed himself to us in the Bible. Thus, we learn the biblical languages so that we can learn of the Triune God of Scripture. But as A. M. Fairbairn (1838–1912) once said, "No man can be a theologian who is not first a philologian. He who is no grammarian is no divine."[10] The earliest Hebrew grammarians— Saadia Gaon (882–942), Menahem ibn Saruq (ca. 910–970), Dunash ben Labrat (ca. 929–990), Yehuda Hayyuj (ca. 940–1010), Jonah ibn Janah (990–1050)—argued that a proper knowledge of Scripture depended on Hebrew grammar. According to David Tene, these early grammarians believed that "(1) language is the means for all discernment and linguistics is the means for all investigation and wisdom; (2) the fulfillment of the commandments depends upon the understanding of the written word, and in turn, the proper knowledge of the language is impossible without the aid of linguistics."[11]

> "True theology and precise exegesis are, to use modern jargon, systemically dependent upon one another."
> —Bruce K. Waltke[e]

The earliest scholarly Hebrew grammarians understood that the end goal of grammatical study was gaining proper wisdom and behaving as those who love God (fulfillment of the commandments). Even so, those goals were dependent on linguistic study of the "written word." Our goal is to know the Bible so that we can know the God we love and serve, and subsequently live as those who believe that what he has said in his word matters.

Hebrew Is a Ministry Time-Saver

On average, pastors are extremely busy, with many important issues vying for their time. Preparing sermons, counseling church members,

---

10. Address before the Baptist Theological College at Glasgow, reported in *The British Weekly*, April 26, 1906, quoted in A. T. Robertson, *A Grammar of the Greek New Testament in the Light of Historical Research* (Nashville: Broadman, 1934), x. Also cited in Robertson, *Minister and His Greek New Testament*, 81.

11. David Tene, "Hebrew Linguistic Literature," in *Encyclopedia Judaica*, ed. Fred Skolnik and Michael Berenbaum (Jerusalem: Keter, 1971), 1360–61.

visiting the sick, attending various meetings, and answering phone calls and emails are just some of the things that fill a pastor's schedule. With all of these responsibilities, is it realistic for someone in ministry to spend valuable time in the original languages of the Bible?

Learning Hebrew well enough to use it effectively, however, can save time in sermon or teaching preparation. In my opinion, many pastors shy away from preaching the Old Testament because of the time it takes to carefully study large swaths of Old Testament narrative. Often, application points may not come for several chapters as one considers the flow of the narrative and the overall message of the Old Testament author. If the pastor is going to work from the original Hebrew, translating (or even just referencing) large portions of Hebrew narrative will prove to be time consuming. Consider, though, how empowering it would be to translate large sections of the Old Testament, precisely because you have devoted yourself in earlier years to learning the language well. The time you spend now to learn Hebrew well will pay off in future studies. With enough study on the front end, pastors can begin to enjoy the preparation of an Old Testament passage from the original Hebrew rather than dreading it.

In addition to helping you translate long sections of Scripture quickly, a knowledge of Hebrew can help you save time when navigating commentaries. The danger of relying on commentaries is that they often do not agree at certain points. Thus, when preparing a message, the pastor is often compelled to read commentary after commentary to make sure all bases are covered. It would be better—

> "One hour in the text [in the original languages] is worth more than ten in secondary literature."
>
> —Scott Hafemann[f]

and much quicker—for pastors to be like the Bereans and check the Scriptures for themselves to see if these things are so (Acts 17:11), instead of only reading the opinions of others.

In his inaugural address at Southern Seminary on October 3, 1890, titled "Preaching and Scholarship," A. T. Robertson observed, "If theological education will increase your power for Christ, is it not your duty to gain that added power? Never say you are losing time by going to school. You are saving time, buying it up for the future and storing it away. Time used in storing power is not lost."[12] The time you spend "storing power" in the biblical languages will not be wasted time.

Hebrew Emphasizes the Value of God's Word

For the Christian, the ultimate source of authority is God's word. One of the ways a pastor communicates to the congregation that the Bible is the foundation of all we believe is by carefully preaching and teaching it weekly. Additionally, when a pastor labors in the original languages to carefully exegete the text, it highlights that the pastor's authority is found in the Bible. Hafemann explains this reality: "Learning the languages affirms the nature of biblical revelation, restores the proper authority of the pastor as teacher, and communicates to our people that the locus of meaning and authority of the Scriptures does not reside in us, but in the text, which we labor so hard to understand. We learn the languages because we are convinced of the inerrancy, sufficiency, and potency of the Word of God."[13]

Our authority is not our favorite scholar or commentary series or the commentary that happens to be in our library. As Enoch Okode notes, "It is hard to maintain the centrality of the word if we view biblical languages as a non-essential and optional extra. Similarly, if preachers don't invest in Hebrew and Greek, their hearers will be deprived of some of the treasures of the word as well as the informed and informative exposition that they deserve."[14]

Objections to Studying Hebrew

Hebrew Is Excessively Difficult

I must agree that Hebrew is difficult. However, I would argue that Hebrew is more *intimidating* than difficult. If you can overcome the intimidation of the language, then learning Hebrew can

12. S. Craig Sanders, "A. T. Robertson and His 'Monumental Achievement,'" Baptist Press, September 22, 2014, http://www.bpnews.net/43400/at-robertson-and -his-monumental-achievement.
13. Hafemann, "Profiles in Expository Preaching," 88.
14. Enoch Okode, "A Case for Biblical Languages: Are Hebrew and Greek Optional or Indispensable?," *African Journal of Theology* 29, no. 2 (2010): 92.

actually be a delight. I have a dear friend who lives in Sioux Falls, South Dakota. Bruce was an information technology professional for nearly forty-five years and has recently retired. In 1980, Bruce began studying New Testament Greek in order to interact with members of the local Kingdom Hall (Jehovah's Witness). After seeing the rewards of learning Greek, Bruce desired to learn Hebrew, but as a result of supporting and raising a young family, he was unable to return to school that following year for his Hebrew studies. As a layman, Bruce had no plans for pastoral ministry; he simply wanted to know God's word in order to share it accurately in doctrinal conversations.

In 2008, Bruce decided to give Hebrew a run—on his own initiative! He purchased an introductory grammar and began to work through it slowly. After years of learning Hebrew and reading the Hebrew Bible, Bruce and his wife, Bonny, now attend a weekly reading group on Saturday mornings to read Hebrew and Greek alongside other faithful believers. The reading group is made up largely of nonclergy. Bruce and his wife are part of a group of people who read the original languages simply because they love the God of the Bible and they cherish the inspired Scriptures in the original languages. Each Saturday around 6:45 a.m., the group begins with a Hebrew reading followed by some discussion from whatever intermediate grammar they are studying. They then move to a Greek reading, all the while helping one another read and translate God's word in the original languages.

> "If my wife did not speak English, and sent love letters to me, I would not be satisfied with using an interpreter to find out what she said. I'd want to understand each nuance of the language and why she picked certain words."
> —Bruce Steventon[g]

Since Bruce and Bonny joined the reading group in 2013, the group has studied several Hebrew and Greek grammars in addition to their Scripture reading in the original languages. The point to understand here is not that every Christian must study Hebrew to this degree to be a good Christian. The point is that learning Hebrew is doable. Yes, it is difficult, but many people with varying abilities and vocations have accomplished the goal of learning Biblical Hebrew, and some of those people have done it from their own volition.

Why don't pastors keep up their Hebrew? One reason is that they never learned enough Hebrew to be confident in their skills. We would recommend at least one semester of syntax *beyond* the foundational semester or year of elementary Hebrew. Because Hebrew is intimidating, many pastors-in-training opt to take only the minimum amount of Hebrew, and even then they devote minimal effort to it. The time you spend in the beginning to learn Hebrew well can produce years of competence and joy while using Hebrew in ministry.

> "I still argue that a student should be required to take at least one year of Hebrew. . . . It takes that amount of time to develop a minimal competency in using the language."
> —Bruce K. Waltke[h]

Another reason pastors don't keep up their Hebrew is the time it takes to review and retain. The objection that Hebrew is difficult is true! However, something being difficult doesn't mean that it is impossible—or that it's not worth every moment of effort devoted to it. Pastors are busy with many other worthwhile responsibilities, and keeping up with an ancient language can often take the back burner. Even though Hebrew takes time and effort to retain, we cannot succumb to laziness while blaming our busyness. A. T. Robertson voiced this indictment regarding Greek students, but it might apply even more to Hebrew students: "The chief reason why preachers do not get and do not keep up a fair and needful knowledge of the Greek New Testament [add also the Hebrew Bible] is nothing less than carelessness, and even laziness in many cases."[15] To be fair, most pastors are not lazy, but if they lack a purposeful and strategic plan to use their Hebrew, it will certainly fall by the wayside. Hebrew is difficult, but proficiency is definitely attainable for most people if given the proper amount of time and attention.

I Can Serve the Lord without Hebrew

With over fifty English translations of the Bible and hundreds of good commentaries that rely on the original languages, is it really necessary to spend years learning the biblical languages? This is perhaps one of the most common objections offered. While this objection

---

15. Robertson, *Minister and His Greek New Testament*, 16.

may initially seem to have teeth, it can easily be shown that its bark
is far worse than its bite. Hafemann explains,

> It is precisely because there are so many excellent commentaries avail-
> able today that the use of the biblical languages in preaching becomes
> more important, not less. The proliferation of commentaries and
> resource materials simply means a proliferation of opinions about the
> biblical text. The same reality confronts us with the expanding number
> of English translations, since every translation is the embodiment of
> thousands and thousands of interpretive decisions; a translation is a
> commentary on the Bible without footnotes. What this means is that
> the busy pastor will be confronted with an ever expanding mountain
> of secondary literature on the Bible, not to mention different render-
> ings of the Bible itself. Thus, given the many commentaries and Bible
> resources available today, not to use the languages in our preaching
> will either cost us too much time and cause frustration in the end,
> redefine our role as pastors altogether, or deny the very Bible we are
> purporting to preach.[16]

In other words, there is no perfect translation of the Bible, and
there are no perfect commentaries. Multiple translations and commentaries may make our library look well stocked, but it does not
assure that our interpretation of the Bible will be correct. Our point
is not to out-translate the translations (or out-comment the commentaries) but to see for ourselves how exegetical decisions are made
by others and why.

One of the first things missionaries do when entering the mission
field is learn the language of the area in which they will be working. This may seem like a purely practical task, but the goal of this

16. Hafemann, "Profiles in Expository Preaching," 86–87.

task is fundamental to effective communication. Missionaries could spend the rest of their ministries serving, preaching, and counseling through a translator. However, meaningful communication will only occur when they speak the language of the people they're serving. The parishioners will be able to understand (at a heart level) what the missionary is preaching and applying from God's word to them. Once missionaries learn the language, they will be able to hear (and perhaps feel) the pain and hurt in the inflection of the people's voices as they express their spiritual needs. At the end of the day, learning the language is not just necessary to convey information, but it is necessary for significant communication to take place. If missionaries are willing to go through that year (perhaps years) of language school in order to genuinely communicate with their target people group, shouldn't we be willing to work hard to understand God's word to us in its original languages?

> "Something is always lost in the process of making translational or interpretive decisions."
>
> —Enoch Okode[i]

Another illustration is provided by Jacques B. Doukhan. He writes, "Who would question the pertinence of learning the English language in order to understand the world of Shakespeare? Or, to be more up-to-date, who would ignore the need for learning English to be able to understand and handle the current intricacies of the political and economic life in America?" He continues, "Yet, when it comes to the Bible, it seems that ignorance is allowed and even recommended."[17]

It is abundantly clear that the English language possesses many helpful tools that aid one in using the original languages of the Bible. Consequently, some argue that students should not spend their time and resources learning the grammar and syntax of Hebrew. Instead, in one semester (or less) they can simply learn to use the most important tools. But according to Okode, such an approach is misguided: "It is a mistake to introduce students to [the] 'tools-approach' after one semester of Hebrew and/or Greek. Tools are for experts who

---

17. Jacques B. Doukhan, *Hebrew for Theologians: A Textbook for the Study of Biblical Hebrew in Relation to Hebrew Thinking* (New York: University Press of America, 1993), ix–x.

have gone through the required training. Without adequate training tools can be dangerous."[18]

To illustrate an inefficient (and dangerous) use of tools, my wife and I decided to install a large pull-up bar in our yard. We have a ceiling-mounted pull-up bar in our garage, but I am such a large man that I nearly pull the garage ceiling down with each pull. In order to install a pull-up bar in the yard large enough for me, I had to use four-by-six-inch posts that were twelve feet long. To get the uprights sturdy in the ground, I had to bury about four feet of the post. This required my wife and me to venture into our first attempt at using an auger. I was getting ready to use a *tool* with which I was neither familiar nor trained.

I went to a local hardware store to rent the auger, and being a man's man, I didn't let the workers know I was a novice. I must have worn the concern on my face, though, because they even showed me how to start the thing. It was a pull start like a lawnmower; they must have assumed I didn't even know how to do that! (For the record, I know how to start a lawnmower.) As I was putting the auger in the truck, the store associates continued to give me pointers on how to use it, and in about thirty-five seconds I was "fully trained" on using this auger to dig four feet down in my rock-hard yard. As we began digging, the auger repeatedly locked up on hard ground or embedded rocks. It pulled my wife and me around in circles like a Disney Tilt-A-Whirl. All in all, our venture at using this new tool looked like a Tennessee hoedown while holding on to a gas engine with a massive drill bit protruding from the middle of it. We accomplished the goal, but it was inefficient. If we were honest with ourselves, we had no idea what we were doing.

This story illustrates how tools, without adequate foundational knowledge, can be dangerous. At one point in our hole-digging adventure, the auger spun around quickly after ratcheting loose from a rock and wrenched our wrists. Thankfully, no one was hurt, but using this tool without proper training was dangerous. The same is true for using tools in biblical languages without the proper training. Not only can those who are trained use the tools more efficiently, but they can use more advanced tools to accomplish more precise tasks with

18. Okode, "Case for Biblical Languages," 93.

greater efficiency. Just because you have a tool doesn't mean you know how to use it, nor does it mean you can use it efficiently or correctly. In fact, language professors often talk about the time when students know just enough to be dangerous in their exegesis. They usually say this about students who are taking Hebrew! How much more, then, is this true of those who neglect the study of the language for the sake of using tools?

> "Our primary concern must be with the grammar of the original language, not the English translation, and for this we must know the original Biblical language. A text simply *cannot* mean what the grammar of that text does not support."
> —Rob Starner[k]

Hebrew Is Not Practical

A final objection that we will consider is the charge that the study of Hebrew is not practical but merely consists of memorizing vocabulary, paradigms, and complex grammatical rules. Now, I have no doubt that some professors are guilty of teaching Hebrew as a dry, lifeless academic exercise. But it certainly shouldn't be this way! Furthermore, those who teach Hebrew cannot simply assure students that somewhere down the road (in a semester or two), they will see the payoff of learning Hebrew. Indeed, it is the job of the teacher to demonstrate *from the first week* that Hebrew is not only immensely important but also extremely practical.

> "The primary work of a teacher is to motivate students to love, not hate, to be attracted to, not repulsed by, to be enthusiastic for, not bored by, his subject. . . . A teacher who bores students should have a millstone tied around his neck and be cast into the sea."
> —Bruce K. Waltke[l]

Learning Hebrew is practical for the following reasons. First, it can be the source of personal spiritual blessing. After all, the very reason for learning Hebrew is to be able to read the Old Testament in its original language. Since when is reading and studying the Bible not practical? David Mathis provides the illustration of "digging for gold" in the Scriptures versus "raking for leaves."[19] The deeper we mine into the depths of the biblical languages, the more rewarding our studies will be. Our spiritual affections

---

19. David Mathis, "More Than Just Raking," Desiring God, November 25, 2013, https://www.desiringgod.org/articles/more-than-just-raking.

will soar as we delight in God's word in the original Hebrew. Psalm 19:7–10 says that God's "law," "testimony," "precepts," "command-ments," and "rules" are "more to be desired . . . than gold, even much fine gold; sweeter than honey and drippings of the honeycomb." Surely, as we devote ourselves to the study of the biblical languages, we will personally reap the rewards of this fruitful labor.

> "What is more important and more deeply *practical* for the pastoral office than advancing in Greek and Hebrew exegesis by which we mine God's treasures?"
> —John Piper[m]

Second, the knowledge and use of He-brew gives confidence to one who preaches or teaches the Bible. Piper argues that when "the original languages fall into disuse . . . the confidence of pastors to determine the precise meaning of biblical texts diminishes. And with the confidence to interpret rigorously goes the confidence to preach powerfully."[20] In addition, when we become less dependent on others, and consequently borrow less from the thoughts of others, our preaching will become increasingly fresh and original. Luther believed this to be true when he said, "Although faith and the gospel may indeed be proclaimed by simple preachers without a knowledge of languages, such preaching is flat and tame; people finally become weary and bored with it, and it falls to the ground. But where the preacher is versed in the languages, there is a freshness and vigor in his preaching. Scripture is treated in its entirety, and faith finds itself constantly renewed by a continual variety of words and illustrations."[21]

> Knowing the biblical languages "provides a sustained freshness, a warranted boldness, and an articulated, sure, and helpful wit-ness to the truth."
> —Jason S. DeRouchie[n]

Indeed, "Preaching without original language exegesis is like wielding a blunt sword."[22] E. Earle Ellis tells of a pastor who confided in him that he never made use of the biblical languages in his preaching. Ellis comments, "Having heard him preach, I have no doubt that he was telling the truth."[23]

20. Piper, *Brothers, We Are Not Professionals*, 99.
21. Luther, "To the Councilmen," 365.
22. DeRouchie, "Profit of Employing the Biblical Languages," 49.
23. E. Earle Ellis, "Language Skills and Christian Ministry," *Reformed Review* 24, no. 3 (1971): 163.

Third, the Hebrew language is practical in ministry because it helps those who use it to defend the truth of the gospel. To adequately and compellingly refute false teachings, one must have a knowledge of the original languages. This includes not only the ability to defend the truth against cults like the Jehovah's Witnesses but also protection against the subtler

> Knowing the biblical languages "equips one to defend the gospel and hold others accountable in ways otherwise impossible."
> —Jason S. DeRouchie[o]

intrusions of pharisaical tradition or liberal theology. Piper explains, "Weakness in Greek and Hebrew also gives rise to exegetical imprecision and carelessness. And exegetical imprecision is the mother of liberal theology." He elaborates, "Where pastors can no longer articulate and defend doctrine by a reasonable and careful appeal to the original meaning of biblical texts, they will tend to become close-minded traditionalists who clutch their inherited ideas, or open-ended pluralists who don't put much stock in doctrinal formulations. In both cases the succeeding generations will be theologically impoverished and susceptible to error."[24]

> "Once students grasp how essential precise exegesis is to sound theology, they tune in [to study the original Hebrew]."
> —Bruce K. Waltke[p]

This Marvelous Privilege

Not everybody who desires to study Hebrew has the opportunity. My PhD supervisor reports that prison inmates have written him to ask for a copy of his introductory Hebrew grammar. They request it, and he's glad to send it. Those who have the opportunity to study with all the tools and qualified teachers need to take their privilege seriously. I tell my students that to squander this opportunity to learn Hebrew is a display of foolishness and ingratitude. Though the illustration is not exact, I'm reminded of the prodigal son, who "squandered" his inheritance in "reckless living" (Luke 15:13 ESV). If we have been afforded such a marvelous privilege of learning Hebrew, we ought not to squander it in reckless affections or imprecise preaching that is not grounded in the text of Scripture. Like the prodigal son, let's

24. Piper, *Brothers, We Are Not Professionals*, 100.

return to the Giver of this privilege and start studying Hebrew once again. There are many people who wish they were in such a situation to learn the biblical languages. Luther exhorts believers by stating,

> Since it becomes Christians then to make good use of the Holy Scriptures as their one and only book and it is a sin and a shame not to know our own book or to understand the speech and words of our God, it is a still greater sin and loss that we do not study languages, especially in these days when God is offering and giving us men and books and every facility and inducement to this study, and desires his Bible to be an open book. O how happy the dear fathers would have been if they had had our opportunity to study the languages and come thus prepared to the Holy Scriptures! What great toil and effort it cost them to gather up a few crumbs, while we with half the labor—yes, almost without any labor at all—can acquire the whole loaf! O how their effort puts our indolence to shame! Yes, how sternly God will judge our lethargy and ingratitude![25]

If Luther could make such a statement in the sixteenth century, how much more could we make it in the twenty-first century? Luther not only exhorted Christians generally to know the languages, but he put a special emphasis on those who are to be "prophets." Luther says,

> There is a vast difference therefore between a simple preacher of the faith and a person who expounds Scripture, or, as St. Paul puts it, a

"Students who assume that a high level of competency is required before Hebrew can be utilized in ministry are more likely to quit before they ever start. Likewise, busy pastors may not retain an idealistic level of language fluency, and because they also assume a higher level is mandatory, they may not attempt to do the exegetical homework necessary to undergird sound exposition of the Scriptures. Neither one realizes that there are levels of proficiency in the study of biblical Hebrew. Moving from one level to another takes time and practice. But it can be done, for it is far better to use Hebrew at any level than to have never used it at all."
—Stephen J. Andrews[q]

25. Luther, "To the Councilmen," 364.

prophet. A simple preacher (it is true) has so many clear passages and texts available through translations that he can know and teach Christ, lead a holy life, and preach to others. But when it comes to interpreting Scripture, and working with it on your own, and disputing with those who cite it incorrectly, he is unequal to the task; that cannot be done without languages. Now there must always be such prophets in the Christian church who can dig into Scripture, expound it, and carry on disputations. A saintly life and right doctrine are not enough. Hence languages are absolutely and altogether necessary in the Christian church, as are the prophets or interpreters; although it is not necessary that every Christian or every preacher be such a prophet, as St. Paul points out in 1 Corinthians 12 and Ephesians 4.[26]

In other words, for those of us who have been given the privilege to study the original languages, there seems to be a special onus to use those languages to interpret Scripture rightly, to expound it powerfully, to dispute false claims accurately, and to feed the sheep with this gift of God's grace.

Those who study the Bible, especially in a theological college or seminary, should make the most of the opportunity that God has given them. We must be good stewards of the gifts that God has given to us and remember that the purpose of studying the Hebrew language is to draw us closer to the one who spoke the

> "Excelling at our vocation as expositors of the Bible and champions of the gospel correlates with having a strong handle on the original languages. Luther is onto something: to competently 'dig into Scripture, expound it, and carry on disputations' we must maintain the gifts God has given us through the original texts."
>
> —Jeremy Bouma[r]

Scriptures. Benjamin B. Warfield, in a lecture titled "The Religious Life of Theological Students," delivered to the students of Princeton Seminary on October 4, 1911, made this impassioned plea to the students:

> Are you alive to what your privileges are? Are you making full use of them? Are you, by this constant contact with divine things, growing in holiness, becoming every day more and more men [and women] of God? If not, you are hardening! And I am here today to warn you to

26. Luther, "To the Councilmen," 363.

take seriously your theological study, not merely as a duty, done for
God's sake and therefore made divine, but as a religious exercise, itself
charged with religious blessing to you. . . . You will never prosper in
your religious life in the Theological Seminary until your work in the
Theological Seminary becomes itself to you a religious exercise out of
which you draw every day enlargement of heart, elevation of spirit,
and adoring delight in your Maker and your Savior.[27]

——————————— **Chapter Reflections** ———————————

1. Are you convinced that a knowledge of Biblical Hebrew can
   provide a lifetime of fruitful study of God's word?

2. What reason do you find most compelling for learning Hebrew? What other reasons can you think of?

3. What are some examples of how knowing Hebrew aids in
   proper interpretation of the Bible?

4. Have you ever heard someone tell you that they never use
   their Hebrew? What strategies can you put into place so that
   this doesn't happen to you?

5. Do you truly believe that studying Hebrew is a privilege?
   Does your resolve to study Hebrew reflect that reality?

27. Benjamin B. Warfield, *The Religious Life of Theological Students* (Phillipsburg, NJ: P&R, 1992), 7.

The Causal כִּי Clause in Nahum 2:2[3]

Adam J. Howell

─────────○─────────

"For the Lᴏʀᴅ is restoring the majesty of Jacob just as the majesty of Israel; for those who empty (plunder) have emptied (plundered) them and their branches they have destroyed."

כִּי שָׁב יְהוָה אֶת־גְּאוֹן יַעֲקֹב כִּגְאוֹן יִשְׂרָאֵל כִּי בְקָקוּם בֹּקְקִים
וּזְמֹרֵיהֶם שִׁחֵתוּ׃

—Nahum 2:2[3]

In the book of Nahum, the Lord delivers an oracle against the Assyrians, one of Israel's primary enemies.[28] The book is chock-full of woes and curses on Assyria because of the devastation they caused to their neighbors, including Israel. However, in Nahum 2:2[3],[29] we get a כִּי clause that provides the ground or reason for why the Lord will destroy Assyria.

Two כִּי clauses occur in Nahum 2:2[3], but the first one is the one we are interested in here. In Nahum 2:1[2], the Lord tells the Assyrians that the scatterer has come against them and they should prepare for battle even though they will be utterly destroyed. The Lord has already told Israel that someone stands on the mountain who brings good news and publishes peace (Nah. 1:15[2:1]), so the message of Assyria's devastation already implies rescue and peace for Israel. However, in Nahum 2:2[3], the Lord provides this explicit ground for why he will destroy Assyria: "For/because (כִּי) the Lᴏʀᴅ is restoring the majesty of Jacob just as the majesty of Israel" (כִּי שָׁב יְהוָה אֶת־גְּאוֹן יַעֲקֹב כִּגְאוֹן יִשְׂרָאֵל).

כִּי clauses can come in several forms. Russell Fuller and Kyoung-won Choi say that כִּי expresses result rather than purpose. They say,

28. This devotional originally appeared at https://adamjhowell.wordpress.com on October 25, 2016.

29. The verse nomenclature here indicates that the versification in Hebrew differs from the versification in English. In English Bibles, this is Nah. 2:2, but in the Hebrew Bible, this is Nah. 2:3. The bracketed number indicates the Hebrew verse number.

"The result clause, by contrast [to the purpose clause], expresses outcome, eventuality, or effect of another action or situation."[30] Indeed, the effect of God destroying Assyria is to restore the majesty of Jacob. Purpose and result clauses are therefore closely related and sometimes difficult to distinguish. Ronald Williams begins his discussion of the כִּי clauses with the causative כִּי clause.[31] The causative is likely the best grammatical identifier for the clause we have in Nahum 2:2[3]. Why does the Lord warn Assyria to "man the ramparts"? "Because" he is restoring the majesty of Jacob. Gesenius says that the conditional clause with the perfect tense (שָׁב) "refers to clauses already brought fully into effect."[32] So, while most English translations communicate a progressive aspect of the verb ("is restoring"), the perfect within the causal כִּי clause indicates the surety of God's work on behalf of his people.

In Nahum 2:2[3], we see that the Lord restores his people by destroying their enemies. Paul tells New Testament believers that our primary struggle is not against flesh and blood but "against the cosmic powers over this present darkness, against the spiritual forces of evil in the heavenly places" (Eph. 6:12 ESV). We know that our primary enemy is sin and death, but in the same way that the Lord destroyed Nineveh in order to restore the majesty of Jacob, he also will destroy our enemies of sin and death in order to restore the majesty of those who trust in Christ. Indeed, he has already conquered sin and death at the cross; therefore, we can be confident that he will gain the victory for his people when he returns again.

God's desire is that his people would reflect his glory. For Israel, that primarily meant living as a holy nation. For New Testament believers, reflecting God's glory also comes by living holy lives under the direction and aid of the Holy Spirit. As we walk according to the Spirit, we are made more and more Christlike and subsequently reflect more and more of the majesty of our Savior. Indeed, when

30. Russell Fuller and Kyoungwon Choi, *Invitation to Biblical Hebrew Syntax: An Intermediate Grammar* (Grand Rapids: Kregel, 2017), §51.

31. Ronald J. Williams, *Williams' Hebrew Syntax*, 3rd ed., rev. and exp. John C. Beckman (Toronto: University of Toronto Press, 2007), §444. See also GKC §158b and Joüon §170d–da.

32. GKC §158d.

the Lord conquers our enemies of sin and death, he is restoring the majesty of his people and displaying his ever-present glory through the church. We can, with confidence, ask the Lord to scatter "the spiritual forces of evil in the heavenly places," accessing the same vengeance with which he destroyed Assyria.

Weighed in the Balances and Found Wanting

In 1914 William James wrote, "Just as, if we let our emotions evaporate, they get into a way of evaporating; so, there is reason to suppose that if we often flinch from making an effort, before we know it, the effort-making capacity will be gone. . . . Keep the faculty of effort alive in you by a little gratuitous exercise every day."[1] How about you? Are there daily "efforts" you practice such that they become a healthy habit? Are you a daily Bible reader? Someone who is likely to read the Hebrew Old Testament for life?

Though each one of us has his or her own personality, predilections, and background, we all can learn how to manage our time better and commit more faithfully to things we truly value. I worked in the fitness industry for over ten years as a manager of a gym while in seminary (yes, I was in seminary that long!). I was always mesmerized by the number of people who would pay big money for a personal trainer only to find out that they were hiring a "friend." Not only did these people want fitness training, but they wanted a life coach. They needed someone to help them organize their life and manage

1. William James, *Habit* (New York: Holt, 1914), 64–65.

their time, including the time they committed to go to the gym. While
we may not all need to hire a life coach, with the right input and accountability, most people are able to improve in managing their time
and organizing their lives. Additionally, the key
to developing a healthy habit is having a plan.

"Excellence is an art
won by training and
habituation. . . . We are
what we repeatedly do.
Excellence, then, is not
an act but a habit."
—Will Durant[a]

My wife and I began dabbling in CrossFit
in 2011. We both played college sports, and we
wanted a workout routine that was similar to
the intensity we experienced in college athlet-
ics. We considered ourselves to be highly disciplined and motivated people, but we found that
when we went to the gym, we stood around
asking each other what we wanted to do. Inevitably, we couldn't
agree. My wife played soccer, and so she could run for days. I played
football, so I could watch her run for days (my training consisted of
eight- to ten-second bursts followed by forty-five seconds of rest).
CrossFit gave us a mutual plan and accountability to go to the gym
and get something done rather than standing around doing nothing.

As our bodies have aged, the intensity of CrossFit is simply uncom-
fortable. We sometimes give in to the fatigue and soreness and decide
to sleep in . . . six days in a row. To combat this temptation to laziness,
we will sometimes sign up for local competitions. The competition
(and the registration fee!) gives us an added incentive to keep up the
discipline of training. It becomes a new, and more focused, plan to
accomplish our goals of fitness. Rather than succumbing to laziness,
we force ourselves to compete so that we train consistently. The sharp
focus of our *plan* helps us to accomplish our *goal*.

A plan . . . accountability . . . a partner/team mentality . . . motivating fear. The clear focus of our plan along with the joy of accomplishing goals with my wife and the fear of failure on the competition
floor transformed meandering college athletes into fitness "competi-
tors." Now, don't misunderstand. You won't see us on TV anytime
soon throwing hay bales or dragging dump trucks. We are not *that*
serious about this aspect of our lives. Even so, the principles still fit.
Without a plan and accountability, we failed to even have an end goal.
Once we had a plan, and now that we continue to adjust our plan,
we have been attaining our fitness goals since 2011.

A Biblical Look at Laziness and Diligence

Consider for a moment digital assistants like Siri or Alexa. These "brilliant" apps are brilliant only insofar as a human being has created an algorithm that will point the digital assistant to the information you're asking for. Circuits and software don't have knowledge independent of the computer programmer, so in order for Alexa to obtain "new" knowledge, a programmer has to rewrite a computer script such that she now has either new information or a new means of getting the information. Need new information? Just rewrite your software script.

Unfortunately, life and Hebrew don't work that way. The world is broken. Though learning can be a great joy, our knowledge is partial and our memories weak. Because of the noetic effects of sin, not only do humans resist knowledge of God, but the use of the mind for other cognitive endeavors is weakened as well. When Adam and Eve rebelled against God, sin tainted all of creation, including our abilities to memorize and understand. That fragility and fracturing of creation even extends to the sphere of studying the Hebrew Old Testament.

Throughout Scripture, we read about "futile thinking" and "darkened hearts" (e.g., Rom. 1:21). Proverbs 28:26 says, "Whoever trusts his own mind is a fool, but he who walks in wisdom will be delivered" (ESV). After Adam's sin, there is an incapacity in the human mind to think rightly about God and his creation that makes trusting our own minds "foolish." Following Adam's disobedience, God cursed the created order (Gen. 3:17–19), and while this "curse" is most obviously seen in the thorns and thistles that compete with agricultural crops, the life of the mind must also now engage in painful toil. Vocabulary is forgotten. There is never enough time to learn. You or your children catch the flu so that you are not able to study sufficiently for the exam. Or perhaps you find yourself at the end of the semester regretting wasted hours playing video games or watching Netflix—hours that, if filled with study, not only would have prepared you to ace an exam but would have equipped you to read the Bible more faithfully for a lifetime.

Təqel (תְּקֵל). This is one of the words that the Lord wrote on the wall at Belshazzar's feast in Daniel 5. As the Lord's hand departed

from the room, Daniel was left to interpret these words for Belshazzar in light of the genetic hubris inherited from his father, Nebu-
chadnezzar (Dan. 5:17–23). The word *təqel* is the Aramaic word for
"to weigh," and with the שׁ/ת interchange between Aramaic and
Hebrew, it is related to the Hebrew word שָׁקַל. From this root, you
may recognize the monetary unit שֶׁקֶל (shekel). Daniel interprets
this word for Belshazzar as "you have been weighed in the balances
and found wanting" (Dan. 5:27 ESV). To be "found wanting" is to
be diminished, to be imperfect. If we are honest with ourselves, we
are all "found wanting" in certain areas, and many of us are "diminished" or "imperfect" particularly in our motivation to learn language
skills. To some degree, that's normal. It is simply a result of the curse
issued after Adam sinned. We will never be able to know all things
perfectly or to remember everything we learn. Studying Hebrew will
be difficult. Nevertheless, we cannot let pride or laziness diminish
our goal of knowing God better through deep study of Hebrew.

In this life, we will never be able to fully gain the skills, expertise,
or performance we desire. We will constantly fall short. And, figura-
tively speaking, when we die, we will be "found wanting." However,
unlike Belshazzar, who worshiped his own glory, we offer up our
incomplete labors as an act of worship to our Lord. We give ourselves
to studying God's word with the hope that we will fall more in love
with the glory of God in the face of Jesus Christ, and we pray that,
while our studies will be imperfect, they will not go unrewarded.

In working hard to study Hebrew, we demonstrate that we value
God and his word above all things. We read and study the Hebrew Old
Testament to know his word, understand it, teach it faithfully, and
ultimately know God better and lead others to know him better too.

The curse guarantees the incompleteness of our work, yet we
don't want to be blameworthy builders who have squandered our
opportunities. The apostle Paul warns about such poor stewardship
in the church. He writes, "If anyone builds on this foundation using
gold, silver, costly stones, wood, hay or straw, their work will be
shown for what it is, because the Day will bring it to light. It will
be revealed with fire, and the fire will test the quality of each person's work. If what has been built survives, the builder will receive
a reward. If it is burned up, the builder will suffer loss but yet will

be saved—even though only as one escaping through the flames" (1 Cor. 3:12–15 NIV).

Especially in Proverbs, we find repeated warnings about laziness.[2] In Proverbs 24:30–34, Scripture provides an illustration of a sluggard allowing his field to be overcome with thorns and nettles. As the author passes by the field of the sluggard, he sees the protective wall broken down and recognizes that this field belongs to a sluggard, "a man lacking sense" (v. 30). After considering the field and its condition, the author says he (the author) "received instruction" (v. 32). The instruction he received was that "sleep," "slumber," and "a little folding of the hands" (laziness) will bring poverty and want (vv. 33–34). While that was the direct instruction received by the main character walking by the garden, the instruction for us is "Do not be like that sluggard!"

For some of us, incomplete knowledge and anemic motivation to learn Hebrew is a part of our sinful disposition living in a fallen world. For others of us, that sinful disposition can be labeled as outright laziness. In the same way that this sluggard in Proverbs needs to pick up the pieces of his wall, tend his garden, and reap the riches of the garden he has been blessed with, so also we need to rebuild the Hebrew wall around our studies of Scripture and reap the blessings of digging for gold in God's word.

> "To subdue [the promptings of sin] I put myself in the hands of one of the brethren who had been a Hebrew before his conversion, and asked him to teach me his language. Thus . . . I now began to learn the alphabet again and practice hard and guttural words. . . . I thank the Lord that from a bitter seed of learning I am now plucking sweet fruits."
> —Jerome (ca. 342–420)[b]

Dispositions and Discipline

We all have different personalities. Some people are extremely organized and predictable. They awake at 5:30 a.m. every day and have their quiet time, which includes readings in Hebrew. That routine may seem like the perfect standard to some readers of this book,

---

2. Prov. 6:6–11; 10:4, 5, 26; 12:24, 27; 13:4; 15:19; 18:9; 19:15, 24; 20:4; 21:25; 22:13; 23:21; 24:30–34; 26:13–16.

Testimony of a Homeschooling Mom

Having been a graduate of a secular university, I was sadly slighted the luxury of being exposed to the classes of Biblical Greek and Hebrew. Unfortunately for me, I did not fully understand or grasp what I was missing back then.

As the next few years placed me in the new roles of wife and then mom, I realized that my relationship with the Lord was important for living well and that my study of God's word directly affected my relationship with the Lord. So I began to study the word of God deeply.

Through the years as my husband and I learned more and more theology, we began to understand that looking at the whole counsel of God's word was a key part of being good spouses and parents. This is because our orthodoxy determines our orthopraxy. In other words, our theology, or lack thereof, determines our life practices. So we set out to make it our mission to understand good theology. The more we studied and learned, the more we understood how much we didn't know. As I dug deeper in my personal study, I learned the value of the Old Testament in seeing Jesus. This is because in the Old Testament, the redemptive story of Jesus is woven through every chapter and every story.

While the Bible is definitely a book for any and every person, my expository studies led me to feel incapable at times of correctly interpreting the text, because I didn't know the original language. I became dependent on my pastors, teachers, and commentators to help me understand the depth of the hermeneutics. While these are all great things, I began to hunger for the ability to do these things on my own. I decided to take this one step at a time.

When my daughter decided to choose Hebrew for her high school foreign language credit, I decided to take the course with her. We have begun this adventure together. Oh, how grateful I am that she as a young woman is learning what has taken me twenty-five years to learn: the value of learning God's word in the language in which it was written. I am so thankful for this new journey!

—Jodi Hiser[c]

but if such an organized person cannot interrupt the schedule to help someone in need (Luke 10:29–37), what good is all that biblical knowledge and self-discipline? It's possible for organized and diligent people to lack the love, grace, compassion, and mercy that are the distinguishing marks of God's people (Matt. 23:23; John 13:35).

Laziness appears differently depending on a person's culture, personality, and background. But laziness *is* an objective behavior condemned in Scripture as unwise and disgraceful. To not be lazy is to be a responsible person before God and others in the work and opportunities put before us. For a Bible college student, seminary student, or minister, that means faithfully seizing the opportunity to learn Hebrew so you can read, study, believe, obey, and teach the Hebrew Old Testament. It is insufficient to say, "I can't learn Hebrew because I'm not good at learning a new language." If God has provided this opportunity to know his word deeply, then we cannot blame our personality tendencies for genuine laziness creeping into our lives. With enough work, studying, learning, and reading, Hebrew might actually become a delight.

Many of my first-year Hebrew students arrive to class on the first day intimidated by the language. Their defense mechanism is to let me know that they are not naturally good at learning languages. Their knee-jerk reaction is to think their personality will hinder their learning of Hebrew. My goal at that point is to remind them that hard work each week of the semester will pay off in the end. I give them a plan and daily assignments to stay on pace, and before long these same students express their joy of the language. In fact, they usually begin to act like they enjoy Hebrew by the end of the first week of class when we are reading Genesis 1:1 in Hebrew. They can't translate it, but having learned the alphabet and vowels, they can read it. This kind of early payoff can often turn a person with a hesitant disposition into a motivated, disciplined warrior.

The Psychology of Habits

Given your own unique personality and background, what will it look like for you to develop a more faithful habit of reading or studying Hebrew? Phillippa Lally and a group of psychology researchers at

University College London followed ninety-six people who each chose a new behavior to adopt as a habit. How long would it take each person to form a habit? The shortest time it took was 18 days. The longest time was 254 days. The average was 66 days. Lally's results were published in the *European Journal of Social Psychology*. From this study, we learn that no habits are formed overnight and some of us must work longer and harder to form a habit. Where are you on the spectrum? If it takes you 100 days to form a habit, what specifically are you going to do to prevent yourself from giving up before meeting the habit-forming threshold?[3]

Can you put disincentives in place to "punish" yourself when you fail to keep your habit that day (no dessert, no cup of coffee, or no using your phone until you complete your habit, for example)? What incentives can you put in place to encourage you to stick with your new habit (perhaps a chocolate candy, a walk around the block, or permission to use your phone after you perform your new habit that day)? For the most effective application of incentives and disincentives, it's best to have another person aware of your accountability system—and it's even better to turn over control of the incentives/disincentives to another person to prevent you from cheating. For example, you can give your phone to your roommate or spouse at night, and commission them to not give it back until you have read your Hebrew Bible for ten minutes in the morning. Over time, as you form a habit, the incentives/disincentives will be less needed. Eventually, you will form a habit, though it may take you 254 days!

In a 2007 article in *Psychological Review*, Wendy Wood and David Neal interact with what they call the "habit-goal interface." They point out there is a massive crossroads of habits and goals, but they specifically explore the way that these two psychological features (habits and goals) interact. Wood and Neal summarize that "goals can (a) direct habits by motivating repetition that leads to habit formation and by promoting exposure to cues that trigger habits, (b) be

---

3. Phillippa Lally, Cornelia H. M. van Jaarsveld, Henry W. W. Potts, and Jane Wardle, "How Are Habits Formed: Modelling Habit Formation in the Real World," *European Journal of Social Psychology* 40, no. 6 (2010): 998–1009. For an abstract of the article, see http://onlinelibrary.wiley.com/doi/10.1002/ejsp.674/abstract. Caleb Spindler helpfully summarized Lally's research for me (as part of a missionary collaboration) in January 2015.

inferred from habits, and (c) interact with habits in ways that preserve the learned habit associations."[4] In other words, goals motivate the formation of habits, and habits help reinforce and confirm established goals. If we consider the goals discussed in chapter 1, knowing God more through knowing his word better should be a primary motivator to establish routines that will support our goal. What about being a better preacher of God's word? What about having a better understanding of the biblical text for the sake of counseling? What is your end goal regarding knowledge of the Bible that will motivate your disciplined study of Hebrew?

We certainly don't put all of our eggs in the psychology basket, but it is true that our brains, personality, and attitudes affect our behaviors. Likewise, the inverse is true. Sometimes our behaviors affect our attitudes. In articles from *Psychology Today* and *Business Insider*, authors argue that healthy routines and habits affect our moods, resulting in how meaningful we believe our lives to be.[5] Setting goals, developing habits, and accomplishing those goals can lead to satisfaction and joy. It may be too strong to invoke a Hebrew curse ("May the LORD do so to me and more also"; כֹּה יַעֲשֶׂה יְהוָה לִי וְכֹה יֹסִיף [Ruth 1:17]) if we don't consciously devote ourselves to creating goals and developing habits to accomplish those goals. Even so, for the sake of knowing God's word better, many of us would be more motivated if we disciplined ourselves to create habits, accomplished small goals of learning Hebrew, and experienced the joy of achieving those goals a little at a time.

Time Management, Effectiveness, and Efficiency

Matt Perman offers countless helpful reflections on time management in his book *What's Best Next*. Although many elaborate

4. Wendy Wood and David T. Neal, "A New Look at Habits and the Habit-Goal Interface," *Psychological Review* 114, no. 4 (2007): 843–63, here 843.

5. Meg Selig, "Routines: Comforting or Confining?," *Psychology Today*, September 14, 2010, https://www.psychologytoday.com/us/blog/changepower/201009/routines -comforting-or-confining; Shana Lebowitz, "A New Psychological Insight Makes Me Feel Much Less Boring," *Business Insider*, June 16, 2016, https://www.businessinsider .com/daily-routines-help-you-feel-life-is-meaningful-2016-6.

time-management systems employ some permutation of to-do lists, Perman says the best thing one can do is form routines or habits.[6] In other words, it is much more important for a pastor to form the habit of reading the Hebrew Bible every day at a particular time than it is to have that task on a meticulously organized to-do list. What would it look like for your study of the Hebrew Bible to become a routine or habit, such as flossing your teeth? How could portions of your day or week be organized into routines or habits? Might you be able to schedule your life to guard study times from the intrusion of competing concerns?

Complementing Perman's study, Cal Newport, in his book *Deep Work: Rules for Focused Success in a Distracted World*, reports that most people have so many distractions that they cannot do "deep work." For humans to thrive in creative thinking and mental processing, Newport tells us, they must be able to focus without distractions for extended periods of time. One way to do this, says Newport, is to bundle numerous mentally superficial tasks into the same time slot, apart from one's "deep work." Newport warns that you must not let "the twin forces of internal whim and external requests drive your schedule."[7]

One technique that I will often recommend to students is to study in smaller, more frequent chunks of time. We have weekly quizzes in my Hebrew classes, and very often I find that students will study for hours on Monday before the quiz on Tuesday. When they come to me in week eight because they can't remember rules or concepts we learned in week two, I will remind them to review a little bit every day, say thirty to forty-five minutes, rather than trying to cram three or four hours in on Mondays. This lit-

> "[I] feel 'poured out' over a great many interests with intense desire to do but so little power and time to accomplish. . . . Hebrew: I can think of nothing I'd like better than to be able to pick up a page of the Hebrew Old Testament and read it at sight. Greek loses a lot of its challenge when one gets to know a little."
>
> —Jim Elliot[d]

---

6. Matthew Perman, *What's Best Next: How the Gospel Transforms the Way We Get Things Done* (Grand Rapids: Zondervan, 2016).

7. Cal Newport, *Deep Work: Rules for Focused Success in a Distracted World* (New York: Grand Central, 2016), 228.

tle trick for time management can be quite beneficial for students and often proves to be more effective for long-term retention. Likewise, shorter chunks of study time can be more efficient for an already busy life. It is easier to find thirty minutes in a day than to find three or four hours.

A Sports Example

Some of the most faithful readers of the Hebrew Bible have learned discipline and perseverance from other areas of their lives. Musicians know what it means to practice every day and see transformed skills over the long haul. Athletes understand regular practice, hard work, and sacrifice for a greater goal. In *Runner's World* magazine, Jeff Galloway offers the following training advice.[8] (The application to Hebrew study is, of course, our own contextualization of his advice.)

- *Vary Your Hebrew Reading.* Like running, reading the Hebrew Bible can benefit from some variety. Perhaps some
  mornings you will pick apart one or two verses—looking up
  rare forms and slowly reading through the lexicon entries.
  Another morning you may choose to race through a longer
  text and not be bogged down by difficult constructions.
  Maybe you read narrative for a season and then turn to poetry in the Psalter.
- *Meet with a Group.* Last year I began a Hebrew reading
  group at the college where I teach. We met on Wednesday
  mornings simply to read the Hebrew Bible. We began by
  reading through Deuteronomy a few verses each day, discussing the grammar, parsing verbs, and reviewing syntax.
  The skill level in the group was incredibly varied, but it was
  easy to allow students to participate at their own level. For
  some, that meant only reading the Hebrew text. For others,
  that meant me asking them questions about parsing difficult
  weak verb forms. If you are a pastor, you may think this kind
  of group reading is impossible, but if you can find another

8. Jeff Galloway, "The Starting Line," *Runners World*, June 2015, 40.

pastor in the area who shares your love for Hebrew, you can keep each other accountable, even if you only meet once per month. Or you can check out the Facebook page "Nerdy Language Majors" to find an online reading group.

- *Practice Semitic Cross-Training.* If you are a runner, cross-training is swimming, biking, or lifting weights. If you are a reader of the Hebrew Bible, perhaps cross-training would be reading from the Mishnah, Talmud, or Targums (Aramaic). Or cross-training may mean taking a week to study vocabulary lists or review syntactical categories as an alternative to your daily reading plan.

Honestly Evaluate Your Behaviors

In many ways, money management is like time management. When a person or couple comes to a financial counselor for help, one of the first things the counselor needs to understand is how much money is coming in, how much money is going out, and where that money is going. Financial counselors encourage counselees to keep a written record of all the money they are spending over the course of a month. People are often shocked to see how much of their money is spent on eating out, or coffees at Starbucks, or snacks at the gas station. Many small purchases can fritter away a great amount of cash.

> "Know the true value of time; snatch, seize, and enjoy every moment of it. No idleness, no laziness, no procrastination: never put off till to-morrow what you can do today."
> —Lord Chesterfield[e]

We all have twenty-four hours in a day, but we spend it very differently. Some things cannot be changed. Your body needs a good night's sleep, which means at least seven or eight hours in bed. You may have highly inflexible work obligations that consume forty or more hours of your week. But what about all the time in between? Do you watch TV? Do you watch movies on Netflix or Amazon Prime? How much time do you spend on Facebook, Snapchat, or Instagram? How much time per week do you spend playing video games? Do you really even know where all of this time goes?

"I spent seven years reading replies to my tweets, and more than a decade reading comments on my blog posts. I have considered the costs and benefits, and I have firmly decided that I'm not going to be held hostage to that stuff anymore. The chief reason is not that people are ill-tempered and dim-witted—though Lord knows one of those descriptors is accurate for a distressingly larger number of social-media communications—but that so many of them are blown about by every wind of social-media doctrine, their attention swamped by the tsunamis of the moment, their wills captive to the felt need to respond *now* to what everyone is responding to *now*."

—Alan Jacobs[f]

In a recent article in *Harvard Business Review*, Hugh McGuire notes that neuroscientific research shows that humans have a preference for "new information"—which can result in almost addictive behavior to check one's email, see the most recent tweet, or not miss the Instagram photos that were just posted. McGuire explains,

> The promise of new information, spurred by, say, pressing the refresh button in your email, or the ding of a Twitter DM alert, triggers the release of a neurotransmitter—dopamine—in the brain. Dopamine makes us more alert to the promise of potential pleasure, and our brains are wired to seek out things that generate dopamine.
>
> There is a learning loop to this process—new information + dopamine = pleasure—that lays down neural pathways that "teach" your brain that there is a reward for pressing the email refresh button (even if that reward is nothing but another message from Dave from accounting).
>
> This loop is reinforced every time you watch a second, third, or fifth, cat video on Facebook. And it's a very hard loop to break. It's almost—almost—as if hundreds of billions of dollars of engineering and product design have gone into building the perfect machine for keeping us distracted; the perfect system to tickle certain wiring in how our brains are set up.[9]

To accomplish his own goal of reading from traditional print books every day and not frittering away his time in an information-induced

---

9. Hugh McGuire, "How Making Time for Books Made Me Feel Less Busy," *Harvard Business Review*, September 1, 2015, https://hbr.org/2015/09/how-making-time-for-books-made-me-feel-less-busy.

dopamine stupor, McGuire imposes the following strictures on his own time: (1) laptop and smartphone are completely put away when he gets home from work; (2) after dinner during the week, he does not watch Netflix or TV, or mess around on the internet; and (3) no glowing screens are allowed in the bedroom.

Before instituting new strictures on yourself, you should first take stock of where your time is being spent. Use a notebook feature on your phone, or better yet, carry a small paper notebook to record the duration of your various activities throughout the day. You will certainly fail to record some things and record other things inaccurately, but over time a clearer picture of how you spend your time will emerge. You will be surprised.

I am consistently reminded how many projects I begin and either never finish or take months to return to. I walk outside my garage and see a wooden wall hanging that I began to build and haven't completed. I open my word processor and see all of the folders full of Hebrew worksheets and summary pages that I've never polished or completed. My wife pokes fun at me when I dream about home renovations. While I am (usually) capable of doing whatever the renovation will entail, it takes me months to do what a contractor can do in an afternoon because I find myself distracted by other obligations. Hence, if I begin a household project, whatever room I'm working on will look like a disaster for weeks or months. Certainly, it is understandable that I would be slower than a professional contractor, but when it comes to the "project" of learning God's word, none of us should delay that pursuit.

Sometimes, keeping that pursuit requires us to ask hard questions about our own personalities and tendencies so that we can leverage our positive inclinations toward accomplishing our goals and put to death the distractions that keep us from attaining our goals. We have to be brutally honest with ourselves about where we fall short on the motivation spectrum and then put a plan in place to overcome that deficiency. We may even have to spend a little time discovering where our time is going. When it comes to the way you spend your time, are you willing to see where the hours really go, develop a plan, and genuinely change your behavior to focus your time on doing the things you truly value most?

Technological Jujitsu

In the martial art of jujitsu, you use the strength of your opponents against them. Technology offers ever-present distractions. But technological innovators also offer various applications and programs to inform us about our use of time and keep us focused on what most concerns us. Below are three ideas on using technology against itself—technological jujitsu—to defeat the distractions of technology.

- Unfollow persons or social media feeds that are not pointing you toward the things you want to value most. The Daily Dose of Hebrew and Daily Dose of Greek send out daily tweets, Facebook posts, and emails to invade social media with matters of eternal value.

- Install a software program or smartphone app that prevents you from surfing the internet according to the specifications that you set. Most humans find it very difficult to not be distracted by the occasional news story, viral video, or friends' social media photos. These sorts of distractions prevent one from "deep work" by keeping one at a superficial, distracted cognitive level. In a blog post titled "The Complete Guide to Breaking Your Smartphone Habit," Brett and Kate McKay suggest smartphone apps for both auditing your smartphone use (Android: Checky, RescueTime, BreakFree, Quality Time; iPhone: Moment) and restricting it (iPhone or Android: Freedom; Android only: FocusOn, Focus Lock, Clear Lock, Stay Focused).[10] Citing various sociological and psychological studies, the McKays discuss how overuse of smartphones can result in (1) loss of empathy, (2) loss of sleep, (3) loss of focus and the ability to do deep, meaningful work, and (4) loss of ability to be fully present in one's life.

- Turn off notifications when you need to get focused work done. I could not live without notifications as I would forget at least half of what I need to get done. However,

10. See *The Art of Manliness*, February 22, 2016, https://www.artofmanliness.com/articles/break-smartphone-habit/.

notifications are also incredibly distracting. I will be working diligently, making wonderful headway on a project, and then I hear the ever-alluring *ding*. Most people cannot just ignore it. While these notifications can be helpful in certain contexts, we would do well to silence them during focused study.[11]

When I was writing my dissertation, my wife would sometimes go out of town with our kids to visit my family and give me focused time to write. This wasn't a regular trend, but she probably made this trip four or five times during the writing phase. When it was time for me to crank out a new chapter, she would pack up the kids and head out. One of the things that held me accountable to write while they were gone was that I knew when they got back, I would have to show my family that I had been working diligently during the time they sacrificed for me to get that project completed. When my wife would leave, she would say, "Be diligent, and let's get this thing finished." Her confidence in me gave me a boost of writing fervor, but her exhortation also informed me that the family expected me to be working while they were gone. I couldn't stand the thought of them returning home and being disappointed that I could/should have gotten more done but instead was lazy. For me, the potential disappointment of my family was enough to keep me motivated; you may need different motivators. Maybe you set financial penalties if you aren't diligent. Perhaps you ask your kids to keep you accountable at the expense of five dollars per occurrence for dillydallying.

"Although [mobile phone] notifications are generally short in duration, they can prompt task-irrelevant thoughts or mind wandering, which has been shown to damage task performance. We found that cellular phone notifications alone significantly disrupt performance on an attention-demanding task, even when participants did not directly interact with a mobile device during the task."
—Cary Stothart, Ainsley Mitchum, and Courtney Yehnert[g]

11. For those who cannot work because you are distracted by the worry of missing a call or text from a family member or in an emergency situation, most cell phones have settings that will silence certain notifications or will allow family members to still make contact.

"I'd say the biggest digital challenge is using our digital devices for good purposes instead of for purposes that are wasteful or even outright evil. Technology—digital technology included—is a good gift from God that he expects us to use, to faithfully steward, for his purposes. We do not carry out the Great Commission apart from technology but with it and through it. These amazing new digital technologies allow us to take God's Word and God's gospel farther and faster than ever before. They allow us to read, study, and know God's Word. Unfortunately, they also bring a world of distraction and all kinds of moral ugliness. As Christians, we need to ensure we are using them for the best purposes, putting them to the best and highest uses."

—Tim Challies[h]

Find what works for you so that you set up a situation in which you can be productive with your language studies.

Assess What You Really Love

Perhaps one of the benefits of assessing our time is to cause us to face up to what we really love. We say we wish we had more time to read the Bible and pray, but it is what we actually do that shows what we want to do. James K. A. Smith, in his provocative book *You Are What You Love*, writes,

> To be human is to be animated and oriented by some vision of the good life, some picture of what we think counts as "flourishing." And we *want* that. We crave it. We desire it. This is why our most fundamental mode of orientation to the world is love. We are oriented by longings, directed by our desires. We adopt ways of life that are indexed to such visions of the good life, not usually because we "think through" our options but rather because some picture captures our imagination. Antoine de Saint-Exupéry, the author of *The Little Prince*, succinctly encapsulates the motive power of such allure: "If you want to build a ship," he counsels, "don't drum up people to collect wood and don't assign them tasks and work, but rather teach them to long for the endless immensity of the sea." We aren't really motivated by abstract ideas or pushed by rules and duties. Instead some panoramic tableau of what looks like flourishing has an alluring power that attracts us, drawing us toward it, and we thus live and

work toward that goal. We get pulled into a way of life that seems to be the way to arrive in that world. Such a *telos* works on us, not by convincing the intellect, but by allure.[12]

When you see the way you choose to spend your time, what does it say about what you actually love? In light of God's word, what is he calling you to do about these loves? Are they in proper relationship with the following instructions of Moses? "And now, Israel, what does the LORD your God require of you, but to fear the LORD your God, to walk in all his ways, to love him, to serve the LORD your God with all your heart and with all your soul, and to keep the commandments and statutes of the LORD, which I am commanding you today for your good?" (Deut. 10:12–13 ESV).

One of the most indicting things for most of us is that our greatest love is often ourselves. We make plans that suit our schedules. We devote ourselves to tasks we're interested in. Perhaps we even devote ourselves to those tasks to the exclusion of others. Likewise, this hubris manifests itself alarmingly through the technology-saturated world in which we live. We mentioned earlier the need to set our phones aside, turn off notifications, and use apps that help us avoid time on glowing screens. In a podcast hosted by Brett McKay of the *Art of Manliness*, he interviewed author Adam Alter about what makes our phones so addictive.[13] Alter argues that app developers put into their apps a feature similar to slot machines. The behavioral addiction to gambling is one thing, but slot machines are also built to keep you coming back. App developers know this and exploit it to our harm. For social media, it's not that Facebook or Twitter is so engaging in and of itself. In fact, most would probably say we despise everyone's self-bloviating and "blowing their own shofar" on those platforms. Alter argues that the allure of many apps is the excitement associated with how the world will respond to what we post. As with the slot machine, we don't know when that Twitter post will "hit the jackpot" and go viral, but that *possibility* is what

12. James K. A. Smith, *You Are What You Love: The Spiritual Power of Habit* (Grand Rapids: Brazos, 2016), 11–12.

13. "Podcast #420: What Makes Your Phone So Addictive & How to Take Back Your Life," *The Art of Manliness*, July 5, 2018, https://www.artofmanliness.com/articles/podcast-420-what-makes-your-phone-so-addictive-how-to-take-back-your-life/.

continues to draw us in. In other words, we are distracted by the possibility that someone will virtually "like" what we've had to say. If that isn't self-love, then I'm not sure what is.

One way that we can put away distractions is to reorient our loves. Rather than loving ourselves and hoping for a certain number of "likes" or "shares," we need to set our hearts on a love for God in the word of God. When that happens, running to other (lesser) loves will fall to the wayside, and we will be more diligent to devote ourselves to those things that capture our hearts. My prayer for myself and for you is that God would give us such a deep love for his word that we are not only willing but eager to put aside distractions and laziness for the sake of knowing him through the original languages.

Chapter Reflections

1. Given your current life situation (student, pastor, new parent, etc.), what's a realistic goal for how much time you want to be reading or studying the Hebrew Bible every day?

2. Are you willing to assess where you really spend your time? How and when are you going to do that? Are you willing to put monitors on your computer or smartphone to keep up with how you spend your time or to block you from wasting time?

3. What's a realistic next step in your life in moving toward greater efficiency and focus? Reading a book on time management? Arranging accountability to friends? Taking a course? Hiring a life coach? Perhaps prayerfully skim back through the chapter and choose one step.

4. Over the next few decades, do you want to fritter away thousands of hours of your life in mindless distractions? If not, what are you going to do to focus your time and abilities on what really matters?

5. How can you reorient your life so that you begin to develop new loves? What would it look like if your love for God's word eclipsed lesser joys?

God May Providentially Answer Our Prayers . . . Way beyond Our Imagination!

RUTH 1:8–9

Tom Blanchard

───────○───────

Since we already know the end of the story of the book of Ruth, it's difficult for us to feel the heart-wrenching emotions felt by Naomi as she stands somewhere on the road between Moab and Bethlehem. Naomi understands that from any human point of view, it makes absolutely no sense for these two young widows to continue with her on this return to her homeland. They have been faithful wives to her now-deceased sons. But Moabite women are not likely to be highly sought after by any godly men living in Israel during these turbulent times of the judges. And Moabite widows? Probably even less likely. Naomi sees no future for them there, so she encourages them to return to Moab (Ruth 1:8a). But as she does, she prays for them: "May the Lᴏʀᴅ deal kindly. . . . [May] the Lord grant that you may find rest" (1:8b–9a ESV).

Now, this is an indirect prayer, addressed to God obliquely using the third-person jussive, invoking a blessing. I'm sure Naomi's prayer for them was sincere. But I'm also pretty sure that she never would have imagined how her prayer, at least for one of these women, would be answered. Indeed, in the providence of God, her prayer became an integral part of the Lord's plan of salvation for the entire world. And in the Hebrew text of Ruth, this jumps out at us especially with two words: חֶ֫סֶד and מְנוּחָה, which most of our versions translate as "kindness" and "rest." We can follow the connections with these words in some English versions but not all. But it's unmistakable in the Hebrew.

In Ruth 1:8, Naomi asks for the Lord to "do חֶסֶד." Fast-forward to 2:19–20, where Naomi learns from Ruth the name of the man who dealt so kindly with Ruth and apparently realizes that this man has unique legal connections to Naomi's family as a *redeemer*. And in this she sees "his" חֶסֶד, either *Boaz's* expression of godly kindness and family loyalty, or *God's* expression of kindness in arranging this "random" event. In either case, Naomi, and our narrator, seems to be connecting this providential meeting of Ruth and Boaz with Naomi's prayer of 1:8. (The word חֶסֶד will make a third and final appearance in 3:10 as Boaz recognizes the manifestation of חֶסֶד in the character and action of Ruth.)

If Naomi believes that she has seen God's providential answer to her prayer of 1:8, she doesn't hesitate to imagine that the answer to her prayer of 1:9, מְנוּחָה, isn't far away. So when we read of her little plan to secure מָנוֹחַ (from the same root as מְנוּחָה) for Ruth in 3:1, we can see what she's thinking: "God providentially answered my prayer for חֶסֶד; this has got to be his answer for מְנוּחָה." Well, it might be (3:11). Or not (3:12). Ruth and Naomi will spend an agitated night and day before they have confirmation (3:13, 18). Now it's all up to their גֹּאֵל (redeemer, 3:9).

The connection between 1:8 and 2:20 is fairly obvious in English. The link between 1:9 and 3:1 might be less so, depending on your translation. But in the Hebrew, the connection jumps out at you.

Yes, God does hear our prayers. He sometimes answers prayer in Scripture with spectacular miracles. But here he answers with quiet, ordinary providence—daily living in humble, trusting obedience. Ruth received the blessings of Naomi's prayer. But what neither Ruth nor Naomi (nor Boaz) ever realized in their lifetimes is that the blessings of Naomi's prayer (Obed, Jesse, David, and generations on to Jesus) would continue into the twenty-first century and into eternity.

Review the Fundamentals Often

The 1991 movie *The Pistol: Birth of a Legend* is an inspiring presentation of the eighth-grade basketball season for Pete Maravich, also known as "Pistol Pete." The film depicts the story of Pete, who is only five feet two, making the 1959 basketball team at D. W. Daniel High School in Clemson, South Carolina. Like any good sports drama, there are ups and downs in Pete's story. However, the one thing consistently portrayed throughout the movie is Pete's diligence to practice the fundamentals of basketball in order to achieve his goal of making the team. In certain montages, you see Pete endlessly dribbling a basketball or shooting foul shots in the rain. No matter the situation, Pete was focused on his goal and practiced the fundamentals necessary to make the team. For Pete, repetition of these fundamentals was the key to success.

Like sports fundamentals, repetition is also essential for a language learner to survive the onslaught of terms and forms that come our way. At first it might seem like Biblical Hebrew is a behemoth or leviathan too big to conquer. However, by reviewing and memorizing vocabulary words and grammatical forms, we slowly begin to gain the upper hand, surviving and even thriving in our pursuit of Hebrew. When a random Hebrew term or phrase is hurled our way, we will not panic, because we have seen something like it before. Through our repetitive practice of the fundamentals, our repertoire of terms and forms will help us accurately identify what may seem like an alien word before us. Mastering the Hebrew language is possible, but it will take effort—and once again, repetition is the key.

My younger two children are learning to read, and one of the exercises they have to do is read lists of words that have the same letter combination of sounds with different consonantal beginnings—for example, *an, van, can, ran, man, Dan, Stan.* The idea is that they repeat (by seeing, saying, and hearing) the letter combination "-an" so much that it sets into their brain's subconscious. The next time they see the combination "-an," they will read it without thinking much about it. Repetition generates that kind of internalized knowledge.

I used to work as a personal trainer, and one thing I would teach my clients is that most people begin performing functional movements with *unconscious dysfunction.* They don't perceive that their squat is bad for their knees because they don't know what a correct squat feels like. Once we worked on their squat form and it improved, they began to perform the workout with better form and progressed to a *conscious dysfunction.* While the movement still needed practice (repetition), they at least were aware when they were performing the movement incorrectly, because they had done enough proper squats that they knew what a good squat felt like. The next phase these clients would enter was *conscious function,* where they performed the movement flawlessly but really had to think about it. They had to consciously tell themselves to push the knees out, squeeze the abs, and keep the chest up. The final phase of developing a proper squat was *unconscious function.* In this last phase, due to hundreds of repetitions, clients preformed the squat flawlessly and without thinking about it. The movement patterns that generated a certain functional goal became second nature.

Like functional fitness, Hebrew takes hundreds (or thousands) of repetitions for the language to become second nature. For that valiant goal to become a reality, repetition will be necessary.

Some may wonder if it is even necessary to memorize Hebrew vocabulary and paradigms since there are resources to aid the modern interpreter. With so many resources, including Bible software and apps, is it worth going through the hard work of learning these fundamentals of a language? We addressed this question in chapter 1. From practical experience, we know that if students do not have a basic foundation in the language, they are not likely to use it. It is simply too time consuming for a pastor (or anyone studying the Bible using Hebrew) to have to look up every word and every form in order to read the text. On the other hand, the broader the vocabulary base and the more familiar one is with the grammar of the language, the more likely Hebrew will be used in ministry. This chapter offers four strategies for how to *study* new material, and the following chapter focuses on how to *memorize* new material.

Review Frequently

When you meet someone for the first time, it is likely that you repeat their name after they tell you what it is. If you're determined to learn their name, you may call them by name several times in various sentences in order to reinforce their name and burn it into your memory. Perhaps you even introduce them to someone else so that you force yourself to remember their name again. Why does this use of repetition work? Because repetition is a key building block for effectively memorizing information. But we cannot simply sit down and try to memorize fifty vocabulary words at one sitting. If you have tried to do that in the past, you know that it simply does not work well.

When I was studying for my PhD comprehensive exams, my last exam was the Hebrew language exam. I had put off my final vocabulary review for the night before the exam so that it would be fresh on my mind for the following morning. I had my vocabulary cards out on my desk, scattered in stacks of words that (a) I knew well, (b) I sort of knew, and (c) I didn't remember at all. I didn't make the mistake of trying to learn fifty words at a time; I made the mistake of trying to cram into my working memory hundreds of words. My wife finally came to the office at 3:30 a.m. to tell me I should go to sleep! I can't say that studying those words that night didn't help some, but I can certainly tell you that I don't remember many of those less frequent words even now. Our long-term memory of Hebrew vocabulary and grammatical concepts will come from consistent, short segments of study rather than from sporadic, marathon study times.

Have Short Study Times

The brain cannot absorb massive amounts of new information at once. Research has shown that it is best to take a break after fifteen to thirty minutes of studying. If we continue to study after thirty minutes, our productivity will drop off considerably. Not only can our short-term and working memories not keep up, but our concentration and motivation wane after thirty minutes. Both of these factors directly affect our productivity. One example of a shorter study-time scheme is the Pomodoro technique. This technique suggests that after twenty-five minutes of work or study, you should take a five-minute break. In addition, for every two hours of study you should take a fifteen- to thirty-minute break.[1] Similarly, memory coach Dominic O'Brien maintains that "taking regular breaks is essential. It is much better to divide your time into, say, six 20-minute bursts of study than to try to focus for a full two hours before taking a break."[2]

The point here is that it is impossible to cram in Hebrew vocabulary and expect to retain it. Instead, it is best to have small blocks of time to study intensively, followed by a break to allow your brain to relax and process the information. Processing of the information is key here. To retain our study after the ten to twenty minutes of working memory, we have to move those newly learned items into "storage." This usually takes conscious effort to make mental images of the vocabulary words, use mnemonic devices, or build memory palaces (see chap. 4 for these techniques for memorizing). While we may take a break after twenty-five minutes of studying *new* information, we are still processing and working to move that information to our cerebral hard drive. Sometimes highly motivated students cannot imagine that twenty-five-minute blocks of study can

1. See http://pomodorotechnique.com/.
2. Dominic O'Brien, *You Can Have an Amazing Memory* (London: Watkins, 2011), 159–60.

be effective. However, you may be shocked at how well twenty-five minutes of new information can be retained if followed by five minutes of processing.

During my time as an adjunct Hebrew professor, I realized that I had to make my vocabulary tests cumulative. Each chapter in the textbook had twelve to fifteen vocabulary words, and I found that students did very well on the chapter vocabulary quizzes. When I finally gave them a cumulative vocabulary quiz, the grades plummeted. I found that the students could memorize twelve to fifteen words for a quiz, but without the regular repetition of those same words, they didn't retain them. Repetition, in short study sessions, will not only benefit the intake of new information, but it will also help with long-term retention.

Have Many Study Times

German psychologist Hermann Ebbinghaus (1850–1909) is well known for the so-called forgetting curve, which charts the rate of memory loss after new material has been learned. He discovered that most of the loss occurs within the first two hours of memorization. We lose about 50 percent after the first hour, another 10 percent after the first day, and another 14 percent after the first month. O'Brien notes the results of Ebbinghaus's study: "Ebbinghaus discovered that if we take notes as we listen, and then review the notes immediately following the event, we can retain 80 percent or more of the information we absorbed. . . . For optimal recall, he concluded that we should then follow this first review with a second review a day later, a third one a week later, a fourth one a month later, and a fifth review three to six months later (if the content was particularly complex)."[3]

Just looking at (or listening to) a vocabulary word once is not going to prove effective. The more times we review a word or paradigm, the more etched it becomes in our memory. This means that we should study a word and then leave it for at least an hour before we try to recall it again. You may think you don't have an hour to wait to review words again and again, but one reason vocabulary cards are so helpful is that you can take a small stack in your pocket wherever

---

3. O'Brien, *You Can Have an Amazing Memory*, 161–62.

you go. If you find a few minutes, you can look over them. While I prefer hard-copy vocabulary cards, vocabulary apps on phones make studying vocabulary accessible as well.

O'Brien, a former memory world champion, states he needs to review material at least five times to effectively memorize it: "If I have a limited amount of time to memorize a large amount of data, I know that I need to be able to review it five times for that information to stick. The more reviews I have, the stronger the retention and the longer I can store the memories, but if time is short, such as during a competition or if I have to memorize a series of names in a room quickly, five reviews is the minimum."[4] If an eight-time memory world champion needs to review data five times before he feels confident that he can recall it, then certainly this is true for the rest of us. Research suggests that it takes between ten and twenty repetitions before a student can "own" a particular word. And yet, how many of us have merely glanced over a vocabulary list before an exam only to realize that we did not know the material like we thought we did?

Language teacher Marjory Brown-Azarowicz suggests that words are best learned when (1) memorized in groups of related words (see below); (2) reviewed ten minutes after initial learning; (3) reviewed one hour later; (4) reviewed one day later; and (5) reviewed every two days until mastery is attained.[5] The exact method is not as important as the general principle: we must review vocabulary, morphology rules, and paradigms often. The more times we are able to review the material, the greater our retention of the material will be. But there is more to successfully gaining information than reviewing it often.

Optimize Your Review Times

It is also important to review material at optimal times. Otherwise, we are in danger of wasting, or at least not getting the most out of, our limited time for study. When should you *not* study? First, you should not study after a meal. After we eat, our brains naturally

---

4. O'Brien, *You Can Have an Amazing Memory*, 76.
5. Marjory Brown-Azarowicz, Charlotte Stannard, and Mark Goldin, *Yes! You Can Learn a Foreign Language* (Lincolnwood, IL: Passport Books, 1989), 28.

divert energy to our digestion by sending red blood cells that help break down and metabolize food. Consequently, the rest of our body tends to slow down and relax, making us feel tired and lethargic. Furthermore, we especially should not study after eating large meals or meals with high sugar or carbohydrates since such food can lead to increased levels of serotonin, resulting in sleepiness.

Second, avoid studying while listening to the radio (music, talk radio) or while watching TV. Memorizing new information requires a great amount of concentration and effort. If you are distracted with other information, you will not be able to direct your full concentration toward memorization.[6] Because of how our brains have been influenced by our fast-paced and "loud" society, some people prefer to study with music. The silence, for some, is more distracting than the music in the background. If you must listen to music while you study, choose a genre that doesn't

> "The digestion process impedes brainwork."
> —S. M. Baugh[a]

have lyrics. If your brain is processing (even subconsciously) lyrics to a song in the background, you're using "RAM" that could be devoted to learning the new material. Even though studying with music may be a society-induced preference, you may be surprised at how valuable it can be to study without any distractions, musical or otherwise.

At my school, the library has some musical practice rooms that are acoustically sealed. The idea is to keep the musical rehearsals *inside* the room, but the unintended beauty of these rooms is that they also keep the distractions *outside* the room. I spoke with a student over the summer who had discovered these rooms (they're hidden in our library basement), and he said that he had been down there for nearly four hours. He started and nearly finished an entire paper. While he broke the rule of studying in smaller chunks of time, I think he discovered the value of studying without aural distractions.

Third, avoid studying and memorizing while occasionally checking your email or social media accounts. This one may be especially difficult because we have become so accustomed to checking and responding to updates. Trying to multitask and study Hebrew will not

6. Many competitive mnemonists typically wear industrial grade earmuffs and dark glasses (or even glasses that are blacked out except for a small hole to see through) in order to give their undivided attention to memorizing information.

go well. You must be able to concentrate on the task at hand. If you're using your computer to study, don't even open your email program or web browser. Turn off email notifications so that you're not distracted by the ever-alluring *ding* of new information that only turns out to be the latest online spring catalog for your favorite clothing store.

Finally, avoid studying in crowded places or in locations where you may run into your friends. When I was in college, I would make sure my study times lined up with when a certain beautiful lady would be in the library as well (she later became my wife). Let's just say the distraction proved to be more powerful than the studying. In our fast-paced culture, many people say they prefer to study in a coffee shop where there is hustle and bustle around them where they can plug in headphones and "focus." That environment feels calming to them because that busyness is part of our daily lives. However, that scenario is not optimal for intense studying. Try studying alone and in the quiet in order to avoid distractions.

Stated positively, you must find times when you are most alert and are free from distractions. For some people this might be early in the morning, and for others it might be late at night. Some may have access to a quiet room in the house or a secluded location in the library in which to study midday. Ideally, you will find a primary time that provides the optimal study situation and also find several secondary times throughout the day to review.

Review Only a Few Words at a Time

It is not only important to study at the right time(s); it is also crucial to study in the right way. For vocabulary, one helpful rule of thumb is to study only a few words at a time. This rule is important because our brains can handle only a limited amount of material at once. Studies have shown that the average person can recall only seven discrete things at a time.[7] Thus, it is helpful to group words together (some-

---

7. See George A. Miller, "The Magical Number Seven, Plus or Minus Two: Some Limits on Our Capacity for Processing Information," *Psychological Review* 63 (1956): 81–97. O'Brien comments, "Psychologists have determined that, on average, the human brain can retain around only seven to nine pieces of data in its short-term (working) memory" (*You Can Have an Amazing Memory*, 81).

times called "chunking"). This strategy is used with phone numbers and social security numbers. Notice that when we memorize phone numbers (111-222-3333) or social security numbers (444-55-6666), we divide them into groups.

It has been suggested that a student should work on five to ten words at the same time (five is better for those just beginning to learn the language). For example, if you have fifteen words to memorize, divide them into three groups and start with only the first five. After spending several minutes with the first five, you can then move on to the second group (and then the third group). Another method is to learn five words in the morning, another five at lunch, and the final five at dinner (followed by a review session for all fifteen). Remember that these strategies aren't just given for the sake of passing a quiz on the vocabulary. They're designed for retention and overall Hebrew acquisition. While you may be able to learn all fifteen words at once, it will pay off in the long run to develop the practice of mastering smaller bits of information.

Another way to study smaller lists of words is to group words that have related meanings. The *New International Dictionary of Old Testament Theology and Exegesis* (*NIDOTTE*) contains an "Index of Semantic Fields" that has Hebrew words listed together under their respective English semantic domains.

- Daughter → בַּת (daughter, granddaughter, H1426); → כַּלָּה (bride, daughter-in-law, H3987); see Family[8]
- Dressing → לָבַשׁ (put on, clothe, wear, H4252; לְבוּשׁ, garment, clothing, apparel, vestment, H4230; מַלְבּוּשׁ, garment, H4860; תִּלְבֹּשֶׁת, garment, H9432); see Clothes[9]

You can see in these examples from *NIDOTTE* that additional Hebrew words are related under their respective semantic field headings (e.g., "Daughter" and "Dressing"). This is a good way to sort vocabulary into smaller groups and have the words in those groups naturally related to one another.

8. *NIDOTTE* 5:52.
9. *NIDOTTE* 5:66.

Similar to grouping words with related meanings, Hebrew often builds vocabulary based on the triliteral root. As you can see in the second example from *NIDOTTE* above ("Dressing"), all of those related words are built around the triliteral root לבשׁ. Some vocabulary guides group words together by root to help you learn vocabulary based on this feature of Hebrew.[10]

Working the other direction, it is also sometimes helpful to dissect words to see the triliteral root and see if this word is related to another you may already know. For example, the Hebrew root זבח means "to sacrifice," and other words containing those same letters may be related in meaning. Very often, Hebrew will add a מ to the front of a word to make it the place of that action. For זבח, the מ makes it "the place of the sacrifice" or an "altar" (מִזְבֵּחַ). In addition to focusing on a limited number of words at a time, you can use these helpful tricks when you encounter a word you've never studied before. If you can identify the triliteral root, you may also be able to identify various affixes that can direct you toward the right meaning of a word you've never formally learned.

Use a Multifaceted Review

Our memories include a complex number of intertwined associations. The more associations that we make, the more likely we will be able to recall the needed information. Thus, memory experts stress the importance of using as many senses as possible when learning new data. According to the William Glasser Institute (California), we retain only 10 percent of what we read, about 50 percent of information we see and hear, and about 80 percent of information we gain from personal experience. Furthermore, if we actively teach something, we have about a 95 percent retention rate.[11]

10. George M. Landes, *Building Your Biblical Hebrew Vocabulary: Learning Words by Frequency and Cognate* (Atlanta: Society of Biblical Literature, 2001). See also "Word List 2: Hebrew Words Arranged by Common Root Listed Alphabetically," in Miles V. Van Pelt and Gary D. Pratico, *The Vocabulary Guide to Biblical Hebrew* (Grand Rapids: Zondervan, 2003), 90–137.

11. As cited in O'Brien, *You Can Have an Amazing Memory*, 154.

Reading

Reading the Hebrew text is a skill that should be utilized as soon as the alphabet, vowels, and phonological principles are learned. Even if we can't translate what we're reading, it is helpful to practice the pronunciation of all the letters (including vowel points and cantillation marks) and learn the flow of the language. Unfamiliar words are easiest when learned from context, so it is helpful to read as much as possible. As we read, even if we don't know the meaning of a particular word, we can sometimes guess its meaning on the basis of the surrounding words. If we read a familiar passage and can at least see the difference between a noun and a verb, we can possibly translate small sections of the verse even if we can't translate all of it.

For beginning Hebrew students, reading will often simply be reading the Hebrew text without an attempt to translate. While this may seem like an elementary approach, it is helpful for gaining the flow of the language, the sounds and rhythm. The phonological principles of Hebrew are sometimes difficult to grasp for English speakers, but regular reading of the Hebrew text will prepare a linguistic environment in your mind so that as your vocabulary grows, reading (and translating) will become easier. The key here is to engage more senses, not fewer. Reading the Hebrew text out loud (seeing and hearing combined) will serve that purpose well.

> "We don't remember isolated facts; we remember things in context."
> —Joshua Foer[b]

When I began learning Hebrew, one of the books I purchased was *First Thousand Words in Hebrew* by Heather Amery.[12] This picture book is much like your standard high school language textbook, with pictures depicting a context and vocabulary related to that context. For example, you'll find a picture of a kitchen and then all of the Hebrew vocabulary associated with a kitchen. Next, you'll see a playground and all of its associated vocabulary. I bought the book primarily because I thought it was cool to have a kindergarten-level vocabulary guide, but using it also solidified for me the importance of context. The pictures provided a visual context to remember the vocabulary. As we read more and more of the Hebrew Bible, even if we don't know all the

---

12. Heather Amery, *First Thousand Words in Hebrew* (Tulsa: Usborne, 2014).

vocabulary words, the contexts we *do* know will provide direction as to the meaning of many words.

Alternatively, we sometimes remember vocabulary words *because of* their context in the Hebrew Bible. When I introduce new vocabulary words in my first-year classes, I give the students a familiar Bible story that uses a particular word so that they have a context in which to situate the word. For example, the Hebrew word לָחַךְ (to lick) is not an incredibly common word, and so it helps students to give them the context in 1 Kings 18:38 of the fire God sent on the altar to consume the burnt offering. This fire also "licked up" the water the servants had poured on the offering. Providing this context may not be a game changer for students, but it may help them remember the word. Likewise, reading the Hebrew Bible and seeing vocabulary words in more and more familiar contexts will only add to your proficiency in the language.

Speaking

In addition to reading, it is also helpful to speak Hebrew. By this I don't necessarily mean holding a conversation with someone. In most of our learning environments, especially as beginning students, conversing in Hebrew will be inconsistent at best.[13] But as we are learning vocabulary words, we should say them out loud. It is difficult to memorize a word that you can't pronounce. The same is true for paradigms. As you read or write them, say them aloud, and you will more likely remember them at a later time. When we hear something, we process that information differently than when we read it. The more senses we use, the better we will be able to recall what we are learning. If you combine speaking the word along with seeing it on a vocabulary card, that's even better.

When we first began homeschooling our children, we used a phonetics system that taught the children the various sounds that a letter can make in English. The flashcards for this system had the letter on

---

13. Keep in mind here that some models for learning Hebrew use an immersion model in which you learn Biblical Hebrew by immersing yourself in Modern Hebrew. Some of these models even require several months of living in Israel. Find out more about one of these methods at the Biblical Language Center's immersion courses (https://www.biblicallanguagecenter.com/immersion-courses-2/).

one side and the sounds listed on the other. The goal was for our kids to memorize all the possible sounds the letter could make, but they didn't learn them by staring at the phonetic values listed on the back of the card. They learned them by saying them aloud hundreds of times. Even if you're just working on the alphabet and vowels, saying Hebrew out loud will reinforce what you're learning: בַּ (ba), בֶּ (be), בֵּ (bey), בִּ (bi), בֹ (bo), בֻּ (boo). Challenge yourself to see how many strange looks you can get as you ride public transportation and recite the Hebrew vowel chart to yourself.

Writing

One of the most effective tools for learning Hebrew is to write it (and rewrite it and then rewrite it again!). If you seek to memorize a word, simply staring at it is not very effective. In fact, looking at a word a hundred times is less effective than employing a mnemonic device (see the next chapter). The way you should test to see whether you really have memorized a word is to write it out (from memory, of course—especially after not having looked at the word for at least an hour). If the word doesn't stick for at least an hour, you don't know it. Yes, you might be able to learn it long enough to take a quiz, but after the quiz it will quickly be forgotten. Furthermore, the purpose of learning Hebrew is not simply to pass a quiz or exam but to learn it well enough to utilize it in life and ministry.

I currently have a student who comes to me regularly after class with a word written in his notebook in Hebrew. Sometime during the class, I said a Hebrew word that he didn't know, and he attempted to sound it out phonetically in his notebook. He comes to me to ask if he has spelled it correctly. Many times, I'm correcting differences between an א or ע, but it is encouraging for me to see him trying to "use" the Hebrew he's learning by writing it. Many of us are not using Hebrew by speaking it through an immersive model, but we can still use Hebrew by writing it again and again and again. This applies to all aspects of learning the language, including vocabulary. The more you write vocabulary words, the better they will stick.

The same is true for learning paradigms. An effective way to learn paradigms is to write and rewrite them until you can write them with

no mistakes. Then try to write them an hour later, without looking at the paradigms, to see if you really know them. If you cannot
reproduce an entire paradigm *without any mistakes*, then you need
to look it over and write it out again. Simply looking at a paradigm
will do little good if you don't test your memory by writing it out.

Hearing

Along with reading, speaking, and writing Hebrew, you can also
listen to it. First, you can listen to vocabulary words. A good strategy is to use simple audio files so that you can listen to the words
during a lengthy commute or just when you're studying. Some textbooks now come with access to audio files of the vocabulary words.[14]
Another option is *Basics of Biblical Hebrew Vocabulary*, read by
Jonathan T. Pennington.[15] To hear the Hebrew Bible being read, you
can purchase *The Entire Hebrew Bible in Audio with Music and
Sound Effects* produced by the Bible Society in Israel. This record-
ing is a dramatized reading in Modern Hebrew. Another option for
listening to the Hebrew Bible is to listen online. One of my favorites
is the Hebrew Audio Bible housed at the Academy of Ancient Languages.[16] The audio is recorded by Abraham Shmuelof, born to an
ultra-Orthodox Jewish family in 1913. As a result of his upbring-
ing, his reading of the text sounds delightfully liturgical. Another
free online audio Hebrew Bible is HaKtuvim, which is produced by
the Bible Society in Israel and is another excellent audio Hebrew
Bible that uses modern pronunciation.[17] Listening to audio files is
especially useful for those who have a long commute or spend a significant amount of time driving. For beginning students, it is best to

14. See, e.g., Duane A. Garrett and Jason S. DeRouchie, *A Modern Grammar for
Biblical Hebrew* (Nashville: B&H Academic, 2009).
15. Gary D. Pratico and Miles V. Van Pelt, *Basics of Biblical Hebrew Vocabulary*
(Grand Rapids: Zondervan, 2006). Keep in mind that because of the different systems for pronouncing Hebrew (Classical versus Modern), you will want to find a
vocabulary audio file that matches the pronunciation of your grammar. For the audio
files associated with Garrett and DeRouchie's introductory grammar (*A Modern
Grammar for Biblical Hebrew* [Nashville: B&H Academic, 2009]), visit http://hebrew
grammar.sbts.edu/page5/page5.html.
16. See http://www.aoal.org/hebrew_audiobible.htm.
17. See https://haktuvim.co.il.

follow the pronunciation system employed by your teacher, whether Classical pronunciation or Modern pronunciation. Since Modern Hebrew is spoken in Israel, it may be more difficult to find entire readings of the Hebrew Bible using a Classical pronunciation. Even so, it will be beneficial to hear both vocabulary words and texts to aid your learning of the language.

Singing

Finally, singing is a proven way of memorizing information. Many of us can still remember a phone number that we never called but is etched in our minds because somebody sang it in the song "867-5309" by Tommy TuTone in 1981. We often tell our students that if you can sing it, you can memorize it. Why is this so? Joshua Foer explains, "The brain best remembers things that are repeated, rhythmic, rhyming, structured, and above all easily visualized."[18] This reality is not something that is new to the modern world but something that has been practiced for millennia.

> "If you can burn a set of words into a jingle, they can become exceedingly difficult to knock out of your head."
> —Joshua Foer[c]

Foer again notes, "Finding patterns and structure in information is how our brains extract meaning from the world, and putting words to music and rhyme are a way of adding extra levels of pattern and structure to language. It's the reason Homeric bards sang their epic oral poems, the reason that the Torah is marked up with little musical notations, and the reason we teach kids the alphabet in a song and not as twenty-six individual letters."[19]

The value of teaching Hebrew with songs has been long noted. One strategy is to use tunes that the students already know and then simply replace the lyrics with Hebrew words or paradigms. Another strategy is to use various genres

> "Song is the ultimate structuring device for language."
> —Joshua Foer[d]

of music. The key is for the song to be memorable, and often a genre that is off the beaten path may be more memorable than your favorite

18. Joshua Foer, *Moonwalking with Einstein: The Art and Science of Remembering Everything* (New York: Penguin, 2011), 128.
19. Foer, *Moonwalking with Einstein*, 128.

type of music. A quick search on YouTube will produce the Hebrew alphabet song in a rap version, a rock version, and more. A final strategy for singing Hebrew is to just sing Hebrew, even if it is not directly related to your textbook drills or paradigms. The folks at Biblearc.com have produced an online course to learn Hebrew, and one of the major components of their methodology is to sing. They have various psalms set to music, and in the videos, they display the translation in addition to various parsings of strategic words as you sing. You may not know all the vocabulary or parsing of the psalm you're singing, but as with reading Hebrew (described earlier), you will be exposed to the language in a memorable way. The more you see, hear, and vocalize (sing) the phonetics of Hebrew, the more these fundamentals will stick. Remember, if you can sing it, you can memorize it. In the case of singing the Psalms, you will also be memorizing Scripture in Hebrew!

One final note on singing Hebrew. Many people will not take advantage of this learning methodology because they think their singing is mediocre at best. My family can attest that my singing is subpar. In fact, it's probably some of the worst they hear. My daughters are kind to give me only a look of confusion when I begin to sing. My sons just flat out tell me it's bad. I've had to swallow my pride on several occasions in class as I began the alphabet song in the wrong key and we found ourselves singing a few notes down on the bass clef. Or I've started too high and we were all sopranos by the time we got to ג (*gimel*). The students usually get a kick out of it, and then I can regroup and start on the right note. Once they chime in, the song flows rather nicely. If you're learning to sing Hebrew on your own, then the fear of not singing well shouldn't be a factor. Let's face it; you belt out your favorite songs in the car all the time anyway, no matter how bad it sounds. Don't be afraid to sing Hebrew, and don't let a lack of musical expertise be an excuse to ignore this method of learning Hebrew.

We tend to think this is a novel way to learn an ancient language, but in fact it's how we learn to do many other things too. A similar, though categorically different, analogy is learning to hit a baseball. You cannot learn to hit a baseball by staring at video footage of the best hitters swinging endlessly. You have to go to the field and actually hit a baseball. Whether we are reading, writing, speaking, hearing, or singing Hebrew, we have to actually use the language to learn it. Just staring at it will not accomplish the goal of learning Hebrew.

As a final encouragement, combine as many of these methods for learning as possible. For some methods, they are combined already. Singing is a combination of speaking and hearing (and seeing, if you're looking at the words from a psalm as you sing it). Perhaps you combine reading with hearing and you read out loud while listening to the same passage read by someone else. Perhaps you combine hearing with speaking and you meet with a group to read Hebrew together. You read along quietly, seeing the words, as you hear the others in the group reading out loud. At the end of the day, no single method is absolutely the right way to learn Hebrew, but it is certain that the more of these methodologies you use and combine, the better off you will be. Remember to put in the work ahead of time to develop a plan for how you're going to conquer this language. Using these strategies, you will be well on your way.

Chapter Reflections

1. How important is reviewing in the acquisition of a language?

2. What are the best times of the day for you to study?

3. How many times do you need to review something before you have memorized it?

4. What are some practical ways you can incorporate all of your senses in learning Hebrew?

5. What sense do you think is the most productive or effective in memorizing Hebrew?

Making Sense of שִׂמְחָה

William Fullilove

Well-meaning congregants and preachers often make the mistake of assuming that words and ideas have a one-to-one correspondence. If you think for just a moment, however, you realize that a single word typically corresponds to several ideas. Think of the English word *funny*. It can be positive, as in "a funny joke," or negative, as in "a funny smell." This difference of meaning is what linguists call a "semantic range," the range of ideas that a word can convey, depending on the context.

Words only mean something in context. If I simply say "funny," without any other words or gestures, it's impossible for someone listening to me to understand which meaning of the word I intend. In our native languages, we use all sorts of contexts—situational, literary, tone of voice, and so forth—to quickly clarify the meaning of a word. In other words, we very quickly—so quickly that we often do not even realize we are doing so—scan through the range of potential meanings and mentally pick the one that fits the context and understand the word that way.

For this reason, when a Hebrew word is repeated in a passage, translators generally try to use the same English word to translate it each time it is repeated. If we don't, the reader of our translation might not realize that a word is repeated in the document. So, for instance, the Hebrew word חֶסֶד is tremendously rich in meaning, and because of that richness, it's almost impossible to translate with a single English word. My favorite "translation" of חֶסֶד comes from Sally Lloyd-Jones in *The Jesus Storybook Bible*. To convey the meaning of חֶסֶד in English, she uses the phrase the "never-stopping, never-giving-up, unbreaking, always-and-forever love" of God for us. That's חֶסֶד! In a more traditional translation, of course, the translators can use only a single English term for חֶסֶד. Otherwise the translation would become unwieldy. And translators will therefore—usually with much handwringing—pick a single English term to use to translate חֶסֶד and use that term every time it appears in a passage. At least the reader therefore realizes the repeated concept the author is using.

At times, however, the context forces translators to break that tendency and use different English words to translate the same Hebrew word. When that happens, we can miss the richness and nuance of the Hebrew text. The word שִׂמְחָה in Ecclesiastes presents a good example. As a book, Ecclesiastes is constantly challenging the reader to work out the twists and turns of its author's thought. When is the author quoting someone else and disagreeing? When is the author quoting someone else and agreeing? When is he wrestling with his own—even contradictory—thoughts?

However, the reader of Ecclesiastes in translation may not even realize this is occurring. Consider Ecclesiastes 2:2 and 8:15a. In most English translations, there is little apparent connection between the two verses. For instance, the HCSB translates them as follows:

> I said about laughter, "It is madness," and about pleasure, "What does this accomplish?" (2:2)

> So I commended enjoyment because there is nothing better for man under the sun than to eat, drink, and enjoy himself. (8:15a)

You might get the connection in English—"pleasure" and "enjoyment" are certainly related concepts—but in Hebrew you can't miss it.

לִשְׂחוֹק אָמַרְתִּי מְהוֹלָל וּלְשִׂמְחָה מַה־זֹּה עֹשָׂה: (2:2)

וְשִׁבַּחְתִּי אֲנִי אֶת־הַשִּׂמְחָה אֲשֶׁר אֵין־טוֹב לָאָדָם תַּחַת הַשֶּׁמֶשׁ כִּי
אִם־לֶאֱכוֹל וְלִשְׁתּוֹת וְלִשְׂמוֹחַ (8:15a)

Note the clearly repeated word, שִׂמְחָה, which, because of context, the HCSB was forced to translate with two different English terms. The author of Ecclesiastes is challenging you to work out in what sense שִׂמְחָה is good and in what sense it is insufficient, even a distraction from true meaning. And that gets to the core of understanding the book.

How can the author critique "pleasure/enjoyment" in one verse and commend it in a later verse? Ecclesiastes demands the reader wrestle with God's approach to שִׂמְחָה. It is too simple to say that pleasure/joy/enjoyment (pick your English gloss for שִׂמְחָה) is always bad. Christians are not pure ascetics. But it is also too naive to say that pleasure/joy/enjoyment is always good. Christians are also not pure hedonists. Instead, our approach to joy is more nuanced. Ecclesiastes really means for us to find joy in life—God made this world good, good, good, . . . very good, and therefore there is real joy to be had. But Ecclesiastes simultaneously means for us to see the limits of trying to find joy in this life—that even joyful pursuits are meaningless if they become the goal themselves. At the thematic level of the book, Ecclesiastes forces us to wrestle with joy in this life. It reminds us that we do not find joy when we chase it. Instead, we find joy when we chase God (Eccles. 12:13). That overall theme extends down to the very linguistic level of the book—is שִׂמְחָה good or bad? The reader, in Hebrew, is forced to wrestle with that question and therefore brought face-to-face with the themes of Ecclesiastes as a whole.

Develop a Next-Level Memory

Joshua Foer, the author of the *New York Times* bestseller *Moonwalking with Einstein*, tells his own story of how he went from being a journalist covering the USA Memory Championship one year to winning the championship the next year. How did a person with an average memory become a memory champion? Here's how he describes himself:

> My memory was average at best. Among the things I regularly forgot: where I put my car keys (where I put my car, for that matter); the food in the oven; that it's "its" and not "it's"; my girlfriend's birthday, our anniversary, Valentine's Day; the clearance of the doorway to my parents' cellar (ouch); my friends' phone numbers; why I just opened the fridge; to plug in my cell phone; the name of President Bush's chief of staff; the order of the New Jersey Turnpike rest stops; which year the Redskins last won the Super Bowl; to put the toilet seat down.[1]

After one year of practice, how was he able to memorize the 107 first and last names of random faces in fifteen minutes? How was he able to memorize eighty-seven random digits in five minutes, or a

1. Joshua Foer, *Moonwalking with Einstein: The Art and Science of Remembering Everything* (New York: Penguin, 2011), 6.

pack of playing cards in one minute and forty seconds (breaking the US record)? The answer: by employing certain memory techniques.[2]

Some maintain that they would love to learn Hebrew but simply do not have the ability to do so. In other words, they claim that they do not have a good memory. They have a difficult time memorizing lists by rote, and it makes them fearful even to think about such an activity with all the jots and tittles associated with Hebrew. This chapter is designed to alleviate such fears and give you proven strategies for memorization. The first section of this chapter will

> In an interview with Bill Barrick about his time as a Bible translator in Bengal, he was asked, "Some of us are not built for Hebrew and Greek, but we see the great need for translation work. How can we help?"
>
> His answer: "Don't sell yourself short. Believe me, some of you have the ability through the strength of God to do it, if God should call upon you to do it—I'm convinced of that."[a]

address the objection that some people just don't have a good memory. The second section will offer six strategies for how to effectively memorize new material.

How Good Is Your Memory?

In previous eras, memory (along with grammar, logic, and rhetoric) was an essential part of classical education. Today, however, the average person is not skilled in the art of memorization. This change occurred because we are no longer dependent on memorizing information out of necessity. Do you know your parents' or close friend's phone numbers? I don't. It's stored in my contacts list, and so memorizing it is no longer a necessity. Since the invention of the printing press, the need to remember information has steadily declined. We have access to books and websites, all through our personal computers and phones.

Most people have the capacity to memorize new information (including new vocabulary words and vowel changes) but do not have

2. See K. Anders Ericsson, "Exceptional Memorizers: Made, Not Born," *Trends in Cognitive Sciences* 7, no. 6 (2003): 233–35. Ericsson concludes, "This research provides compelling evidence that ordinary people can dramatically improve their memory performance with appropriate strategies and practice" (235).

the training on how to most effectively use their mind to grasp and retain new information. In fact, memorizing new information may be best served by taking the time to discover your learning style. Just because a certain method works best for one person doesn't mean that same memorization strategy will work for you.

Think back through some things you memorized easily that have stuck with you. Perhaps you remember detailed sports stats or musical lyrics. Perhaps you have a work of art emblazoned in your memory from a trip to the local art gallery. Think of something you remember well. Now, consider *how* you memorized those things. Very often, our best memory strategies go unnoticed in our own brains because we don't have to work hard to remember things by using our *best* memory techniques. We are hardwired for that memory strategy or learning style, and so we are not cognizant of even thinking while using it. Perhaps you easily learned song lyrics because a musical verse and regular rhythm makes the words stick. If so, then put your Hebrew paradigms to music. Maybe that piece of art maintains its details in your mind's eye because you're a visual learner and the visual stimulation of the colors in the frame brought delight to the neurons in your brain to solidify that image. If so, then perhaps your memory of Hebrew will work best when you stimulate brain synapses with visual pictures of Hebrew vocabulary or images that correspond to a Hebrew word's meaning. One word that I did this with was נטע,

Figure 4.1

Artwork by Harvey Howell

"to plant." For whatever reason, I remembered this word because the bottom edge of the *ayin* looked to be digging into the ground like a plow, so the farmer could "plant" seeds. It was a visual cue that I remember to this day.[3] The point is, everyone has the capacity to

3. The sketch of the farmer "planting" with נטע (fig. 4.1) is credited to my dad, Harvey Howell. My dad taught visual arts for over thirty years in Tennessee and continues to help me learn Hebrew visually.

memorize new information, but learning *how* to learn may take some effort up front.

As we begin to think of developing a hearty memory, the goal is to get the data from short-term memory to long-term memory. The process of acquiring new information includes three stages: decoding, storage, and retrieval. Because the brain is constantly inundated with new information, much of the information that we receive is not stored. Most information goes into our short-term memory. But if this information is not frequently accessed, the brain thinks that it is not important and so it focuses on other information. One of the best ways of moving information from our short-term to our long-term memory is to access that information on a regular basis through repetition.

> "There is no such thing as a bad memory. . . . There are only trained or untrained memories."
> —Harry Lorayne[b]

If you are uninterested and unengaged in a topic, then it will be difficult to learn. If you convince yourself that Hebrew is not necessary and that you are studying Hebrew only to get a degree, it will prove to be challenging for you. In contrast, if you are interested, excited, and passionate about Hebrew, your study of the language will be aided. The more you are engaged in the material, the quicker you will assimilate it.

Thomas Hyde and James Jenkins conducted a psychology experiment regarding memory in 1969.[4] Their study demonstrated that making meaningful connections with random words helped the participants recall the words more accurately. For example, those told to merely reflect on the pleasantness of a word (getting their emotions involved) had nearly twice the success of those who were told to recognize if the word contained the letter *E*. In other words, if we can relate what we are memorizing to our emotions (as opposed to merely memorizing by rote), the effectiveness of our labor will increase greatly. Emotions can enhance one's memory.

> "Everyone has a great memory for something."
> —Joshua Foer[c]

---

4. See Thomas S. Hyde and James J. Jenkins, "Recall for Words as a Function of Semantic, Graphic, and Syntactic Orienting Tasks," *Journal of Verbal Learning and Verbal Behavior* 12 (1973): 471–80.

It is also good to eat healthy, exercise, and get enough rest. Eating good foods provides the nutrients needed for your brain to function properly. A healthy diet can help produce a healthy mind. It is also important to keep our body healthy through physical exercise. Dominic O'Brien, the eight-time world memory champion, ramped up his exercise training before a memory competition. We tend to be more alert and have more energy when we exercise regularly. Finally, it is also crucial that we get enough rest. This is often a challenge for students who are also working and have other responsibilities. But without adequate rest, it is difficult to be efficient and productive. If you're tired, you will have a hard time concentrating, something that is crucial for memorization.

> - "To be healthy your brain needs you to follow the general principles of a good, healthy lifestyle."
> - "Physical exercise, good nutrition, intellectual stimulation, and making time for relaxation, all play their part in ensuring that you stay mentally pin-sharp."
> - "Sleep is essential for the proper functioning of your memory."
>
> —Dominic O'Brien[d]

Use Mnemonic Devices

A mnemonic device is a memory technique that helps one encode and later recall information. The key is to associate the new material with something you already know. Although this may take a bit more time up front, the payoff is well worth it. Instead of staring at the same words over and over again because they don't "stick," it is much better to invest a little time so that you actually memorize the word the first time you see it. What are the best practices for effectively memorizing information? Below are seven strategies and techniques that have been proven to aid in the memorization process.

Use Your Imagination and Association

As we mentioned, association is one of the key ways to move information from a short-term or working memory into long-term storage. Like other brain processes, association doesn't happen on its own. We have to be proactive and "think about thinking." Use previously existing images and consciously link them with new words or concepts. You must try to relate the new word to words you already know, either in English or in other languages. Think of things that stand out and are unique. They could be silly, crazy, impossible, or absurd. Typically, the more extreme they are, the more effective they will be.

If we don't associate a piece of new information with something we already know, the information will not find a home and will quickly be forgotten. Once it is associated with a clear mental image, however, it has sticking power. The clearer the picture, the more that image is burned into your memory.

A more specific way to use association in Hebrew is to associate the meaning of words with words you've already learned. This type of association can work within a much larger context of words too. We mentioned earlier the similarities between the זבח word family (זָבַח, "he sacrificed"; זֶבַח, "a sacrifice"; and מִזְבֵּחַ, "an altar"). Another example of this is the word מִדְבָּר (wilderness). However, it's not initially what you may think. If you remove the מ from מִדְבָּר, you have the root דבר. Most of us know this root as "to speak." However, Hebrew has a rarer secondary root of דבר that means "to drive out." This is the cognate root for מִדְבָּר. It is the "place of the driving out"

or "the wilderness." This whole context of association works like this. Most people learn דבר (to speak) and מִדְבָּר (wilderness) pretty early in their Hebrew journey. If you throw in the few occurrences of דבר (to drive out), you can more easily remember מִדְבָּר *and* you can remember a more obscure word like דבר (to drive out). At the end of the day, a good deal of memory work can occur by making these associations. Minimally, you can associate new vocabulary words with words you've learned previously.

Use Substitute Words

When learning a new language, it is often difficult to associate words with something you already know—especially if the words represent abstract ideas. One of the most helpful tools is to pronounce the Hebrew term and try to identify English words (or words from other languages you know) that sound similar. Linking a similar-sounding word or phrase in your native language will help you memorize the new word in a foreign language.

> "All memory, whether trained or untrained, is based on association."
>
> —Harry Lorayne and Jerry Lucas[f]

I usually tell students to say the Hebrew word (which requires them to have learned the proper pronunciation first) and then to associate the word with the first thing that comes to their mind. This will often be an odd association, but since we don't always have a pictorial association with a word in Hebrew, the association of the sound of the word will be the next best thing. So, after saying the word, you can make an association based on what you just said. One that I remember from over a decade ago is כָּתַב, meaning "to write." I always enjoyed carpentry work with my dad when I was young, and one of the fond memories I have is of him whittling off the end of a carpenter's pencil. He would "cut off" (which sounds like כָּתַב) the end of the pencil so that we could "write" with it. That may seem odd to you, but *your* associations will seem odd to me. Find the ones that work for you and employ them to the fullest.

Let's try this with another example. The Hebrew word יָשַׁב means "to sit, dwell, settle." When I was learning this set of vocabulary, the first thing that came to my mind was "shoving" someone off the end of a bench in a baseball dugout in order "to sit." Hence, "ya shove" someone over in order "to sit down." I can't tell you where this image came from in my brain or why it popped up at that moment, but to this day I not only remember יָשַׁב but also remember why I remember יָשַׁב. We tend to forget average, everyday things. Thus, the more outrageous the example becomes, the more likely it will stick.

Use Acronyms

An acronym is simply an abbreviation that is formed from the first letter (or letters) in a phrase or word. For example, Tanakh (TNK, תנך) is the acronym for the sections of the Hebrew Bible:

*T*orah (תּוֹרָה), Nevi'im (נְבִיאִים), and *K*etuvim (כְּתוּבִים). The first letter of each word formed a new word. A well-known acronym is used for teaching children the colors of the rainbow: *R*ed, *O*range, *Y*ellow, *G*reen, *B*lue, *I*ndigo, and *V*iolet. When the first letters are put together, we get ROYGBIV. That doesn't look like anything until we see it as someone's name: Roy G. Biv. Today there are thousands of school children who are familiar with and thankful for Mr. Biv for helping them learn the colors of the rainbow.

One example that I use in class helps students memorize the rules associated with how the vowel points change in noun syllables. The grammar that I use for first-year Hebrew focuses heavily on morphology, and I require students to be able to tell me how a vowel will change if it is in a certain syllable of a given word. This method is helpful when we begin adding suffixed elements such as feminine singular or plural, masculine plural suffixes, or pronominal suffixes. The acronyms for these rules are as follows:

CAPL: Closed Accented Prefers Long

OPRL: Open Pretonic Requires Long

CURS: Closed Unaccented Requires Short

OAPS: Open Accented Prefers Short

OOPPS: Original Open ProPretonic [reduces to a] *Shewa*

These are significantly shortened versions of the rules from the textbook, but along with the full explanation in the textbook, these acronyms help students with all of noun morphology. It sounds crazy up front, but I often hear students reciting these acronyms in the hallways at school. Trying to memorize such rules by brute force (rote) is possible but very difficult and time consuming.

Use Silly Stories

The key here, once again, is to associate something that you already know with something that you are learning, or to develop a creative and memorable story or image in your brain that allows you to make the associative jump to long-term memory. One example that I've borrowed is called the Hebrew Love Story.[5] This story works when trying to memorize the various ways that inseparable prepositions (בְּ, לְ, כְּ) attach to the front of a word with an initial *yod*. The most common example I use is the word יְהוּדָה. I teach students that the inseparable prepositions point "normally" with a vocal *shewa* (לְיְהוּדָה). In יְהוּדָה particularly, this construction now leaves two vocal *shewas* at the beginning of a word, which Hebrew doesn't allow. I teach that when we have two *shewas* at the beginning of a word, they "fight." The first *shewa* becomes a short vowel, often a *hireq*, and the second *shewa* becomes silent (לִיְהוּדָה). Now the students can see the beauty of the relationship between a *hireq* and a *yod* that culminates in the historic love relationship known as a *hireq yod* (לִיהוּדָה)!

I usually spice up the story with some reflections on the love between Ruth and Boaz, and so this rule usually becomes the "Boaz" rule. "Add the 'normal' preposition with a vocal *shewa*; engage the *shewa* 'fight'; then let Boaz work his גִּבּוֹר חַיִל magic." Whether students remember the whole story or not, they usually remember that in the Hebrew Bible "to Judah" looks like לִיהוּדָה and not לִיְהוּדָה.

Use English Cognate Terms

In Hebrew, it is difficult to find English cognates since English vocabulary is a melting pot of languages. In addition, our most common cognates in English are not Semitic. Some words find associations, but I'm not sure if they are true cognates. One example is the Hebrew word for "camel," גָּמָל. You can hear some minor similarities, certainly enough to help with memorization, even though its status as a true cognate is questionable. Most dictionaries say the English *camel* is of Semitic origin but that it entered English through Latin.

Another place where cognates can be helpful for learning Hebrew is in names. Many of the Hebrew words we may recognize are in the form of names in English. For example, my name, Adam, is the Hebrew אָדָם, "man." That alone can be helpful for remembering the word. Another one that I remember is the verb נָתַן, "to give." For

---

5. The Hebrew Love Story comes from Russell Fuller and Kyoungwon Choi's introductory Hebrew grammar, *Invitation to Biblical Hebrew: A Beginning Grammar* (Grand Rapids: Kregel, 2006), 35.

some reason when I was learning Hebrew, I saw this word in relation to Benjamin Netanyahu (נְתַנְיָהוּ). His name is a combination of the verb נָתַן, "to give," and the divine name, יהוה. That association alone helped me remember both of these basic vocabulary words. While these are not what I would consider true cognates, they are ways in which something you already know in English can be associated with the new information you're learning in Hebrew so that it is more easily memorized.

We've mentioned already the value of learning Hebrew vocabulary by seeing the relationship between Hebrew words built off the same root. One particular book that groups Hebrew vocabulary according to roots is *Building Your Hebrew Vocabulary: Learning Words by Frequency and Cognate* by George M. Landes.[6] This book organizes vocabulary words by verbal roots *and* in order of frequency. Along with each verbal root, you get nominal cognates to that root that may or may not occur as many times as the verbal root. The value of this arrangement is that you learn the most common verbal roots (on which other vocabulary is built) while you simultaneously learn more obscure vocabulary that would be difficult to remember if learned in isolation from its verbal root. A good example of this is the verbal root עָלָה. I've copied the vocabulary card that I used when learning the vocabulary in Landes's book for my comprehensive exams (see fig. 4.2).[7] One thing you see immediately is the number of cognates related to the verbal root עָלָה. Some of these may be questionable, as Landes admits. The second thing to notice is that some of these nominal and adjectival cognates on the card occur minimally in the Hebrew Bible.[8] These may be words that, if learned independently of the verbal root, would be difficult to associate with something else. However, because of their association with the verbal root, it at least will give

6. George M. Landes, *Building Your Hebrew Vocabulary: Learning Words by Frequency and Cognate* (Atlanta: Society of Biblical Literature, 2001).
7. The card images displayed here were created for personal study, but the definitions come verbatim from Landes, *Building Your Hebrew Vocabulary*, 50.
8. Landes lists the number of occurrences of the cognates in the book, but they were not transferred over to the cards we used.

Figure 4.2

500~ (17)

עָלָה

1 עַל	2 עַל־כֵּן	3 עֹלָה
4 מַעַל	5 עֶלְיוֹן	6 מַעֲלָה
7 עֲלִיָּה	8 מַעֲלֶה	9 עָלֶה
		10 תְּעָלָה

to ascend, go up; (Hi.) to lead up or out, bring up

1. (prep.) on, over; in front of, before; above, more than; on account of; concerning; against; to, towards; (conj.) because
2. therefore, for that reason
3. sacrifice that is wholly burned, burnt offering
4. (prep.) above, on top of; (adv.) upwards
5. something that is higher, upper; as divine epithet: most high
6. upward movement (of people), ascent; (pl.) pilgrimages; step, stair
7. upper room
8. rising, ascent, climb; podium, platform
9. leaf, foliage
10. watercourse; conduit, channel

you something to which you can connect these potentially obscure nominal cognates.

Use the Method of Loci (Memory Palace)

This particular method of memorization, called *loci* ("places" in Latin), is employed by all the top mnemonists (those who study and

"While a plausible argument can be mounted for learning the vocabulary of Biblical Hebrew solely by frequency arrangements, it has been my experience that the task is somewhat easier when one can see the words in groupings that show their etymological relationships, thus providing a helpful mnemonic device for learning how cognate words are meaningfully linked."

—George M. Landes[g]

practice the art of memorization). The origin of this technique, at least according to legend, goes back to the Greek poet Simonides of Ceos in the fifth century BC. The story states that after he delivered an ode in honor of a nobleman, he was summoned outside the grand banquet hall by two young men on horseback. At the precise moment that he crossed the threshold, the entire building collapsed and everyone inside was killed. Foer explains, "As the poet closed his eyes and reconstructed the crumbled building in his imagination, he had an extraordinary realization: He remembered where each of the guests at the ill-fated dinner had been sitting. Even though he had made no conscious effort to memorize the layout of the room, it had nevertheless left a durable impression upon his memory. From that simple observation, Simonides reputedly invented a technique that would form the basis of what came to be known as the art of memory."[9]

Things that we can see with our mind are easy to memorize. With this technique a person envisions a building (house or palace) or even a route and then places objects to be remembered in various rooms (or along a path). These objects are not usually average or ordinary but are exaggerated, or something abnormal is associated with them. The person places these objects in the house in a particular order that is followed every time. To recall these items, the person then goes room by room through the house seeing the items that were placed there. Foer states, "The idea is to create a space in the mind's eye, a place that you know well and can easily visualize, and then populate that imagined place with images representing whatever you want to remember."[10]

9. Foer, *Moonwalking with Einstein*, 94.
10. Foer, *Moonwalking with Einstein*, 96.

The memory palace can be organized as simply or as complexly as needed to accomplish the goal. For some, a memory "palace" can be made with only one "room/setting" that associates a certain word with its surroundings. If you're working to memorize the word for "wilderness" (מִדְבָּר), perhaps your memory palace can be something as simple as imagining Israel wan-
dering around in הַמִּדְבָּר (the wilderness) for

> "Memory is primarily an imaginative process."
> —Tony Buzan[h]

forty years. If you remember the word "wilderness" by envisioning a *bear* (pronounced with a Southern accent, "bār") in the *mid*dle of the wilderness, then you can now imagine a bear walking around alongside Israel in הַמִּדְבָּר (the wilderness). Make it even more memorable; make it a polar bear. Your memory palace doesn't have to be elaborate to be effective. The goal is to make it personal and make it memorable.

As an example, let's say you need to learn the words יָשַׁב (to sit), כָּתַב (to write), מִדְבָּר (wilderness), and מִלְחָמָה (battle). First, you will need to develop mnemonic devices to help you remember the English glosses of these words. As you build this "palace," imagine the wilderness again, and you know there is a bear in the wilderness because that is how you memorized the word. At this point, you don't see the bear though. The word for "battle," מִלְחָמָה, has the word לֶחֶם (bread) in the middle of it. These words are not related except that you remember that you are willing to get into a "battle" over "bread" (your mnemonic device). As you approach the people of Israel in the wilderness (מִדְבָּר), knowing the bear is near, you sense grumbling from the people because there is no bread. To make matters worse, you visit Joshua's Sandwich Shop, but there are no seats, so "ya shove" (יָשַׁב) Enoch off his chair so you can "sit down." The waitress comes over to take your order, but her pencil is broken. When learning the word כָּתַב, you imagined a flat carpenter pencil that forced you to "cut off" the end of it to sharpen it so that you could "write" with it. The waitress recognizes her need to "cut off" (כָּתַב) the end of the pencil so she can "write" your order, but then the bear arrives at Joshua's Sandwich Shop too. Noticing that there is only one loaf of bread left in the shop, you "battle" (מִלְחָמָה) with the bear over the last loaf.

You can see that it doesn't take long before you have a fairly elaborate picture in your mind, and you are able to continue to add to and reconstruct your "palace" (city or room) around new vocabulary you add to your repertoire. The images need to be clear in your mind. As you seek to recall these words at a later time, you simply walk through the "palace" or story seeing all the images that you have created.

Another way to apply the memory palace logic is to associate the picture in your mind with the context of a story in the Hebrew Bible. Rather than making up a story in your mind, you begin to fit the Hebrew vocabulary into their already-existing biblical contexts.

> "The more vivid the image, the more likely it is to cleave to its locus."
> —Joshua Foer[i]

As I mentioned before, when I'm pronouncing vocabulary for first-year students, I will tell them, "This is the word used in the Bible when . . ." and then give a biblical context with which they are familiar so that they can associate that word with that setting in their mind's eye. It never fails that nearly half the class nods their heads in affirmation once they've made that connection. The more you can connect your memory palace to already established pictures in your mind, the better new elements added to the palace will stick.

Use an Alternative Method of Loci

While talking with some friends, I've discovered another method for memorizing Hebrew vocabulary that is similar to the memory palace in that you develop a "storyboard" in your mind that you can return to time and again in order to memorize vocabulary words.[11]

In this method, the first step is to associate a "story" with each letter of the Hebrew alphabet. Each of these stories must be just one simple sentence with a subject, verb, and object. For example, א may be assigned the sentence "Ox pulling a plow." ב is assigned "Belle singing into microphone." The goal is to associate a sentence with a

---

11. I learned about this alternative method of *loci* while talking to one of my Hebrew students, Richi Hofer. He pointed me to the student who told him about it, Joel Bell, who subsequently pointed me to Daniel Wilson as the source of this memory technique associated specifically with Hebrew. I've corresponded with Daniel via email to get the details of this method, and his ideas are presented here with permission. The examples given in this section are all Richi Hofer's personal examples.

subject, verb, and object to each letter of the Hebrew alphabet. The key for this method to work is to memorize these one-sentence "stories." This method takes some time to set up, but once you have these one-sentence stories memorized, the power of this method starts to take shape. Because the key is memorizing these one-sentence stories, I would encourage you to make them all your own rather than using someone else's.

After memorizing these sentences for each letter of the Hebrew alphabet, you can begin to apply these stories to any triliteral root in the Hebrew Bible. This method is quite effective for learning Hebrew verbal roots since many roots are based on a triliteral word. Let's look at the word עבד as an example. Each letter of the root has a particular sentence that you've already associated in your mind. ע is "Pelican eating fish." ב is "Belle singing into microphone." ד is "Dwight speaking to crowd." These are odd, sometimes weird, and uniquely yours. There is no standard for what sentence has to be associated with a particular letter for this technique to work. After associating the sentences with the Hebrew letters, you will take the *subject* of the sentence for the first letter of the vocabulary word, the *verb* for the second root letter, and the *object* for the third root letter to create a new sentence that is exclusive to this triliteral root. Here's how it lays out:

Pelican (subject) eating fish.	ע
Belle **singing** (verb) into microphone.	ב
Dwight speaking **to crowd** (object).	ד
New sentence: "Pelican singing to the crowd."	עבד

Now that you have created this new sentence that is uniquely related to the triliteral root, the creativity has to kick in again. You take that sentence and make a story associated with the meaning of the triliteral root. For this example, my student remembered, "Pelican singing to the crowd because he is *serving* them."

I realize that after all that, you may wonder if it is worth it. Those who have used this method would say it is. Think about how to remember homonyms, like עבד and אבד. Since you have a different one-sentence "story" associated with אַ and עַ, you have a unique mental image of an ox singing to the crowd for אבד and a pelican singing to the crowd for עבד. Because the mental image you assign the ox singing to the crowd will be different from the pelican singing to the crowd, you will likely be able to remember the difference between these homonyms. Another place where this method can be helpful is with obscure or rare words. You may not encounter these words very often, and so remembering their meanings will prove difficult. However, if you can always go through and associate your sentences and stories to the triliteral root, you will then discover again your unique story associated with that particular root and be ever closer to remembering the meaning of the word. Like most memory techniques, this one takes some diligent creativity up front. But again, once you've put in the preliminary work, this method can work its magic.

These techniques are merely tools to gain proficiency in Biblical Hebrew. Although it will still take planning, practice, and perseverance, using these methods will make the acquisition of Hebrew easier (and perhaps more enjoyable). Everyone has the God-given capacity to memorize new material, even languages! Let's tap into our ability and use it to learn the language of the Old Testament.

─────────────── **Chapter Reflections** ───────────────

1. On a scale of 1–10, how would you rate your memory?

2. Are your eating and sleeping patterns conducive for fostering a good memory? If not, what needs to change?

3. What mnemonic devices do you find the most intriguing?

4. What would it look like for you to employ all the memory techniques in this chapter?

5. Choose three to five Hebrew words and see if you can come up with a way to memorize those words by using the memory palace technique.

Asyndeton and Discourse Grammar

Peter J. Gentry

———————————○———————————

Discourse grammar describes grammatical relations above the boundary of the clause or between sentences in a discourse or text. Asyndeton, a recognized feature of discourse grammar, comes from a word in Greek: *deton* means "bound," *syn* means "together," and *a* means "not." So putting all three morphemes together, asyndeton means "not bound together." Normally, clauses or sentences in texts are connected by particles called conjunctions. In Hebrew literature, almost all clauses or sentences begin with *vav* (and). The conjunction *vav* joins two things at the same grammatical level. So clauses or sentences in a discourse are normally joined by *vav*. When a clause or sentence has no connector or conjunction, we call this situation asyndeton, "not bound together" by the *vav* connector.

According to Stephen G. Dempster, who pioneered discourse grammar study of Biblical Hebrew, asyndeton is quite rare and consequently is noteworthy for the hearer or reader.[12] It functions to mark two things: (1) the beginning of a section or sequence of clauses, much like indentation marks the beginning of a new paragraph; or (2) a clause that functions as a comment on or explanation of the previous sentence.

The first clause in Genesis 1:1 is *not* prefixed by *vav*. This case of asyndeton is marking a new beginning—in fact, it marks the first paragraph or section in the entire text.

We can also see asyndeton in Genesis 1:27. The verse contains three clauses or sentences: (1) and God created man in his image; (2) in the image of God he created him; and (3) male and female he created them. The first sentence has a normal clause pattern: verb-subject-object (וַיִּבְרָא אֱלֹהִים | אֶת־הָאָדָם). The conjunction *vav* is used, and the verb is a *vav*-consecutive imperfect—all standard in Hebrew narrative. The remaining two sentences have a different

---

12. Stephen G. Dempster, "Linguistic Features of Hebrew Narrative: A Discourse Analysis of Narrative from the Classical Period" (PhD diss., University of Toronto, 1985).

clause pattern: modifier-verb-object (זָכָר אֹתוֹ בָּרָא אֱלֹהִים בְּצֶלֶם
אֹתָם בָּרָא וּנְקֵבָה:). Both are also asyndetic—that is, not connected
by the conjunction *vav*; both verbs are perfects. This is a clear discourse grammar signal with pragmatic significance: these clauses
do not advance the narrative but digress and pause to comment on
the first clause in the verse. These two short sentences are grammatically marked as circumstantial information or parenthetical
remarks. The author is *digressing from* the narrative to stress two
particular aspects or features of the creation of humankind. In other
words, the last two clauses are footnotes dealing with the first clause
or sentence:

A. Humankind resembles God in some way.
B. Human sexuality is binary and entails two distinct genders,
   male and female.

By pausing to stress these two things, the author prepares us for
the two commands given to humankind in the very next verse:

A. Be fruitful (three imperatives in Hebrew).
B. Rule over the other creatures (two imperatives in Hebrew).

The actual literary presentation is chiastic in structure. The word
chiasm comes from the letter in the Greek alphabet known as *chi* (χ),
which is shaped like an X. The top half of the letter has a mirror image
in the bottom half. If, for example, a literary piece has four distinct
units and the first matches the last while the second matches the
third, the result is a mirror image, a chiasm. The following diagram
illustrates the chiastic structure of the Genesis passage:

> God created mankind in his image
> > according to his likeness:
> > > A   in the image of God he created him
> > > > B   male and female he created them
> > > > B′   be fruitful and increase in number and fill the
> > > > earth
> > > A′   and subdue it
> > and rule over the fish/birds/animals

Thus, binary sexuality (i.e., duality of gender) is the basis for being fruitful, while the divine image is correlated with the command to rule as God's viceroy. These observations from the discourse grammar of the narrative are crucial. They are decisive in showing that the divine image is *not* to be explained by or located in terms of binary sexuality in humanity.[13]

Asyndeton is also crucial in interpreting the difficult passage in Genesis 6:1–4.

> When man began to multiply on the face of the land and daughters were born to them, the sons of God saw that the daughters of man were attractive. And they took as their wives any they chose. Then the Lord said, "My Spirit shall not abide in man forever, for he is flesh: his days shall be 120 years." The Nephilim were on the earth in those days, and also afterward, when the sons of God came in to the daughters of man and they bore children to them. These were the mighty men who were of old, the men of renown. (ESV)

Note that verse 4 contains two sentences, one verbal (followed by a long relative clause) and one verbless:

הַנְּפִלִים הָיוּ בָאָרֶץ בַּיָּמִים הָהֵם וְגַם אַחֲרֵי־כֵן אֲשֶׁר יָבֹאוּ בְּנֵי הָאֱלֹהִים
אֶל־בְּנוֹת הָאָדָם וְיָלְדוּ לָהֶם הֵמָּה הַגִּבֹּרִים אֲשֶׁר מֵעוֹלָם אַנְשֵׁי הַשֵּׁם:

These mark a new paragraph and a comment on verses 1–3.

The temporal expressions "in those times" and "afterward" are significant. Two main possibilities exist for interpretation of these expressions. If one interprets "those times" to be the times described

---

13. As, for example, in the exposition of M. Smith: "The creation of the human person involves male and female. . . . The imagery of the human in terms of the Divine in Genesis 1 seems to assume a divine couple, male and female, since the human person is created in the image of the Divine, partaking of both maleness and femaleness." M. Smith, "God Male and Female in the Old Testament: Yahweh and His 'Asherah,'" *Theological Studies* 48 (1987): 339. Earlier, Karl Barth promoted an approach to the divine image also based on the duality of gender. Karl Barth, *Church Dogmatics*, III/1, authorized trans. J. W. Edwards, O. Bussey, and Harold Knight (Edinburgh: T&T Clark, 1958), 186; and Barth, *Church Dogmatics*, III/2, authorized trans. Harold Knight, G. W. Bromiley, J. K. Reid, and R. H. Fuller (Edinburgh: T&T Clark, 1960), 203.

in verses 1–3, then what is distinguished are the times before the flood from the times after the flood. The relative clause introduced by "afterward" would seem to indicate that the cohabitation of the sons of God and the daughters of humans continued after the flood. One might possibly conclude that the Nephilim were the product of such unions (cf. Num. 13:22, 28, 33).

Yet a different interpretation is possible. The expression "afterward" (אַחֲרֵי־כֵן) usually occurs in the second of two verbal sentences: the first sentence says that event X did or will happen; the second says that subsequent to the event in the first sentence, event Y did or will happen.[14] Here we must note that the expression אַחֲרֵי־כֵן is modified by a relative sentence that refers specifically to the event in verse 2.[15] Therefore one could assume that "those days" means before the cohabitation of divine and human beings. Verse 4 would then comment that the Nephilim were in the earth before the business of angelic and human beings cohabiting and also afterward and therefore had nothing to do with these unions.

This latter interpretation is strengthened by considerations of discourse grammar. Verse 4 consists of two clauses or sentences, the first verbal, the second verbless. Both are marked by asyndeton (i.e., no conjunction or connector at the beginning of the clause/sentence). In the first, the verb is non-initial, meaning the subject occurs before the verb. This pattern marks a commentary or explanatory digression. The fact that the first sentence is subject initial indicates a new topic. The relative sentence in verse 4 correlates this new topic with the events of verse 2. The verbless clause is a further comment on the Nephilim. They were the heroes from the distant past. This may mean the distant past with reference to the writer, or it may indicate a period long past in reference to the event of 6:2. Therefore the writer would be demythologizing the Nephilim. These heroes of ancient times were there before and after the events of 6:2 and were not necessarily related to them at all. Thus, verse 1 describes

14. Although this pattern is standard or usual, it is not the only kind of construction, as Gen. 41:31 shows.

15. This is apparently the only occurrence of אַחֲרֵי־כֵן where it is modified by a relative sentence. BDB adduces 2 Chron. 35:20, but the parallel is not exact or compelling.

an increase in female humans, verse 2 describes a cohabitation of angelic and human beings, and verse 3 concludes that the result is still human and therefore under God's judgment, while verse 4 states that all this has nothing to do with the well-known Nephilim. Since the word *Nephilim* is not otherwise explained, they must have been well known to the ancient (first) readers of this text.

If Jewish writers in the Second Temple period had properly understood the discourse grammar of their sacred texts, already one thousand years old, they would not have produced their speculations about Genesis 6:1–4 in the Enochic traditions.[16]

16. See Peter J. Gentry and Andrew M. Fountain, "Reassessing Jude's Use of Enochic Traditions (with Notes on Their Later Reception History)," *Tyndale Bulletin* 68, no. 2 (2017): 261–86.

Strategically Leverage
Your Breaks

We have a section of our yard where the kids play kickball or baseball constantly in the summer. Home plate, the pitcher's mound, and the bases are all well established, primarily because those are grassless patches. Last spring, I tilled the ground and planted new grass. We (I) had to nurture and care for these new plots of grass. We (I) had to water them and keep harmful creatures (my children) off the "baby grass" as we called it. One particular week it rained incessantly, so the new grass was both watered and relieved of the Canaanites stomping all over it. After that week, I looked out at the grass, and it was thick and lush because it had been nurtured (by God himself!). We want the results of your efforts to maintain and improve your Hebrew to be "thick and lush" like those baby grass patches in my yard.

Like new grass, houseplants need water, or they will die. If you neglect your Hebrew, your knowledge will also wither, oftentimes faster than you would like. Hebrew students can draw wisdom from the many studies that have been done on elementary school children's reading loss during the summer months. Amazingly, a child who reads *only four or five books* over the course of the summer has no decline in reading-achievement scores.[1] In fact, the children of more involved (and usually affluent) parents make small gains in reading over the summer months, according to studies.[2]

Below are listed the factors that help many kids preserve their reading ability over the summer. For the remainder of this chapter, we will explore these dynamics with specific application to keeping one's Hebrew.

- *Accountability.* Some parents (the more involved ones) provide the resources (books) and accountability (incentives, disincentives) their children need to keep reading over the summer. Good accountability can be hard to swallow at times because it keeps us moving toward a specific goal even if we may want to let that goal slip. As adults, we will have to set up accountability structures for ourselves to learn and retain Hebrew, rather than having our parents set them up for us.
- *A Plan.* Specific written plans help children accomplish reading goals. At my (Rob's) children's school, the summer begins for younger students with a list of "required" and "optional" books and a clear expectation of how many books should be read over the summer.
- *Realistic Goals.* Setting the bar too high discourages students and can cause them to give up. Hebrew is already intimidating enough. We should work to establish realistic goals, and once a few minor goals are accomplished, we'll be motivated to set more elaborate goals down the road.
- *Enjoyment.* Students who enjoy reading read more. If you're a parent, you've likely seen the moment where a child crosses over from doing reading as a chore to reading as a pathway to adventure. It is a bit different analogy, but we will often read to our kids in the evenings. When we first began The Wingfeather Saga by Andrew Peterson, the kids would

1. So reports James Kim of the Harvard Graduate School of Education, who is referenced in Annie Murphy Paul, "Do Kids Really Have 'Summer Learning Loss'?," *Time*, July 1, 2013, http://ideas.time.com/2013/07/01/do-kids-really-have-summer-learning-loss/.
2. Paul, "Do Kids Really Have 'Summer Learning Loss'?"

grumble when we would get the book out and begin reading. It was a chore for them to sit and listen to several short
chapters. However, as the story began to develop and we read
with more consistency, they began to beg for more chapters
to be read each evening. It helped that nearly every chapter
was a cliffhanger, and my wife and I began to see our children actually *enjoy* the story.

- *Competition.* Everyone knows how much fun it is to participate in a summer reading program where there are prizes and
  awards. My children participate in the public library's summer
  reading competition so that they can enter to win any number
  of cool prizes. They get a ticket for each milestone they reach,
  and they can put that ticket into a bucket for a drawing of
  various prizes. A behemoth Lego set is a remarkable motivator
  for an eleven-year-old! What reward(s) will motivate you as
  you set up competitions with your peers to learn Hebrew?

- *Community.* The local library has a party at the end of the
  summer to celebrate students' successes at reading. Even as
  adults, we know how much more likely it is that we finish a
  book and enjoy it when we read it in community.

We will now apply these principles to the maintaining of Hebrew
skills over extended breaks between academic semesters. Of course,

"Another result when pastors do not study the Bible in Greek and Hebrew is that they, and their churches with them, tend to become second-handers. The harder it is for us to get at the original meaning of the Bible, the more we will revert to the secondary literature. For one thing, it is easier to read. It also gives us a superficial glow that we are 'keeping up' on things. And it provides us with ideas and insights which we can't dig out of the original for ourselves.

We may impress one another for a while by dropping the name of the latest book we've read, but secondhand food will not sustain and deepen our people's faith and holiness.

Weakness in Greek and Hebrew also gives rise to exegetical imprecision and carelessness. And exegetical imprecision is the mother of liberal theology."

—John Piper[a]

these principles equally apply to the long-lasting "postgraduation break" (also known as "real life").

Accountability

Before we consider accountability during a break, we need to think about the state of students entering that break—the mental, emotional, and spiritual realities of the students headed into a hiatus. Students are often weary after a long semester, and the excitement of engaging a new language may have waned significantly since week one of the semester. As a teacher of Hebrew, I join other language professors in two main objectives: (1) to take students successfully to the appropriate language competency level and (2) to infect them with my passion for the Hebrew Bible. If you are a professor and have fallen prey to just going through the motions (lecturing from twenty-year-old notes with no new input or passion), then consider what it may take to reignite your initial joys in Hebrew! Otherwise you may be missing your calling and injuring young souls. If you are a student whose teacher is perhaps not instructing or inspiring you effectively, you must supplement your own Hebrew diet. Don't blame a slothful professor for your lack of Hebrew joy, but seek out a more balanced diet of inspiration that you are not currently receiving. Reading through this book will point you to many outside resources that can complement your current Hebrew education so that your end-of-semester burnout can transition into the delight of reading God's word in the original Hebrew.

While one piece of this discussion is recognizing the reality of your emotional state at the end of a semester, the other factor is knowing that you will not likely pursue the joy of reading Hebrew without some accountability structure in place. You may need friends to come alongside you and ask you about your progress. You may need a reading group that is going to work through a few verses each Saturday morning. Whatever that strategy may be, in order to enjoy Hebrew, you must *actually read Hebrew*! For many of us, accountability is necessary in order to reach that level of delight.

So, accountability for the summer (or winter) must reflect the skill and passion of the student entering the break. If skill and passion are lacking, accountability becomes more difficult. It's unlikely that a new runner will faithfully train for a race if he or she has only read about other people's passion for running. I personally have never experienced the mystical "runner's high." That's largely because I have never disciplined myself through accountability structures to run long enough to warrant the release of endorphins associated with this physiological phenomenon. That's not running's fault. That's my fault! If we are going to experience a "reader's high" in Hebrew, we must put ourselves under accountability structures that will move us closer and closer to the desired goal of delight in the Hebrew Bible, and these structures must begin at our current skill level.

There are two main types of accountability: (1) accountability that is authoritatively imposed from the outside and (2) accountability that is self-imposed. We will consider these two categories in succession.

Formal Accountability

Hebrew teachers should make use of class structures, as well as incentives and disincentives, to encourage students to read and study Hebrew during the breaks. Below are some recommended formalized or institutionalized forms of accountability:

- In *quizzes, exams, or other assignments* at the end of the semester, the teacher should ask the students a pointed question: "What specifically are you going to do to keep up with your Hebrew over the break?" Before this question is posed, the professor should have provided some options for how to keep up Hebrew so that students already have concrete ways in their mind to make this happen. If a professor doesn't give these concrete methods ahead of time, it is likely the majority of responses will be a vague, "I'm going to read Hebrew." Make the question worth enough points that students have to develop a substantive answer.
- The professor may give an *assigned paper* in which students are required to map out in detail their plans for staying in Hebrew over the break. Part of the assignment can include

filling in an actual calendar with specific reading plans or
goals. Anything you can do so that the outcome is a clearly
articulated and mapped-out plan will be helpful.

- Students can be *guided in a visualization* of their future lives.
Coaches and advisers in sports, finances, and employment all
testify that visualization methods help people to meet their
goals. Both negative and positive visualization are beneficial.
Thus, for example, the professor can guide students through
visualizing the day that they will be able to open their Hebrew Bibles and simply read, enjoying the language with
all its rich expression. Or the day that they will encounter a
theological or textual conundrum and be able to confidently
open the Hebrew Bible and interact with theological arguments because of their Hebrew competence. Studies have
shown that students with self-efficacy expectations achieve
increased academic success and they persist longer in their
desired field.[3] In other words, if students can visualize the
positive effectiveness of their future use of Hebrew, they
may be more motivated to dive in deeper during their formal
training *and* continue their learning after graduation. When
our goals and desires align with Scripture, we can rightly ask
God to give us lasting vision and perseverance to accomplish
those goals. We can pray, "God, help me to envision a life of
faithful stewardship for the Hebrew instruction and skills
you have allowed me to have."

- The teacher can *pair up students* (or require them to find a
partner) and give them a formalized assignment to check in
with each other weekly over the break. (Such checking in can
be a text, email, or phone call, documented on a standardized worksheet.) As an added incentive, a teacher can offer
an upward adjustment in students' final grades for those
who successfully complete an entire summer (or winter) of
Hebrew-reading accountability. Students can be required to

---

3. E.g., Robert W. Lent, Steven D. Brown, and Kevin C. Larkin, "Relation of
Self-Efficacy Expectations to Academic Achievement and Persistence," *Journal of
Counseling Psychology* 31, no. 3 (1984): 356–62.

submit a record of their work with their accountability partner's affirmation of their faithfulness.

- Most online course management systems (e.g., Canvas,
  Blackboard, Edmodo) allow teachers to *continue communi-
  cating with students* even after the class has formally ended.
  We recommend teachers send a "continue with Hebrew"
  email two weeks after a class ends, another email two weeks
  later, and then another a month later. The email should
  be a short and simple plea for students to not forgo what
  they worked so hard to achieve—with perhaps one specific
  exhortation. A little humor can go a long way in helping
  students favorably receive these email reminders. Perhaps
  the professor can make a fake testimonial video of a former
  student with a bag over his head confessing his shame in
  apostatizing from the language. I (Rob) regularly employ
  puppets in videos for my students (and yes, they are graduate students).

- For students who are continuing with another Hebrew
  class, they can be reminded throughout the summer that
  their next course will *begin with a quiz over the previous
  material*. It's amazing how motivating grades can be. If students know they will fail an upcoming quiz without review,
  they somehow find time to review. One of our (Rob's and
  Adam's) colleagues, Tom Schreiner, has the reputation of
  beginning his upper-level Greek exegesis course on Romans
  with a translation quiz on a passage randomly drawn from
  the letter. In other words, he is setting a very high entry bar.
  Essentially, he is saying, "On the first day of class, you need
  at least a superficial knowledge of the Greek from the entire
  book of Romans. You should be able to sight-translate from
  the book (with rare vocabulary given to you). We will spend
  the rest of the semester delving through the grammatical
  and theological complexities of the book." One might
  think that setting the bar this high would scare off students,
  but every time Schreiner offers his Romans class, it fills to
  maximum capacity. Paradoxically, just as churches with high
  membership requirements are growing much faster than

those churches with no membership requirements, so having high expectations for students seems to be better than having lower ones.

- Perhaps drawing from some of the suggestions in this book, a teacher may choose to give a *detailed reading plan to students*. If a teacher prefers one particular "summer reader" (see below), he or she may go ahead and list that volume as one of the required textbooks. The professor can get students started in the book, providing them with a schedule to finish it over the break. Students generally find it easier to continue a plan they have already started as opposed to starting one from scratch. Figure 5.1 provides an example of a detailed reading plan. I will explain more about this reading plan later in the chapter, but you can at least see the idea now.

Self-Imposed Accountability

If a teacher does not formally impose accountability to keep students in the Hebrew language, or if students have graduated, it will be necessary for the Hebrew students to impose accountability on themselves. Warning—the cliché is true: "The road to failure is paved with good intentions." You may sincerely say, "I plan to read my Hebrew Bible every day," but without accountability, you are likely to fail. Below is a list of suggestions for informal or self-imposed accountability:

- *Sign up for the daily reminders* via email, tweet, or Facebook post at www.dailydoseofhebrew.com. Discipline yourself to watch your daily Hebrew video before you read any other emails or tweets.
- After you commit to a specific reading or study plan (see below), *post a record of your performance* in a prominent public place. Don't get crazy and humblebrag on the internet about how much of the Hebrew Bible you're reading each day. Perhaps you just hang a reading chart on your fridge so that your family or roommate(s) can see it and hold you accountable to reading. If several days go by and everyone

Figure 5.1

Hebrew for Life Summer Reading Plans

Accountability Partner: _____

Accountability Partner's Signature: _____

Day	Jonah	Ruth	Deuteronomy	Day	Jonah	Ruth	Deuteronomy
June 1	1:1–5	1:1–5	1:1–5	July 12	4:5–9	2:20–3:1	1:42–46
June 2	1:2–6	1:2–6	1:2–6	July 13	4:6–10	2:21–3:2	6:1–5
June 3	1:3–7	1:3–7	1:3–7	July 14	4:7–11	2:22–3:3	6:2–6
June 4	1:4–8	1:4–8	1:4–8	July 15	chap. 1	2:23–3:4	6:3–7
June 5	1:5–9	1:5–9	1:5–9	July 16	chap. 2	3:1–5	6:4–8
June 6	1:6–10	1:6–10	1:6–10	July 17	chap. 3	3:2–6	6:5–9
June 7	1:7–11	1:7–11	1:7–11	July 18	chap. 4	3:3–7	6:6–10
June 8	1:8–12	1:8–12	1:8–12	July 19		3:4–8	6:7–11
June 9	1:9–13	1:9–13	1:9–13	July 20		3:5–9	6:8–12
June 10	1:10–14	1:10–14	1:10–14	July 21		3:6–10	6:9–13
June 11	1:11–15	1:11–15	1:11–15	July 22		3:7–11	6:10–14
June 12	1:12–16	1:12–16	1:12–16	July 23		3:8–12	6:11–15
June 13	1:13–2:1	1:13–17	1:13–17	July 24		3:9–13	6:12–16
June 14	1:14–2:2	1:14–18	1:14–18	July 25		3:10–14	6:13–17
June 15	1:15–2:3	1:15–19	1:15–19	July 26		3:11–15	6:14–18
June 16	1:16–2:4	1:16–20	1:16–20	July 27		3:12–16	6:15–19
June 17	2:1–5	1:17–21	1:17–21	July 28		3:13–17	6:16–20
June 18	2:2–6	1:18–22	1:18–22	July 29		3:14–18	6:17–21
June 19	2:3–7	1:19–2:1	1:19–23	July 30		3:15–4:1	6:18–22
June 20	2:4–8	1:20–2:2	1:20–24	July 31		3:16–4:2	6:19–23
June 21	2:5–9	1:21–2:3	1:21–25	Aug. 1		3:17–4:3	6:20–24
June 22	2:6–10	1:22–2:4	1:22–26	Aug. 2		3:18–4:4	6:21–25
June 23	2:7–11	2:1–5	1:23–27	Aug. 3		4:1–5	
June 24	2:8–3:1	2:2–6	1:24–28	Aug. 4		4:2–6	
June 25	2:9–3:2	2:3–7	1:25–29	Aug. 5		4:3–7	
June 26	2:10–3:3	2:4–8	1:26–30	Aug. 6		4:4–8	
June 27	2:11–3:4	2:5–9	1:27–31	Aug. 7		4:5–9	
June 28	3:1–5	2:6–10	1:28–32	Aug. 8		4:6–10	
June 29	3:2–6	2:7–11	1:29–33	Aug. 9		4:7–11	
June 30	3:3–7	2:8–12	1:30–34	Aug. 10		4:8–12	
July 1	3:4–8	2:9–13	1:31–35	Aug. 11		4:9–13	
July 2	3:5–9	2:10–14	1:32–36	Aug. 12		4:10–14	
July 3	3:6–10	2:11–15	1:33–37	Aug. 13		4:11–15	
July 4	3:7–4:1	2:12–16	1:34–38	Aug. 14		4:12–16	
July 5	3:8–4:2	2:13–17	1:35–39	Aug. 15		4:13–17	
July 6	3:9–4:3	2:14–18	1:36–40	Aug. 16		4:14–18	
July 7	3:10–4:4	2:15–19	1:37–41	Aug. 17		4:15–19	
July 8	4:1–5	2:16–20	1:38–42	Aug. 18		4:16–20	
July 9	4:2–6	2:17–21	1:39–43	Aug. 19		4:17–21	
July 10	4:3–7	2:18–22	1:40–44	Aug. 20		4:18–22	
July 11	4:4–8	2:19–23	1:41–45				

in the household sees that you're not checking off boxes, chances are they will ask you if you are still reading. If you have your reading list tucked away somewhere safe from public view, there's no way for someone to easily hold you accountable to that plan. It will help you to know others will see that sheet.

- *Make a formal commitment to another Christian* about your reading or study plan and schedule specific expected communication to keep you accountable. It is not enough to say, "Please keep me accountable." You need to say something like, "Will you please schedule a reminder on your phone for every Friday afternoon? I'd like you to send me a text every Friday. Please ask specifically where I have failed to meet my Hebrew reading goals. I hate to be a pest, but would you schedule it right now while we are talking?" Be specific, and be persistent. Maybe you would join forces with another classmate and you both set the reminder on your phones to hold one another accountable to reading. Perhaps you have another local pastor with whom you can make this treaty. Find someone you know who has a similar desire to enjoy Hebrew, and hold each other accountable.

- *Employ strong incentives and disincentives* to stay with your reading plan. For example, if you stay with your reading plan all summer, give yourself permission to completely goof off one day and eat at whatever restaurant you want. Weekly incentives or disincentives may work better—a soft-serve ice-cream cone on weeks that you stay with your plan, for example. As a disincentive, maybe you commit not to watch any baseball if you haven't maintained your reading plan for that day/week. For even more immediate rewards, you could allow yourself a peanut M&M or Skittle for every verse you translate. We do this at our house during homeschool days, but with Nerds (and yes, they're tiny, so a little box goes a long way!). Or, don't eat breakfast, have a cup of coffee, or get on your phone until you've read Hebrew for ten minutes. Tell your roommates or parents that if you fail to stay on your reading plan, you must clean the bathroom or empty the cat's litter box that week. I guarantee they will hold you accountable!

A Plan

Every late December, nearly all media outlets discuss how to keep your New Year's resolutions. It turns out that one of the key ingredients in successfully keeping one's resolutions is adopting clear and measurable goals. What's true for New Year's resolutions more generally applies directly to keeping your Hebrew. Here is a basic truth that will change your life: *write down* your Hebrew plan with undeniable, measurable specificity. Write it down. Write it down. Write it down. Then, have a method of regularly reminding yourself of that commitment (an automated reminder on your phone, for example, or a handwritten card taped to the shower door). Also, be realistic. For example, commit to read the Hebrew Bible for ten minutes every morning as part of your devotional time. Use a timer and make it a habit.

Dan Wallace recommends employing "the revolving door principle" in your original language reading plan. He explains, "Rotate some chapters in and rotate some out."[4] This is considered an upper-level reading plan, especially if you intend to read/translate whole chapters per day. Yet the "revolving door" approach could be prudently applied to smaller chunks of the Old Testament—say five verses per day. See the chart below for a sample of how overlapping with previous readings can be systematically applied to your daily reading plan. This same structure was used to develop the summer reading plan that was listed previously. In this plan, the student reads five verses per day, but only one new verse is encountered each day (after the first day, of course). From a pedagogical perspective, this repetition is a great way to review vocabulary and syntactical constructions while you continue to branch out into longer and longer sections of the Hebrew Bible. The reading plan above (see fig. 5.1) employs this same concept with options for Jonah, Ruth, and Deuteronomy 1 and 6.

4. Daniel B. Wallace, "Reading through the Greek New Testament," *Center for the Study of New Testament Manuscripts* (blog), December 29, 2013, https://daniel bwallace.com/2013/12/29/reading-through-the-greek-new-testament/.

Day	Reading for the Day
June 1	Ruth 1:1–5
June 2	Ruth 1:2–6
June 3	Ruth 1:3–7
June 4	Ruth 1:4–8
June 5	Ruth 1:5–9
June 6	Ruth 1:6–10
June 7	Ruth 1:7–11

Does this plan seem manageable and appealing? Write it down. Find some level of accountability. Post it humbly in a public place. Now, do it.

Another simple plan is to follow someone else's plan. There are several good "graded readers" that guide students through biblical texts with varying levels of assistance. If a student uses a "summer reader," I recommend committing to a certain amount of daily study time rather than to specific lessons. For example, commit to work in the reader for fifteen minutes of your lunch break, Monday through Friday. After fifteen minutes, stop and close the book. Eat your dessert. Move on. Below are three recommended readers:

- Robert B. Chisholm. *A Workbook for Intermediate Hebrew: Grammar, Exegesis, and Commentary on Jonah and Ruth.* Grand Rapids: Kregel, 2006. Chisholm's workbook moves systematically through the Hebrew text of both Jonah and Ruth, two of the best books for students to begin translating after two semesters of introductory Hebrew. Chisholm includes some notes but also allows room for students to answer questions about grammar and syntax so that it truly functions as a workbook.

- William Fullilove. *A Graded Reader of Biblical Hebrew.* Phillipsburg, NJ: P&R, 2018. Fullilove's reader provides various texts in the Hebrew Bible that are increasingly difficult (hence graded). The book is organized by narrative texts, legal texts, psalms, prophetic literature, and finally wisdom. One of the wonderful features of Fullilove's reader is the simplicity

"Several things happen as the original languages fall into disuse among pastors. First, the confidence of pastors to determine the precise meaning of biblical texts diminishes. And with the confidence to interpret rigorously goes the confidence to preach powerfully. It is difficult to preach week in and week out over the whole range of God's revelation with depth and power if you are plagued with uncertainty when you venture beyond basic gospel generalities. . . . So the preacher often contents himself with the general focus or flavor of the text, and his exposition lacks the precision and clarity which excite a congregation with the Word of God. Boring generalities are a curse in many pulpits."

—John Piper[b]

of it. It genuinely is a graded reader, not an attempt to be a handbook or intermediate grammar. He has included enough helps to keep you moving forward, but he also leaves room for you to do the beneficial work of looking up more complex grammatical discussions.

- Miles V. Van Pelt and Gary D. Pratico. *Graded Reader of Biblical Hebrew: A Guide to Reading the Hebrew Bible*. Grand Rapids: Zondervan, 2006. Van Pelt and Pratico's reader, like Fullilove's, contains readings in biblical texts of increasing difficulty. Rather than tracking through a manageable book of the Old Testament, Van Pelt and Pratico provide small chunks of various texts for students to sample.

If you have already taken a class in Hebrew syntax (for example, you've worked through an intermediate grammar and know what a verbless clause and temporal ב are), then a good prepackaged plan for you might be to read through a volume of the Baylor Handbook on the Hebrew Bible (BHHB) series (see fig. 5.2). These volumes provide detailed, phrase-by-phrase analysis of several books in the Hebrew Bible. They are essentially Hebrew exegesis classes in paperback format. Depending on the author, the Baylor Handbook series offers insights at the level of microsyntax (word and clause structures) as well as macrosyntax (paragraphs and discourse structures). I recommend the Baylor series to anyone who has had a year of Hebrew. Such

Figure 5.2

Jonah 2:4   51

A וַתַּשְׁלִיכֵנִי מְצוּלָה בִּלְבַב יַמִּים   2:4

B וְנָהָר יְסֹבְבֵנִי

C כָּל־מִשְׁבָּרֶיךָ וְגַלֶּיךָ

D עָלַי עָבָרוּ׃

The lines in v. 4 are marked with *Zaqeph parvum, 'Atnah, Tipha,* and
Silluq. Lines A and B are a couplet indicated by the word pair created by
מְצוּלָה (and יַמִּים) in line A with that of נָהָר in line B. Other translations
(NRSV) have understood lines A and B as a triplet (tricolon), interpreting "into the seas" as a separate line. Both construals are possible, but
the couplet (and not triplet) will be retained here, as explained below.
Although the Masoretic accent mark divides lines C and D, the two lines
are continued across the "line boundary" (Dobbs-Allsopp 2001:5) by
means of enjambment.

Line A. וַתַּשְׁלִיכֵנִי מְצוּלָה בִּלְבַב יַמִּים.

וַתַּשְׁלִיכֵנִי. Hiph *wayyiqtol* 2ms + 1cs suffix. The *wayyiqtol* can be
understood as epexegetical in that it explains the events in v. 3 (WO
§32.2.2). Jonah was in distress and cried out (v. 3) because of what is
described in v. 4. The personal pronoun functions as the accusative complement of the verb.

מְצוּלָה. The verb שָׁלַךְ is typically followed by a PP (עַל, בְּ, אֶל) functioning as a verbal complement. As a result, Wolff (1986:126) suggests
that the PP בִּלְבַב יַמִּים fits the typical construction with the verb, thus
leading him to conclude that מְצוּלָה ("deep") is a "subsequent and additional interpretation" of "heart of the seas." BHS suggests deleting either
מְצוּלָה or בִּלְבַב יַמִּים, under the assumption that one is a gloss, although
there is no textual evidence to warrant the emendation. Allen (1976:214)
follows similarly. Further analysis of the syntactic function of מְצוּלָה mer-
its consideration. Some verbs of movement govern adjuncts that function adverbially. Although location can be specified by a prep such as
עַל, בְּ, אֶל (as with בִּלְבַב יַמִּים), in some instances, nouns may follow
certain verbs and function locatively as an "accusative of place" (WO
§10.2.2). In such constructions the verb is followed by a noun (without
a prep) indicating place or location (cf. Gen 18:1; 45:25; Isa 44:13).
Understood this way, Jonah 2:4 may be read as a verb + accusative of
place + PP. The PP בִּלְבַב יַמִּים stands in apposition to the accusative of

students will not know everything they can know about Hebrew, but the handbook gives them a phrase-by-phrase explanation so that they can learn more Hebrew grammar and syntax in an inductive manner.

If you are reading a BHHB volume and syntactical categories are fuzzy in your brain, you should consider having an intermediate grammar or some laminated reference sheets near you. Also, Todd Murphy's *Pocket Dictionary for the Study of Biblical Hebrew* (Inter-Varsity, 2003) provides brief definitions and examples of a variety of grammatical terms. You will never regret buying Murphy's book and having it close at hand. Finally, Miles Van Pelt's *Biblical Hebrew: A Compact Guide*, 2nd ed. (Zondervan, 2019) is a great resource to have on hand while continuing to read your Hebrew Bible.

Realistic Goals

Recently my (Rob's) friend Charles was telling me about his ninety-five-year-old neighbor. When Charles greeted the neighbor and asked, "How are you doing?" the gentleman replied, "Well, I woke up this morning. It's a good day!" Setting realistic goals (like waking up, if you are ninety-five) can go a long way toward preventing discouragement.

Take an honest assessment of your prior ability to form new habits, your time management skills, and your passion about Hebrew. Is the only thing you can commit to two minutes per day? Then do that. If you stick to your commitment for three months, that success will give you momentum to broaden and deepen your goals for reading the Hebrew Bible. The key is to be honest with yourself about your skill level, but not to be discouraged if your goals feel too small initially. For most of us, smaller goals up front will be more beneficial because we might actually reach them. After reaching several reading goals, we can then write down more extravagant goals.

Frank Farley, a specialist in motivation and risk-taking and professor of psychological studies and education at Philadelphia's Temple University, speaks specifically to the importance of making realistic goals when committing to New Year's resolutions. His advice applies equally well to "Hebrew resolutions" over the summer or winter break. Farley gives the following advice:

1. Do not set impossible goals or goals too high to reasonably achieve.

2. Make each resolution as specific as possible and time-stamped. For example, you might set a goal of reading Hebrew every weekday for ten minutes before breakfast for the next two months. That goal is both specific and time-stamped.

3. Keep the number of goals you have small, check your progress often, and reward yourself for small successes along the way. Don't set out to read the entire Hebrew Bible. Set several small, achievable goals so that you're motivated by having obtained them. In addition, include some kind of metric for behavior as well as progress. Perhaps you didn't read as far as you wanted in a biblical book, but you did indeed read ten minutes per weekday. Don't be discouraged. The *behavior* of the goal was met even if the overall progress was slower than expected.

4. Vary your resolutions each year so you don't get stuck in a rut. You might want to adopt different Hebrew resolutions every summer in college or seminary. For example, you could vary the time you read, change between print or digital text, switch up outside study elements (commentaries, Hebrew handbooks), and so on. If you have simply been reading a Hebrew Bible, what about slowly rewriting by hand an entire book of the Hebrew Bible in your journal (with vowel points and cantillation marks!)? Maybe your goal could be to systematically walk through a different introductory grammar than the one you first learned with. This will help you solidify many basic concepts but from a different perspective.

5. Don't beat yourself up for failures. Farley comments, "Don't catastrophize an occasional bad behavior. When you fall off your schedule, it isn't the end of the world. Like Frank Sinatra said, dust yourself off and start all over again."[5]

5. Interview by Heidi Mitchell, "Burning Question: What's the Best Way to Keep Up a New Year's Resolution?," *Wall Street Journal*, January 19, 2016, D2.

Enjoyment

Sometimes students suggest to me that they will review vocabulary and paradigms over the break. Generally, I think this is a bad idea. Unless you are linguistically inclined, bald language review will soon erode your motivation. What will keep you enjoying Hebrew? Staying close to the actual Hebrew Bible. It is through reading, meditating on, believing, loving, and obeying the Spirit-inspired words of the biblical authors that you will feast on food that non-Hebrew readers know not of. You will be able to declare with David, "The law from your mouth is more precious to me than thousands of pieces of gold and silver" (Ps. 119:72; טֽוֹב־לִ֥י תֽוֹרַת־פִּ֑יךָ מֵ֝אַלְפֵ֗י זָהָ֥ב וָכָֽסֶף׃).

Tim Challies discussed in a 2016 article how self-discipline can lead to joy. Very often, "discipline" in our lives gets a negative connotation because we usually think of discipline as forcing ourselves to do the things in life we don't *want* to do. Challies, however, suggests, "We don't just need to discipline ourselves away from unpleasantness but toward joy."[6] He argues that often our self-discipline is designed to help us do less-than-desirable tasks so that we can avoid even more undesirable consequences. We discipline ourselves to do our personal finances so that we don't overspend. We discipline ourselves to avoid sweets in order to fend off the negative consequences of overeating. But what would our lives look like if our self-discipline led to a delight in the task we had been disciplining ourselves to do? Perhaps we shouldn't think of self-discipline as avoiding negative consequences, but maybe we could begin to think of it as a pursuit of joy.

I believe this is especially true with the biblical languages. If developing a joy of reading the Hebrew Bible comes with actually reading the Hebrew Bible, then there will be lots of self-discipline involved to get to that end goal. There will be a lot of sacrifice and hard work. However, we don't put in those long hours of studying Hebrew just to *avoid* the consequences of not knowing Hebrew. In fact, I bet if you polled ten people, only one or two of them could come up

---

6. Tim Challies, "The Joy of Self-Discipline," May 13, 2016, https://www.challies.com/articles/the-joy-of-self-discipline/.

with a tangible negative consequence of not knowing Hebrew (that's unfortunate, I know). Therefore, our self-discipline in Hebrew studies needs to shift from avoiding negative consequences to pursuing the joy of reading God's word in the original language. This will indeed take discipline and a plan, but once that plan is executed, we will find ourselves more on the joy end of the spectrum than on the frustration end.

Competition

The will to win might be one of the strongest motivators in the human person. It motivates perseverance and tenacity while one is playing Monopoly, and it may even motivate survival if someone is trying to "win" against some form of spiritual warfare or persecution. This will to win makes competition a strong asset in learning Hebrew. Let me clarify: let's not induce sinful one-upmanship as we seek to learn Hebrew, but we can set up friendly competitions to see who will have to pay for the meal if he or she loses.

One way to compete is entering a head-to-head contest. Maybe you and a friend decide to hold each other accountable, but rather than just texting each other based on the reminders you set in your phones, you also decide that whoever can recite the largest chunk of the text you were reading that week gets two extra mulligans on the golf course next time you play. Maybe your positive incentive to read Hebrew daily is to get ice cream on Saturday. Join up with a friend (accountability) and decide that if one of you skips a day, that person has to pay for both ice creams. These kinds of friendly wagers can be a fun way to motivate each other to keep moving forward in learning Hebrew.

Another way to generate competition is by having a lofty goal to achieve. I (Rob) am the Grand Poo-Bah of a secret society. It is the A. T. Robertson Secret Society, so named for a famous Greek grammarian who taught at my school. To join the society, you must make 100 percent on one of my Greek exams. Members receive a personal induction letter with instructions about how to obtain the society's secret password—which allows them access to the society's website:

> "A great help for the investigation of truth is the diligent study of the Holy Scriptures in those languages in which they were written by the Holy Spirit. Not only is this the only well from which we can draw the original force and meaning of the words and phrases of Divine utterance, but also those languages possess a weight of their own—a vividness which brings to the understanding fine shades of meaning with a power which cannot survive the passage into another tongue.... There is in the originals of the Scripture a peculiar emphasis of words and expressions, and in them an especial energy, to intimate and insinuate the sense of the Holy Ghost unto the minds of men, which cannot be transduced into other languages by translations, so as to obtain the same power and efficacy.... What perplexities, mistakes, and errors, the ignorance of these original languages hath cast many expositors into, both of old and of late, especially among those who pertinaciously adhere unto one translation."
> —John Owen[c]

www.atrsecretsociety.org. We also have a closed Facebook page, with more than three hundred active members. We have our own secret meetings, T-shirts, a secret handshake, and secret greetings.

This secret society is not formally a head-to-head competition, but it does create in students the impetus to achieve excellence. As an educator, the key is to create competition without discouraging struggling students. Competition can be an intense motivator, but it can also be a discouragement for those who don't achieve the desired, lofty goal. Be careful to find that balance, both in the classroom and in personal competitive relationships. Competition should help motivate us, not help us denigrate one another.

Community

Another sure way to enjoy Hebrew is either to study with others who are laboring to learn the language or to study in Hebrew the passages of Scripture that you are teaching in your ministry to benefit the local community of believers you serve. First, studying in a group may bring joy merely because of the camaraderie and motivation that comes with working in groups. Michael Austin, another member of the Greek and Hebrew reading group in Sioux Falls, said,

The reason I was so excited to join [the group] was because of my love of God and his word. I am no Greek or Hebrew scholar, but I do know enough to be dangerous, so I try to be careful. The fellowship and friendship have become very important to me. Gathering together around Scripture is the key. Randy, Donn, and Bruce have been so generous with their time. I tell my boys that if they ever want to find great friends, look for a Greek or Hebrew reading group! The instant fellowship with other believers who love God's word is a wonderful thing.[7]

In his testimony, Michael highlights the fellowship and joy that can develop when people are gathered around God's word. He also hints at the benefit of studying in groups in order to avoid errors. Both of these are significant reasons to study and read Hebrew with friends.

The second way Hebrew could become a community endeavor is by studying in Hebrew a lesson or passage you are preparing to teach. I never teach students to substitute their devotional Bible reading for academic work in the Bible, but the inverse of that should be encouraged. If you are studying the Old Testament to preach (quasi-academic work), then seek out new and rich devotional insights from the original Hebrew. You may need some additional commentaries or resources beside you so that you don't misunderstand a Hebrew clause and teeter off the exegetical edge. These resources allow you to still wrestle with the text you are teaching, and I'd almost guarantee that you will gain some sort of devotional insight that is refreshing to your soul and will benefit your parishioners.

"The interpreter who interprets Scripture only in his modern language is always working with a linguistic veil between himself and original texts. And he never knows how thin or how thick this veil is."
—Bernard Ramm[d]

Last semester I had a student participate in an independent study on Hebrew exegesis of the Minor Prophets. One of the assignments was for him to write an exegetical paper on a passage of his choice. He chose Joel 2, and during the course of his exegetical work, he prepared a block diagram of the structure of Joel 2 using Biblearc .com. Only a month later, he was asked to preach at the church

7. Michael Austin, email correspondence with Adam J. Howell, August 9, 2018.

where he now serves. He sent me the sermon on Joel 2, and I was incredibly encouraged to hear his grammatical diagram in his sermon. The church members didn't know he was thinking Hebrew in his mind or that he was visualizing the block diagram as he preached. He didn't reference Hebrew or the grammatical structure. But I could hear it. I had seen him labor with the Hebrew text so as to produce an exegetical diagram, and I could hear how he was walking through that structure as he preached. He told me later that his work in the Hebrew made that sermon so much more enjoyable because he was confident that he delivered a solid message that was based on the text itself, not on someone else's commentary on the text.

No matter how much work we put into making our desires to know Hebrew a reality, we can all do more. We can have one more goal, or one more plan in place, to know and enjoy Hebrew. Many of us need to take the first step toward developing a plan to leverage our academic breaks to our advantage. Develop a plan, write it down, and then let your breaks work for you as you continue this journey of learning to love the Hebrew Bible.

Chapter Reflections

1. Do you have a break coming up in your formal academic studies (e.g., a winter or summer vacation)? Take some time to prayerfully visualize (a) how you want to stay in your Hebrew Bible and (b) what failure and regret would look like.

2. Skim back over some of the reading plan ideas. Which approach appeals to you? Wallace's revolving door? One of the "summer readers" or Hebrew exegetical guidebooks with a commitment of fifteen minutes each day? Consider writing down your commitment to one of these reading plans right now. Write it down. Write it down. Write it down. Right now. What's the next step? Ordering a book? Entering a daily reminder on your smartphone calendar?

3. Where are you employing your Hebrew in your ministry to others? If you currently are not doing so, where can you start connecting your reading of the Hebrew Bible with your practical study?

4. Is there someone else to whom you can teach Hebrew? A group at church? Your children? A homeschooling cooperative?

5. Jot down three forms of increased accountability for your study and reading of Hebrew (e.g., certain incentives or disincentives, a public record of your habits, or the active involvement of a friend or fellow student).

The Double-Edged Sword of Biblical Languages: The Case of Job's "Repentance"

Dominick Hernández

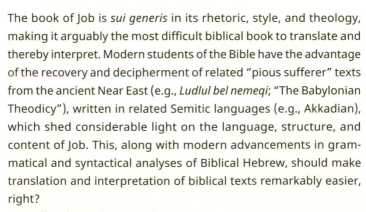

The book of Job is *sui generis* in its rhetoric, style, and theology, making it arguably the most difficult biblical book to translate and thereby interpret. Modern students of the Bible have the advantage of the recovery and decipherment of related "pious sufferer" texts from the ancient Near East (e.g., *Ludlul bel nemeqi*; "The Babylonian Theodicy"), written in related Semitic languages (e.g., Akkadian), which shed considerable light on the language, structure, and content of Job. This, along with modern advancements in grammatical and syntactical analyses of Biblical Hebrew, should make translation and interpretation of biblical texts remarkably easier, right?

Well, it depends on which text.

Sometimes knowledge of biblical languages clarifies previously challenging texts, facilitating interpretation and consequently permitting readers to apply the principles of the text to their lives in relevant ways. On other occasions, however, proficiency in biblical languages calls traditional interpretation into question, demanding that the reader reexamine the text, reconsider its meaning, and perhaps dissent from a previously long-standing interpretation. As readers, we generally prefer the first option over the second—that is, we prefer clarification over complication. However, as Bible students who are bound to the authoritative words of the biblical text, an improved knowledge of the biblical languages compels us to perpetually reconsider even those deeply rooted interpretations of passages. In this sense, knowledge of biblical languages is functionally a double-edged sword: it permits the reader to profoundly engage with and understand intricacies of the biblical text, yet it simultaneously humbles the reader by forcing a perpetual reexamination of conclusions relating to the text.

The book of Job requires more reexamination than any other book in the Bible. Edward L. Greenstein concisely states one of the primary reasons this is the case: "The greatest obstacle before the translator of Job, however, is the necessity to overcome the many presuppositions that have accompanied the book since antiquity."[8] One of the most common assumptions concerning Job relates to 42:6:

"Therefore I despise myself, and repent in dust and ashes." (ESV, NIV)	עַל־כֵּן אֶמְאַס וְנִחַמְתִּי עַל־ עָפָר וָאֵפֶר׃

Following the above translations, many commentators suggest that Job repents of the comments that he made about God during the dialogues with his companions. If this is the case, then why does God, twice in 42:7–8, speak favorably about Job's speech?

8. Edward L. Greenstein, "Challenges in Translating the Book of Job," in *Found in Translation: Essays on Jewish Biblical Translation in Honor of Leonard J. Greenspoon*, ed. James W. Barker, Anthony Le Donne, and Joel N. Lohr (West Lafayette, IN: Purdue University Press, 2018), 189.

"The Lord said to Eliphaz the Te-
manite: 'My anger burns against
you and against your two friends,
for you have not spoken of me
what is right, as my servant Job
has.'" (42:7 ESV)

וַיֹּאמֶר יְהוָה אֶל־אֱלִיפַז הַתֵּימָנִי
חָרָה אַפִּי בְךָ וּבִשְׁנֵי רֵעֶיךָ כִּי לֹא
דִבַּרְתֶּם אֵלַי נְכוֹנָה כְּעַבְדִּי אִיּוֹב׃
(42:7)

"For you have not spoken of me
what is right, as my servant Job
has." (42:8b ESV)

כִּי לֹא דִבַּרְתֶּם אֵלַי נְכוֹנָה כְּעַבְדִּי
אִיּוֹב׃ (42:8b)

These positive comments relating to Job's speech appear in the
context of God's rebuke of Job's companions' speeches. This fact
precludes the suggestion that God is commending Job's statement
of "repentance" in 42:6. God is actually endorsing Job's speech from
the dialogues, in which he engages in a discussion with his friends
about their view of an incontrovertible system of just retribution.
While Job's friends direct their comments toward Job—initially striv-
ing to convince Job to return to God and then condemning Job as
one of the wicked—Job directs his complaints (mostly) toward God.
It is apparently this speech that God is commending.

For readers familiar with Job's complaints toward God, this is a
hard sell. It is unquestionably more theologically comfortable to
somehow conclude that Job said "sorry" about the bad things he
said when he was complaining about his tragic situation. So don't
take my word for it! Let us briefly take a look at the facts of the
case.

As Job directs his complaint toward God, his speech is filled with
hostile comments relating to how Job perceives God acting toward
him. Job's comments in chapter 9 are a perfect example of what *not*
to say to God about God. For example, in Job 9:5–10, Job appears
to be praising God for his immense power exhibited through his
authority over creation. God can move mountains (v. 5), can shake
the earth (v. 6), commands the sun and the stars (v. 7), stretches out
the heavens, and creates constellations (vv. 8–9). At first glance, Job
appears genuinely awestruck by the greatness of God . . . that is,
until verse 10. In verse 10, it becomes evident that Job is not amazed
by God's power but is actually parodying one of his companion's

(Eliphaz's) statements in order to assert that God's "marvelous deeds" (נִפְלָאוֹת) are manifested in God's abuse of creation. This is evident through the almost exact quotation of Eliphaz's words relating to God's "marvelous deeds":

Eliphaz in 5:9	עֹשֶׂה גְדֹלוֹת וְאֵין חֵקֶר נִפְלָאוֹת עַד־אֵין מִסְפָּר:
Job in 9:10	עֹשֶׂה גְדֹלוֹת עַד־אֵין חֵקֶר וְנִפְלָאוֹת עַד־אֵין מִסְפָּר:

Job proceeds to explicitly state that God is more interested in continually mistreating him for no apparent reason than in helping him in his pathetic state (9:14–19). As if this were not enough, Job then claims that God is indiscriminate in judgment (9:22), bringing the righteous and the wicked to the same end (תָּם וְרָשָׁע הוּא מְכַלֶּה). Since Job's fate in the present life is not contingent on his righteousness, he concludes that God is apathetic about the fates of human beings in the afterlife. All must meet the same fate, whether righteous or wicked (cf. 3:13–15). According to Job, God is a violent and capricious mocker, who heartlessly scoffs at the innocent in their times of greatest need (9:23).

Not only is God indiscriminate in judgment according to Job, but God actively perverts justice (9:24)! God permits the wicked to inherit the earth, blessing them with dominion over all things (9:24: אֶרֶץ | נִתְּנָה בְיַד־רָשָׁע). Job's assertion utterly contrasts with traditional biblical wisdom that indicates that the wicked are cut off from the face of the earth (cf. Ps. 37:9). To Job, God bestowing the land on the wicked demonstrates God's arbitrariness, which is exemplified by God actively impairing judgment on the earth by "covering the faces of its judges" (פְּנֵי־שֹׁפְטֶיהָ יְכַסֶּה; Job 9:24).

Now, does this sound like a person ready to "repent"? Even after the whirlwind speeches, Job lacks the answers to the issues that he repeatedly presents throughout the dialogues. Job never finds out why he is suffering and is apparently never privy to the details of the prologue. Job is essentially left in ignorance with regard to why his tragic circumstances came upon him. Thus, even after the whirlwind speeches, Job is disheartened and prepared to make a statement expressing his wretched emotional condition. Lo and behold, taking a fresh look at Job 42:6 discloses a statement that fits this context. In fact, an analysis of the Hebrew of 42:6 demonstrates that its traditional interpretation is anything but obvious.

First, translators seem to have an issue with the verb מאס being used intransitively (i.e., without a direct object). Since this verb frequently appears with a direct object (i.e., it is used transitively), translators tend to supply a direct object, rendering the conjugated form אֶמְאַס as something akin to "I despise *myself*." This is obviously interpretive, as "myself" is simply nowhere to be found in the Hebrew text. In fact, a cursory look at Job 7:16 demonstrates that מאס can mean something like "to be fed up" when used intransitively in the *qal* (מָאַסְתִּי לֹא־לְעֹלָם אֶחְיֶה ["I am fed up! I will not live forever!"]).[9] Job being fed up with his circumstances after being humbled by God through the whirlwind speeches and still not receiving any answers regarding his personal situation seems to distinctly fit the context of Job 42.

Second, translators grapple with the meaning of the word נחם in the *niphal*, which is frequently translated "to repent." A cursory look at the dictionary reveals that this verb is multivalent (see, e.g., BDB, 636–37, *niphal*). For example, in 1 Samuel 15:29, the writer indicates that God does not lie or "repent" (וְלֹא יִנָּחֵם יְשַׁקֵּר וְלֹא), and in verse 35 of the very same chapter, presumably the same author asserts that God does indeed "repent" that he made Saul king over Israel (וַיהוָה נִחָם כִּי־הִמְלִיךְ אֶת־שָׁאוּל). So, wait, does God repent or not?

Clearly, the word נחם is being used differently in these two neighboring verses. In the case of 1 Samuel 15:29, נחם means to confess some sort of wrongdoing—which God cannot do. In the case of 1 Samuel 15:35, the word represents God as being "sorry"—a sentiment reflecting Israel's unfortunate situation resulting from Saul's poor leadership. In fact, the translators of the Septuagint of 1 Samuel understood that נחם was being used differently in these verses, rendering the word in 1 Samuel 15:29 as μετανοέω, "to re-

9. Translators also frequently supply a direct object to the verb in this context, despite the fact that it is clearly being used intransitively (cf. ESV, NIV, NRSV).

pent" (LSJ, 1115), and in 1 Samuel 15:35 as μεταμέλομαι, "to regret" (LSJ, 1114).

Third, translators wrestle with the phrase עָפָר וָאֵפֶר in Job 42:6. Many translations render this phrase literally as "dust and ashes," perhaps depicting Job's condition at the beginning of the book (cf. 2:8). However, עָפָר וָאֵפֶר can also simply refer to the human condition. For example, Job seems to use this phrase in this manner in 30:19, while Abraham makes clear that he is only a human being in the presence of the deity by using this exact phrase (Gen. 18:27).

Perhaps instead of the understanding that Job "repents" in the sense of asking for forgiveness, a better understanding of Job 42:6 in the context of God's commendation of Job's speech (42:7–8) portrays Job as fed up and feeling sorry about the human condition. This makes sense in light of God's revelation through the whirlwind speeches leaving Job without any semblance of a reason for his calamitous situation. In this context, Job does not appear to repent but, rather, states:

"Therefore, I am fed up. I am sorry about dust and ashes" (i.e., the human condition).	עַל־כֵּן אֶמְאַס וְנִחַמְתִּי עַל־עָפָר וָאֵפֶר:

This is admittedly a difficult verse with weighty theological implications. Nevertheless, regardless of where one stands on this issue of Job's "repentance," this matter is more intricate than most translations portray, which pragmatically demonstrates the necessity to utilize biblical languages in preaching and teaching the Scriptures. As teachers, it is impossible to sufficiently explicate the message of a text unless we first engage with the critical issues therein.

One final point must be accentuated: upon encountering difficult biblical texts, it is especially important to refrain from importing traditional understandings of the text, despite the fact that they might facilitate a simplified translation and fortify established interpretation. The student of the Bible must recognize the nature of the double-edged sword of biblical languages and appropriately divide the text, even if that same sword slashes our traditional interpretation and chisels a new understanding.

Read, Read, Read

I've mentioned before that I worked at a fitness center while completing my graduate degrees. While there, I saw many life-changing journeys related to weight loss and overall health. I remember one particular guy well. When he began coming to the gym, he had difficulty walking because of his weight. He would get on the treadmill and use the handrails to walk for as long as he could. At the beginning, it wasn't a long walk, but it was a start. When he first joined the gym, he came in occasionally; when you saw him, you wondered if his gym membership was worth it. Then he began to come in every day. That was when our staff knew that something was about to change. He went from needing the handrails to walking slowly without them. He then progressed to a brisk walk, and his consistent efforts culminated in him jogging periodically. Over several months, his consistency, more than the type of exercise he was doing (walking, jogging, weight training, etc.), helped him make the most progress. The key to his success was that he exercised every day. After he lost well over one hundred pounds—a significant physical change—we decided as a staff *not* to retake his photo for our gym computer system. We wanted him to take pride in how far he had come, enjoying the results of his daily work over those months.

Perhaps the most important practice for maintaining and increasing your facility in Biblical Hebrew is similar to this exercise success story. Read Hebrew daily. I cannot stress that enough: read it daily. From the very beginning of the learning process, it is key to develop the habit of reading the Bible in Hebrew. At first it may involve only a few minutes or a few verses—but the key is consistency. When I say "read Hebrew," I want to be clear that in week one of your first Hebrew class, you won't be able to read very much, if anything. However, from that day forward, you need to find yourself in the Hebrew Bible practicing whatever concept you're learning. Over time you can increase your Hebrew fitness and spend more time actually reading and less time identifying whether a *shewa* is silent or vocal. The key is to develop the habit of engaging daily with the Hebrew text. In this chapter, we will discuss the practice of reading Hebrew daily, including what to read, how to read, how long to read, and how to use Hebrew while memorizing verses in English.

What to Read

One of the biggest mistakes a new Hebrew student can make is to begin reading a book of the Hebrew Bible with difficult syntax and vocabulary. Choosing the right book to read is important. If a zealous Hebrew student decides to start off by reading the Book of the Twelve (Minor Prophets) or Job, frustration and disappointment will surely result. Instead, it is better to begin with easier books, making reading more enjoyable while giving you confidence in your developing skills.

But which Old Testament books are easy to read and which ones are difficult? At least two factors contribute to a book's difficulty: vocabulary and syntax. While vocabulary can be categorized somewhat scientifically on the basis of the frequency of vocabulary used, it is more difficult to rate a book on the basis of its style and syntax. One other factor to consider when deciding what to read in the Hebrew Bible is the length of the book. Remember what we said about generating manageable goals? It might be discouraging to begin with the Kings narratives even if the vocabulary "ease" is in the top three. Many Hebrew students begin with Jonah or Ruth because of size and (relative) ease of syntax. Even though the vocabulary in these two books is slightly more difficult, if you complete a whole book of the Hebrew Bible, your "emotion meter" will max out with excitement and joy.[1]

In the following chart, the first column lists books according to vocabulary alone[2] and the second according to unique vocabulary.[3] The third list was produced by John Wayne Coatney and uses a fairly complex (but helpful) spreadsheet and "scoring" system to rank books by both vocabulary *and* syntax.[4]

Vocabulary Alone	Unique Vocabulary	Vocabulary and Syntax
2 Chronicles	Deuteronomy	Haggai
1 Samuel	Exodus	Malachi
Deuteronomy	1–2 Kings[a]	Ruth
1 Kings	Leviticus	Jonah
Exodus	Jeremiah	Joshua
2 Kings	1–2 Samuel	Nehemiah

1. Use discretion even with the size of the book. Obadiah is merely twenty-one verses long, but the vocabulary and syntax might leave you feeling like you were punched by a heavyweight prizefighter.

2. This list is based strictly on the number of words in the book that occur five hundred or more times. This data was compiled by Andrew Yates using Logos Bible Software based on the Anderson-Forbes Analyzed Text (http://amyates.blogspot.com /2015/05/old-testament-hebrew-reading-list.html).

3. For Andrew Yates's definition of "unique vocabulary," see his blog posts on this list: "Old Testament Hebrew Reading List," May 18, 2015, http://amyates .blogspot.com/2015/05/old-testament-hebrew-reading-list.html; and "OT Hebrew Reading List—Part Dux," November 21, 2016, http://amyates.blogspot.com/2016 /11/ot-hebrew-reading-list-part-dux.html. He offers a printable reading plan in both PDF and spreadsheet forms if you're a box checker like me.

4. This list is from a Facebook post by John Wayne Coatney, dated April 3, 2015 (https://m.facebook.com/groups/224415954327748?view=permalink&id=58336323 5099683&_rdr). This list shows a lot of promise by way of statistical analysis, but it may be slightly off as it relates to actual "ease of reading." The statistical analysis used by Coatney includes categories for vocabulary words occurring fewer than seventy times in the Hebrew Bible, hapax legomena, unique vocabulary forms, *ketiv/qere* forms, and a percentage of poetry. The percentage of poetry gives this list an element of syntactical organization since poetry is generally more difficult syntactically to translate. In Coatney's spreadsheet, each of these categories has a relative weight in the scoring and can be manipulated if you think the amount of poetry should carry more weight than unique vocabulary. So you can use this list as a starting point, but then perhaps tweak it depending on which of the analyzed categories you think would more accurately reflect the order of syntactical difficulty. I personally would begin this list with Deuteronomy, then Samuel, Ruth, and Jonah, but I don't have any statistical data to support that conclusion.

Vocabulary Alone	Unique Vocabulary	Vocabulary and Syntax
Leviticus	Zechariah	Ezra
Jeremiah	Haggai	Exodus
2 Samuel	Judges	Numbers
Zechariah	Numbers	Joel
Haggai	Jonah	Leviticus
Judges	Ruth	Zechariah
Numbers	Ezekiel	Esther
Jonah	Genesis	Chronicles
Ruth	Malachi	Daniel
Ezekiel	Daniel	Judges
Genesis	Ecclesiastes	Amos
Malachi	Amos	Zephaniah
Daniel	Psalms	Obadiah
Ecclesiastes	Joshua	Genesis
Amos	Esther	Kings
Psalms	Hosea	Ecclesiastes
Joshua	Micah	Micah
Esther	Joel	Samuel
Hosea	Zephaniah	Deuteronomy
Micah	Obadiah	Hosea
Joel	Nehemiah	Habakkuk
Zephaniah	Isaiah	Song of Songs
Obadiah	Lamentations	Nahum
Nehemiah	Proverbs	Ezekiel
Isaiah	Ezra	Jeremiah
Lamentations	Job	Job
Proverbs	Habakkuk	Proverbs
Ezra	1–2 Chronicles	Lamentations
Job	Nahum	Isaiah
Habakkuk	Song of Songs	Psalms
1 Chronicles		
Nahum		
Song of Songs		

[a]In his list, Yates separates Kings, Samuel, and Chronicles to get the full list of thirty-nine books. For space reasons, I've combined them here. These books can be understood as single compositions; the vocabulary is consistent throughout.

Based on these lists, I would recommend a new Hebrew learner to start reading something like Ruth, Jonah, or Deuteronomy. The vocabulary in these books is relatively easy, and the syntax is primarily narrative prose. In addition, these narratives are familiar to most who would be reading the books in Hebrew, so if you encounter some obscure vocabulary or syntax, you may be able to work through it because of your familiarity with the English text already.

How to Read

Now that you know which books to read (at least initially), what is the best way to actually read the Old Testament? As you begin (or continue) to read the Hebrew Bible, it is important to use the appropriate tools to facilitate this process. Below we discuss several categories of tools, ranging from those offering the most help to those offering the least help. Someone who has sprained an ankle needs a crutch and not necessarily a wheelchair. If you use a method that provides you too much assistance, your Hebrew skills may actually begin to erode. The goal is to consider how you can exercise your Hebrew muscles so that you can be less reliant on assistance.

Reading with an Interlinear or Reverse-Interlinear Bible

An interlinear Bible (see fig. 6.1) has the Hebrew text on one line and the English text directly below it with the English word under the Hebrew word to which it corresponds (a reverse interlinear has the English text on top).

This tool may be helpful for some but probably should be avoided by most serious Hebrew students. Interlinears are not the best method because they do not allow you to determine whether you actually know the Hebrew text since you can see the English words at the same time. For example, if you don't know a particular word at first, it is helpful to force yourself to try to recall the word. Maybe you know it, but you just need to remember your mnemonic device to bring the meaning of the term to your mind. That momentary struggle is healthy, and without it you will not know if you have adequately memorized a word or not. If your goal is to be able to read the Hebrew Bible independently, then an interlinear will be a crutch (or a wheelchair) that will stifle your long-term progress.

One situation in which I may recommend an interlinear for a short time is when you are first beginning to translate Hebrew, maybe in the first few weeks of your first semester. Hebrew word order and syntax can be a challenge, and sometimes an interlinear can at least let you

Figure 6.1

Genesis | בראשית

Hebrew interlinear (read right-to-left), Genesis 1:1–14a

Verse 1: בְּרֵאשִׁית (in-beginning) בָּרָא (he-created) אֱלֹהִים (God) אֵת (—) הַשָּׁמַיִם (the-heavens) וְאֵת (and—) הָאָרֶץ׃ (the-earth)

Verse 2: וְהָאָרֶץ (and-the-earth) הָיְתָה (she-was) תֹהוּ (formlessness) וָבֹהוּ (and-emptiness) וְחֹשֶׁךְ (and-darkness) עַל־ (over) פְּנֵי (face-of) תְהוֹם (the-deep) וְרוּחַ (and-Spirit-of) אֱלֹהִים (God) מְרַחֶפֶת (hovering) עַל־ (over) פְּנֵי (face-of) הַמָּיִם׃ (the-waters)

Verse 3: וַיֹּאמֶר (and-he-said) אֱלֹהִים (God) יְהִי (let-him-be) אוֹר (light) וַיְהִי־ (and-he-was) אוֹר׃ (light)

Verse 4: וַיַּרְא (and-he-saw) אֱלֹהִים (God) אֶת־ (—) הָאוֹר (the-light) כִּי־ (that) טוֹב (good) וַיַּבְדֵּל (and-he-separated) אֱלֹהִים (God) בֵּין (between) הָאוֹר (the-light) וּבֵין (and-between) הַחֹשֶׁךְ׃ (the-darkness)

Verse 5: וַיִּקְרָא (and-he-called) אֱלֹהִים (God) לָאוֹר (the-light) יוֹם (Day) וְלַחֹשֶׁךְ (and—the-darkness) קָרָא (he-called) לָיְלָה (Night) וַיְהִי־ (and-he-was) עֶרֶב (evening) וַיְהִי־ (and-he-was) בֹקֶר (morning) יוֹם (day) אֶחָד׃ (one)

Verse 6: וַיֹּאמֶר (and-he-said) אֱלֹהִים (God) יְהִי (let-him-be) רָקִיעַ (expanse) בְּתוֹךְ (in-midst-of) הַמָּיִם (the-waters) וִיהִי (and-let-him-be) מַבְדִּיל (separating) בֵּין (between) מַיִם (waters) לָמָיִם׃ (to-waters)

Verse 7: וַיַּעַשׂ (and-he-made) אֱלֹהִים (God) אֶת־ (—) הָרָקִיעַ (the-expanse) וַיַּבְדֵּל (and-he-separated) בֵּין (between) הַמַּיִם (the-waters) אֲשֶׁר (that) מִתַּחַת (from-under) לָרָקִיעַ (to-the-expanse) וּבֵין (and-between) הַמַּיִם (the-waters) אֲשֶׁר (that) מֵעַל (from-over) לָרָקִיעַ (to-the-expanse) וַיְהִי־ (and-he-was) כֵן׃ (so)

Verse 8: וַיִּקְרָא (and-he-called) אֱלֹהִים (God) לָרָקִיעַ (—the-expanse) שָׁמָיִם (Heaven) וַיְהִי־ (and-he-was) עֶרֶב (evening) וַיְהִי־ (and-he-was) בֹקֶר (morning) יוֹם (day) שֵׁנִי׃ (second)

Verse 9: וַיֹּאמֶר (and-he-said) אֱלֹהִים (God) יִקָּווּ (let-them-be-gathered) הַמַּיִם (the-waters) מִתַּחַת (from-under) הַשָּׁמַיִם (the-heavens) אֶל־ (into) מָקוֹם (place) אֶחָד (one) וְתֵרָאֶה (and-let-her-appear) הַיַּבָּשָׁה (the-dry-ground) וַיְהִי־ (and-he-was) כֵן׃ (so)

Verse 10: וַיִּקְרָא (and-he-called) אֱלֹהִים (God) לַיַּבָּשָׁה (—the-dry-ground) אֶרֶץ (Earth) וּלְמִקְוֵה (and—collection-of) הַמַּיִם (the-waters) קָרָא (he-called) יַמִּים (Seas) וַיַּרְא (and-he-saw) אֱלֹהִים (God) כִּי־ (that) טוֹב׃ (good)

Verse 11: וַיֹּאמֶר (and-he-said) אֱלֹהִים (God) תַּדְשֵׁא (let-her-produce) הָאָרֶץ (the-earth) דֶּשֶׁא (what-is-green) עֵשֶׂב (vegetation) מַזְרִיעַ (yielding) זֶרַע (seed) עֵץ (tree-of) פְּרִי (fruit) עֹשֶׂה (making) פְּרִי (fruit) לְמִינוֹ (according-to-kind-of-him) אֲשֶׁר (which) זַרְעוֹ־ (seed-of-him) בוֹ (in-him) עַל־ (on) הָאָרֶץ (the-earth) וַיְהִי־ (and-he-was) כֵן׃ (so)

Verse 12: וַתּוֹצֵא (and-she-brought-out) הָאָרֶץ (the-earth) דֶּשֶׁא (what-is-green) עֵשֶׂב (vegetation) מַזְרִיעַ (yielding) זֶרַע (seed) לְמִינֵהוּ (according-to-kind-of-him) וְעֵץ (and-tree) עֹשֶׂה (making) פְּרִי (fruit) אֲשֶׁר (which) זַרְעוֹ־ (seed-of-him) בוֹ (in-him) לְמִינֵהוּ (according-to-kind-of-him) וַיַּרְא (and-he-saw) אֱלֹהִים (God) כִּי־ (that) טוֹב׃ (good)

Verse 13: וַיְהִי־ (and-he-was) עֶרֶב (evening) וַיְהִי־ (and-he-was) בֹקֶר (morning) יוֹם (day) שְׁלִישִׁי׃ (third)

Verse 14: וַיֹּאמֶר (and-he-said) אֱלֹהִים (God)

The Creation of the World

1 In the beginning, God created the heavens and the earth. 2 The earth was without form and void, and darkness was over the face of the deep. And the Spirit of God was hovering over the face of the waters.

3 And God said, "Let there be light," and there was light. 4 And God saw that the light was good. And God separated the light from the darkness. 5 God called the light Day, and the darkness he called Night. And there was evening and there was morning, the first day.

6 And God said, "Let there be an expanse[1] in the midst of the waters, and let it separate the waters from the waters." 7 And God made[2] the expanse and separated the waters that were under the expanse from the waters that were above the expanse. And it was so. 8 And God called the expanse Heaven.[3] And there was evening and there was morning, the second day.

9 And God said, "Let the waters under the heavens be gathered together into one place, and let the dry land appear." And it was so. 10 God called the dry land Earth,[4] and the waters that were gathered together he called Seas. And God saw that it was good.

11 And God said, "Let the earth sprout vegetation, plants[5] yielding seed, and fruit trees bearing fruit in which is their seed, each according to its kind, on the earth." And it was so. 12 The earth brought forth vegetation, plants yielding seed according to their own kinds, and trees bearing fruit in which is their seed, each according to its kind. And God saw that it was good. 13 And there was evening and there was morning, the third day.

14 And God said, "Let there be

[1] Or a canopy; also verses 7, 8, 14, 15, 17, 20
[2] Or fashioned; also verse 16
[3] Or Sky; also verses 9, 14, 15, 17, 20, 26, 28, 30; 2:1
[4] Or Land; also verses 11, 12, 22, 24, 25, 26, 28, 30; 2:1
[5] Or small plants; also verses 12, 29

From *The Hebrew-English Interlinear ESV Old Testament: Biblia Hebraica Stuttgartensia and English Standard Version*, © 2014 by Crossway, a publishing ministry of Good News Publishers. BHS-text, © 1977 and 1997 Deutsche Bibelgesellschaft.

see how the Hebrew becomes English syntactically. You can see where words occur in the Hebrew sentence and how they get put together into an English translation. This is a rather restricted use of an interlinear, and you should make sure you're not relying on the interlinear when you should be doing your own translation work. As soon as you can move beyond an interlinear, you should, but if it helps you engage with the Hebrew text, then it can be a starting place. A top-selling, user-friendly interlinear is Crossway's *Hebrew-English Interlinear ESV Old Testament*, shown above. Bible software like Accordance and Logos also can generate interlinear and reverse-interlinear texts.

Reading with a Diglot

A diglot version of the Bible offers the Hebrew text on one page and an English Bible translation on the facing page. Crossway, once again, has an excellent resource here. Their *ESV Hebrew-English Old Testament* (2015) offers the ESV on one page and *BHS* on the facing page (see fig. 6.2). Alternative options are the *Hebrew-English Diglot Bible* (American Bible Society, 2001), offering the NKJV as the English translation, and the *Hebrew-English Bible* (The Bible Society in Israel, 2014), which has the NASB paralleling the Hebrew text.

While giving less help than an interlinear Bible, a diglot also provides too much help for the average Hebrew student. If you are unsure of a Hebrew word, you can simply glance at the opposing page to find the meaning of the word. In addition, you also see the words in the surrounding English context that you may not want to see. In essence, then, this method gives the reader too much information (i.e., assistance).

Reading with a Reader's Hebrew Bible

Recognizing that inexperienced readers of the Hebrew Bible are often frustrated by unfamiliar vocabulary words, several publishers are now offering a "reader's edition" of the Hebrew Bible, with uncommon vocabulary words listed verse by verse at the bottom of each page (see fig. 6.3). Two good Hebrew reader's editions are available. The first is Zondervan's *A Reader's Hebrew Bible*.[5] This

5. *A Reader's Hebrew Bible*, ed. A. Philip Brown II and Bryan W. Smith (Grand Rapids: Zondervan, 2008).

Figure 6.2

LEVITICUS   24:10–25:6

Punishment for Blasphemy

¹⁰Now an Israelite woman's son, whose father was an Egyptian, went out among the people of Israel. And the Israelite woman's son and a man of Israel fought in the camp, ¹¹and the Israelite woman's son blasphemed the Name, and cursed. Then they brought him to Moses. His mother's name was Shelomith, the daughter of Dibri, of the tribe of Dan. ¹²And they put him in custody, till the will of the LORD should be clear to them.

¹³Then the LORD spoke to Moses, saying, ¹⁴"Bring out of the camp the one who cursed, and let all who heard him lay their hands on his head, and let all the congregation stone him. ¹⁵And speak to the people of Israel, saying, Whoever curses his God shall bear his sin. ¹⁶Whoever blasphemes the name of the LORD shall surely be put to death. All the congregation shall stone him. The sojourner as well as the native, when he blasphemes the Name, shall be put to death.

An Eye for an Eye

¹⁷"Whoever takes a human life shall surely be put to death. ¹⁸Whoever takes an animal's life shall make it good, life for life. ¹⁹If anyone injures his neighbor, as he has done it shall be done to him, ²⁰fracture for fracture, eye for eye, tooth for tooth; whatever injury he has given a person shall be given to him. ²¹Whoever kills an animal shall make it good, and whoever kills a person shall be put to death. ²²You shall have the same rule for the sojourner and for the native, for I am the LORD your God." ²³So Moses spoke to the people of Israel, and they brought out of the camp the one who had cursed and stoned him with stones. Thus the people of Israel did as the LORD commanded Moses.

The Sabbath Year

25 The LORD spoke to Moses on Mount Sinai, saying, ²"Speak to the people of Israel and say to them, When you come into the land that I give you, the land shall keep a Sabbath to the LORD. ³For six years you shall sow your field, and for six years you shall prune your vineyard and gather in its fruits, ⁴but in the seventh year there shall be a Sabbath of solemn rest for the land, a Sabbath to the LORD. You shall not sow your field or prune your vineyard. ⁵You shall not reap what grows of itself in your harvest, or gather the grapes of your undressed vine. It shall be a year of solemn rest for the land. ⁶The Sabbath of the land¹ shall provide food for you, for yourself and for your male

¹ That is, the Sabbath produce of the land

399

Figure 6.2

ויקרא   24,10—25,6

10 וַיֵּצֵא֙ בֶּן־אִשָּׁ֣ה יִשְׂרְאֵלִ֔ית וְהוּא֙ בֶּן־אִ֣ישׁ מִצְרִ֔י בְּת֖וֹךְ בְּנֵ֣י

11 יִשְׂרָאֵ֑ל וַיִּנָּצוּ֙ בַּֽמַּחֲנֶ֔ה בֶּ֚ן הַיִּשְׂרְאֵלִ֔ית וְאִ֖ישׁ הַיִּשְׂרְאֵלִֽי׃ 11 וַיִּקֹּ֣ב בֶּן־

הָאִשָּׁ֨ה הַיִּשְׂרְאֵלִ֤ית אֶת־הַשֵּׁם֙ וַיְקַלֵּ֔ל וַיָּבִ֥יאוּ אֹת֖וֹ אֶל־מֹשֶׁ֑ה וְשֵׁ֥ם אִמּ֛וֹ

12 שְׁלֹמִ֥ית בַּת־דִּבְרִ֖י לְמַטֵּה־דָֽן׃ 12 וַיַּנִּיחֻ֖הוּ בַּמִּשְׁמָ֑ר לִפְרֹ֥שׁ לָהֶ֖ם עַל־

13 פִּ֥י יְהוָֽה׃ פ 13 וַיְדַבֵּ֥ר יְהוָ֖ה אֶל־מֹשֶׁ֥ה לֵּאמֹֽר׃ 14 הוֹצֵ֣א אֶת־
14

הַֽמְקַלֵּ֗ל אֶל־מִחוּץ֙ לַֽמַּחֲנֶ֔ה וְסָמְכ֧וּ כָֽל־הַשֹּׁמְעִ֛ים אֶת־יְדֵיהֶ֖ם עַל־

15 רֹאשׁ֑וֹ וְרָגְמ֥וּ אֹת֖וֹ כָּל־הָעֵדָֽה׃ 15 וְאֶל־בְּנֵ֥י יִשְׂרָאֵ֖ל תְּדַבֵּ֣ר לֵאמֹ֑ר

16 אִ֥ישׁ אִ֛ישׁ כִּֽי־יְקַלֵּ֥ל אֱלֹהָ֖יו וְנָשָׂ֥א חֶטְאֽוֹ׃ 16 וְנֹקֵ֤ב שֵׁם־יְהוָה֙ מ֣וֹת

יוּמָ֔ת רָג֥וֹם יִרְגְּמוּ־ב֖וֹ כָּל־הָעֵדָ֑ה כַּגֵּר֙ כָּֽאֶזְרָ֔ח בְּנָקְבוֹ־שֵׁ֖ם יוּמָֽת׃

17 וְאִ֕ישׁ כִּ֥י יַכֶּ֖ה כָּל־נֶ֣פֶשׁ אָדָ֑ם מ֖וֹת יוּמָֽת׃ 18 וּמַכֵּ֥ה נֶֽפֶשׁ־בְּהֵמָ֖ה
18

יְשַׁלְּמֶ֑נָּה נֶ֖פֶשׁ תַּ֥חַת נָֽפֶשׁ׃ 19 וְאִ֕ישׁ כִּֽי־יִתֵּ֥ן מ֖וּם בַּעֲמִית֑וֹ כַּאֲשֶׁ֣ר עָשָׂ֔ה

20 כֵּ֖ן יֵעָ֥שֶׂה לּֽוֹ׃ 20 שֶׁ֚בֶר תַּ֣חַת שֶׁ֔בֶר עַ֚יִן תַּ֣חַת עַ֔יִן שֵׁ֖ן תַּ֣חַת שֵׁ֑ן כַּאֲשֶׁ֨ר

21 יִתֵּ֥ן מוּם֙ בָּֽאָדָ֔ם כֵּ֖ן יִנָּ֥תֶן בּֽוֹ׃ 21 וּמַכֵּ֥ה בְהֵמָ֖ה יְשַׁלְּמֶ֑נָּה וּמַכֵּ֥ה אָדָ֖ם

22 יוּמָֽת׃ 22 מִשְׁפַּ֤ט אֶחָד֙ יִהְיֶ֣ה לָכֶ֔ם כַּגֵּ֥ר כָּאֶזְרָ֖ח יִהְיֶ֑ה כִּ֛י אֲנִ֥י יְהוָ֖ה

23 אֱלֹהֵיכֶֽם׃ 23 וַיְדַבֵּ֣ר מֹשֶׁה֮ אֶל־בְּנֵ֣י יִשְׂרָאֵל֒ וַיּוֹצִ֣יאוּ אֶת־הַֽמְקַלֵּ֗ל אֶל־

מִחוּץ֙ לַֽמַּחֲנֶ֔ה וַיִּרְגְּמ֥וּ אֹת֖וֹ אָ֑בֶן וּבְנֵֽי־יִשְׂרָאֵ֣ל עָשׂ֔וּ כַּאֲשֶׁ֛ר צִוָּ֥ה יְהוָ֖ה

אֶת־מֹשֶֽׁה׃ פ   קנד

25 1 וַיְדַבֵּ֤ר יְהוָה֙ אֶל־מֹשֶׁ֔ה בְּהַ֥ר סִינַ֖י לֵאמֹֽר׃ 2 דַּבֵּ֞ר אֶל־בְּנֵ֤י פרש

יִשְׂרָאֵל֙ וְאָמַרְתָּ֣ אֲלֵהֶ֔ם כִּ֤י תָבֹ֙אוּ֙ אֶל־הָאָ֔רֶץ אֲשֶׁ֥ר אֲנִ֖י נֹתֵ֣ן לָכֶ֑ם

וְשָׁבְתָ֣ה הָאָ֔רֶץ שַׁבָּ֖ת לַיהוָֽה׃ 3 שֵׁ֤שׁ שָׁנִים֙ תִּזְרַ֣ע שָׂדֶ֔ךָ וְשֵׁ֥שׁ שָׁנִ֖ים

תִּזְמֹ֣ר כַּרְמֶ֑ךָ וְאָסַפְתָּ֖ אֶת־תְּבוּאָתָֽהּ׃ 4 וּבַשָּׁנָ֣ה הַשְּׁבִיעִ֗ת שַׁבַּ֤ת שַׁבָּתוֹן֙

יִהְיֶ֣ה לָאָ֔רֶץ שַׁבָּ֖ת לַיהוָ֑ה שָֽׂדְךָ֙ לֹ֣א תִזְרָ֔ע וְכַרְמְךָ֖ לֹ֥א תִזְמֹֽר׃ 5 אֵ֣ת

סְפִ֤יחַ קְצִֽירְךָ֙ לֹ֣א תִקְצ֔וֹר וְאֶת־עִנְּבֵ֥י נְזִירֶ֖ךָ לֹ֣א תִבְצֹ֑ר שְׁנַ֥ת שַׁבָּת֖וֹן

יִהְיֶ֥ה לָאָֽרֶץ׃ 6 וְֽהָיְתָ֞ה שַׁבַּ֤ת הָאָ֙רֶץ֙ לָכֶ֣ם לְאָכְלָ֔ה לְךָ֖ וּלְעַבְדְּךָ֥

13 2 S 14,6. 14 Mm 3746. 15 Mp sub loco. 16 Mm 802. 17 Mm 585. 18 Mm 590. 19 Mm 804. 20 Mm 803. 21 Mm
210. 22 Mm 2610. 23 Mm 470. Cp 25 1 Mm 793. 2 Mm 1181. 3 Mm 805. 4 Mp sub loco. 5 Mm 806.

10 ᵃ יש׳ ‖ 11 ᵃ 𝔊⁵⁹(𝔄𝔗ᴹˢ) τὸ ὄνομα κυρίου cf 16 ‖ 15 ᵃ 𝔊ᴮᴬ θεόν ‖ 16 ᵃ 𝔊(𝔙) τὸ
ὄνομα κυρίου cf 11 ᵃ ‖ 17 ᵃ 𝔊 + καὶ ἀποθάνῃ, it 18ᵇ.21ᵇ ‖ 18 ᵃ > 𝔈 pc Mss 𝔊𝔙 ‖
ᵇ cf 17ᵃ ‖ 21 ᵃ⁻ᵃ > 𝔊 ‖ ᵇ cf 17ᵃ ‖ 22 ᵃ 1 לָכֶם ut Nu 15,16 ‖ 23 ᵃ 𝔖 + wmjt = וַיָּמָת ‖
Cp 25,5 ᵃ ᵃ 𝔊𝔖 וְאֵת ‖ ᵇ ᵃ 𝔖 ספחי cf 11 ‖ ᶜ nonn Mss דְרִיך ‖ 6 ᵃ⁻ᵃ pl it 44ᵃ⁻ᵃ.

reader's edition is based on the Westminster Leningrad Codex, and footnotes gloss definitions for vocabulary occurring fewer than one hundred times. It also gives stem-specific glosses for verbal stems (often an interpretive decision, so be aware of that), and it provides the glosses from *HALOT* and BDB. For verbs, the respective stems are given in the footnotes, but not full parsing. For words that occur *over* one hundred times, this reader's edition offers a glossary just in case some of those words escape your memory too.

The second reader's edition I would recommend is *Biblia Hebraica Stuttgartensia: A Reader's Edition*.[6] This edition provides glosses for vocabulary occurring less than seventy times, and it parses all weak verbs. You will have to get used to the parsing nomenclature for this feature to be helpful, but once you understand the abbreviations the editors use, you will also have that information footnoted for you. This *BHS* reader's edition also provides a glossary of terms that are not already glossed in the footnotes throughout the text. Either of these reader's editions would be an excellent resource in this category.

We highly recommend that beginning students (really any student) use one of the above readers (I favor the Hendrickson edition). These readers provide just enough information to help the student without providing too much information to stifle growth. In fact, such reader's editions often motivate students to actually use and read their Hebrew Bibles. Many professors will deter students from using a reader's edition, and at some point you should set it aside. But if a reader's edition can provide enough help in the early stages of your learning to get you reading your Hebrew Bible daily, then go for it.

Reading with a Reader's Lexicon

If students don't mind having a second print volume open alongside their Hebrew Bible, a "reader's lexicon" can provide the necessary vocabulary help. Unlike a typical lexicon that lists words in alphabetical order according to their lexical form, a reader's lexicon provides words according to their canonical usage. For example, as a person is reading

6. *Biblia Hebraica Stuttgartensia: A Reader's Edition*, ed. Donald Vance, George Athas, and Yael Avrahami (Peabody, MA: Hendrickson, 2015). This reader's edition is hardback, so for the sake of longevity (wear and tear) this may be the preferred volume.

Figure 6.3

Obadiah עובדיה

1 חֲזֹ֖וןᵃ עֹבַדְיָ֑הᵇ

כֹּֽה־אָמַר֩ אֲדֹנָ֨י יְהוִ֜ה לֶאֱד֗וֹם

שְׁמוּעָ֨הᶜ שָׁמַ֜עְנוּ מֵאֵ֤ת יְהוָה֙ וְצִיר֙ᵈ בַּגּוֹיִ֣ם שֻׁלָּ֔חᵉ

ק֛וּמוּ וְנָק֥וּמָהᵉ עָלֶ֖יהָ לַמִּלְחָמָֽה׃

2 הִנֵּ֥ה קָטֹ֛ןᵃ נְתַתִּ֖יךָᵇ בַּגּוֹיִ֑ם בָּז֥וּיᵃ אַתָּ֖ה מְאֹֽד׃

3 זְד֤וֹןᵃ לִבְּךָ֙ הִשִּׁיאֶ֔ךָᵇ שֹׁכְנִ֥י בְחַגְוֵי־סֶ֖֫לַעᶜ מְר֣וֹם שִׁבְתּ֑וֹ

אֹמֵ֣ר בְּלִבּ֔וֹ מִ֖י יוֹרִדֵ֥נִיᵉ אָֽרֶץ׃

4 אִם־תַּגְבִּ֣יהַּᵃ כַּנֶּ֔שֶׁרᵇ וְאִם־בֵּ֥ין כּֽוֹכָבִ֖יםᶜ שִׂ֣יםᵈ קִנֶּ֑ךָ

מִשָּׁ֥ם אוֹרִֽידְךָ֖ נְאֻם־יְהוָֽה׃

5 אִם־גַּנָּבִ֤ים בָּֽאֽוּ־לְךָ֙ᵃ אִם־שֽׁוֹדְדֵ֣י לַ֔יְלָה

אֵ֣יךְ נִדְמֵ֔יתָהᵃ הֲל֥וֹא יִגְנְב֖וּ דַּיָּ֑םᵍ

אִם־בֹּֽצְרִים֙ᵇ בָּ֣אוּ לָ֔ךְ הֲל֖וֹא יַשְׁאִ֥ירוּ עֹלֵלֽוֹתᵉ׃

6 אֵ֚יךְᵃ נֶחְפְּשׂ֣וּ עֵשָׂ֔ו נִבְע֖וּ מַצְפֻּנָֽיוᵈ׃

7 עַֽד־הַגְּב֣וּל שִׁלְּח֗וּךָᵈ כֹּ֚ל אַנְשֵׁ֣י בְרִיתֶ֔ךָᵇ

הִשִּׁיא֛וּךָ יָכְל֥וּ לְךָ֖ אַנְשֵׁ֣י שְׁלֹמֶ֑ךָᵈ

לַחְמְךָ֗ יָשִׂ֤ימוּ מָזוֹר֙ᶜ תַּחְתֶּ֔יךָ אֵ֥ין תְּבוּנָ֖הᵍ בּֽוֹ׃

8 הֲל֛וֹא בַּיּ֥וֹם הַה֖וּא נְאֻם־יְהוָ֑ה

וְהַאֲבַדְתִּ֤יᵃ חֲכָמִים֙ מֵֽאֱד֔וֹם וּתְבוּנָ֖הᵇ מֵהַ֥ר עֵשָֽׂו׃

Obadiah 1

1 ᵃS72 חָזוֹן *vision, revelation.* ᵇPN *Obadiah.* ᶜS71 שְׁמוּעָה *news, report.* ᵈS70 ᵢ צִיר *envoy, messenger.* ᵉDp10 ᵢ שׁלח. ᶠG37, ᵍG49 קום.

2 ᵃS70 קָטֹן *small; insignificant; young.* ᵇG14s2 ᵢ נתן. ᶜGp50 בזה *despise.*

3 ᵃS72 זָדוֹן *arrogance, pride.* ᵇH10s2 ᵢᵢ נשׁא *trick, deceive.* ᶜS77 חַגְוָה (or וְהָגוּ) *refuge, shelter; cleft in rock.* ᵈS70 סֶלַע *rock; cliff.* ᵉS72 מָרוֹם *height; elevated site.* ᶠS72s0 שֶׁבֶת *home, dwelling.* ᵍH20s4 ירד.

4 ᵃH22 גבה *go high, soar.* ᵇS70 נֶשֶׁר *eagle; vulture.* ᶜS75 כּוֹכָב *star.* ᵈGp50 (G65?) ᵢ שׂים. ᵉS72s2 קֵן *nest.* ᶠH24s3 ירד.

5 ᵃS75 גַּנָּב *thief.* ᵇG15 בוא. ᶜG57 שׁדד *destroy,* devastate. ᵈinterr. אֵיךְ *how?* ᵉN12 ᵢᵢᵢ דמה *be ruined.* ᶠG25 ᵢ גנב *steal.* ᵍS72s0 דַּי *sufficient, enough.* ʰG55 ᵢ בצר *pick grapes.* ⁱS76 עֹלֵלוֹת *gleanings.*

6 ᵃinterj אֵיךְ *how!* ᵇN15 חפשׂ *be searched out, ransacked.* ᶜN15 ᵢᵢᵢ בעה *be grazed until bare.* ᵈS77s0 מַצְפּוּן *private collection, hidden treasure.*

7 ᵃD15s2 ᵢ שׁלח. ᵇ⁻ᵇ= *treaty partners, allies.* ᶜH15s2 ᵢᵢ נשׁא *trick, deceive.* ᵈ⁻ᵈ= *those who are at peace with you.* ᵉS72s2 לֶחֶם; *or rd* לַחֲמֶיךָ G57s2 ᵢᵢ לחם *those who eat with you.* ᶠG25 ᵢ שׂים. ᵍS70 ᵢᵢ מָזוֹר *ambush; trap.* ʰS71 ᵢᵢ תְּבוּנָה *reason, rationality.*

8 ᵃHrl4 ᵢ אבד. ᵇS71 ᵢᵢ תְּבוּנָה *reason, rationality.*

through a particular book of the Bible, the words will be given in the chapter(s)/verse(s) in which they occur in the text. Words found in Genesis 1 are under the lexical heading for Genesis 1. Words occurring in Genesis 2 are under the lexical heading for Genesis 2, and so on.

The best Hebrew Bible reader's lexicon available is *A Reader's Hebrew-English Lexicon of the Old Testament* by Terry A. Armstrong, Douglas L. Busby, and Cyril F. Carr.[7] Definitions (drawn from BDB) are provided for all words that occur fewer than fifty times. The authors of this volume also provide additional statistics regarding the usage of each word listed. Up to three numbers are provided as frequency data. For nouns and adjectives, the first number indicates how many times that word occurs in the book you are reading (e.g., Genesis). The second number indicates how many times that word occurs in the entire Hebrew Bible. For verbs, the first number tells you how many times the word occurs *in the given stem* (e.g., *qal*) in the book you're reading. The second number indicates how many times the word occurs *in that stem* in the rest of the Hebrew Bible. The third number indicates how many times the word is used in the Hebrew Bible in all verbal stems combined.

Reading with a Lexicon or Dictionary

Using only a lexicon or dictionary may prove to be more of a challenge than you want. However, the benefits (and encouragement) of sitting down with nothing but your Hebrew Bible and a dictionary will be worth it. The hard work of flipping pages in a lexicon to get to the right word, and then scouring the word's entry, will pay dividends that you never dreamed of. It will be slow work at first. If there is a word you don't know, you are forced to either skip it (not ideal) or pause your reading to look up the inflected word in the dictionary. If you are just learning Hebrew, there is a slight chance that you will not be able to even find the word since you typically have to look up the lexical form of the word. Verbs are especially difficult since they

---

7. Terry A. Armstrong, Douglas L. Busby, and Cyril F. Carr, *A Reader's Hebrew-English Lexicon of the Old Testament* (Grand Rapids: Zondervan, 2013). This lexicon was originally published in 1980 as a three-volume set. Zondervan reprinted a single-volume edition in 2013.

often have weaknesses in the roots (gutturals, *vavs*, *yods*, geminates, etc.) that obscure the root you are trying to find in the lexicon. In the end, what began as an exercise in reading turns into an exercise in the alphabet and using a dictionary (though not a bad thing in itself). Such an approach can easily lead to disappointment and discouragement. Even so, be encouraged by the testimony of John Newton, the author of "Amazing Grace":

> You must not think that I have attained or ever aimed at, a critical skill in any of these: . . . In the Hebrew, I can read the Historical Books and Psalms with tolerable ease; but, in the Prophetical and difficult parts, I am frequently obliged to have recourse to lexicons, etc. However, I know so much as to be able, with such helps as are at hand, to judge for myself the meaning of any passage I have occasion to consult.[8]

Because of some of these difficulties, lexicons and dictionaries are recommended for those who have a vast vocabulary and at least a couple of years of practice reading the Hebrew Bible.

Reading with Digital Texts

The ability to read the Hebrew Bible and access Hebrew resources digitally is now a reality for virtually every student. In fact, the majority of students who will continue faithfully to read their Hebrew will do so in digital format because of the ease of access and resources that link to the text. While it can be inconvenient to carry a printed edition of the Hebrew Bible, one can easily access a digital text on one's computer, tablet, or smartphone. Currently, the smartphone has become the ubiquitous digital assistant—replacing cameras, books, wallets, and even printed Hebrew Bibles!

In addition, many digital texts have search features that mirror concordance capabilities and are linked with lexicons, parsing information, and even grammatical diagrams so that students can quickly gain assistance with the text. We realize that any digital recommendations

---

8. Richard Cecil, *Memoirs of the Rev. John Newton*, in *The Works of Rev. John Newton*, vol. 1, 49–50, quoted in John Piper, *Brothers, We Are Not Professionals: A Plea to Pastors for Radical Ministry*, updated and expanded ed. (Nashville: B&H, 2013), 104.

will quickly become outdated, but we tentatively offer the following recommendations. For the computer, we recommend Accordance or Logos. For tablets and smartphones, we recommend the Olive Tree Bible Study app or the Accordance or Logos apps. Also, on tablets, Biblearc has an excellent app that provides modules for arcing, block diagramming, and discourse analysis, all similar to what's available at their website.

One word about digital texts must be included here. Like the interlinears above, if digital texts get you reading the Hebrew Bible, then by all means use them. In order to learn Hebrew, *you must read* Hebrew. If the convenience of the digital texts provides the opportunity for you to read Hebrew while getting an oil change or waiting at the salon, then certainly use them. However, be aware that convenience is not the best way to learn Hebrew. We will talk more about this in the next chapter, but for now, be aware that there are some significant drawbacks to relying solely on digital Hebrew Bibles and all the bells and whistles those digital versions usually provide.

How Long to Read

In the story about the guy from the gym at the beginning of this chapter, notice that he began exercising according to his abilities. He was not physically able to exercise for long periods of time or do any sort of strenuous activity. Walking with the help of the treadmill handrails was where he began. He started slowly, but he was consistent. For newly minted Hebrew students, the key is not the amount of time they spend reading the Hebrew Bible but how *consistently* they read it. Often, if our goals are too lofty, we will fail to reach them. Also, we must remember that it is better to read a little every day rather than to read for an extended period of time once (or twice) a week. We would suggest reading the Hebrew Bible for at least ten minutes a day. For the beginning student this may amount to only a few verses. Over time, however, your goal should be to read Hebrew for at least thirty minutes every day. Again, don't be discouraged by how few verses you may read in that thirty minutes. The key is consistency. Read. Read. Read. Is thirty minutes a day worth a lifetime of delight and joy in the Hebrew Bible?

Testimonial of a Renewed Hebrew Reader

I had learned Hebrew and Greek in my late teens and early twenties. I had gained a solid foundation of the grammar and vocabulary of both languages.

Somehow, however, I had left the knowledge of the languages at some rest stop along the highway of life. Maybe they had jumped out of the car when I wasn't looking. All I could say was it was forty years later, and it seemed I knew less than I did before. I knew I should be much farther along than I was. I was frustrated and disappointed in myself, wondering if I should just accept what had happened or maybe, just maybe, do something about it.

Was it possible to go back to that rest stop and pick Hebrew and Greek up again? Would they be waiting for me when I went back to get them?

Three life occurrences caused me to reach this disquieting moment. First, I had a son in seminary who was learning the original languages. He was excited and wanted to share that excitement with me. Wanting to encourage dear old dad, he purchased for me first a reader's Greek New Testament and later a reader's Hebrew Old Testament.

That's when I first realized my language skills were back at the rest stop.

Reader's editions are wonderful gifts that weren't available when I was younger. In the "old days" it was difficult to "just" read Hebrew by oneself as there were frequently rare words or forms that required breaking out the lexicon. Sometimes the most difficult part was figuring out what the dictionary form of the word was! Personal computers and helpful websites didn't exist, so it took a lot of dedication and commitment (as well as time) to look things up in a bulky book every sentence or two.

I also felt pressured by time. I was impatient, and reading in the original took a lot more time than reading in English. While I had made a commitment to read in the original before preaching on a passage, that was about the only time I did so. Consequently, I didn't progress in my skills as I should have. And when opportunities to preach diminished because of my circumstances, even less time was spent in the original languages.

So, having reader's editions was marvelous. I could read anywhere, and more scriptural ground could be covered because I was not stopping every few words to look something up. All I had to do was look at the bottom of the page at the appropriate note, get the sense, and continue reading. And yes, I am aware that there are apps and websites that make all this possible on a smartphone, but we're talking about someone who is old school and likes the feel of a real book in his hands.

A second push came from leading the five hundredth anniversary celebration of the Reformation at my church. I was aware that it was coming long before it got there, and I immersed myself in reading about the Reformers. Their writings and stories of their lives inspired and challenged me. At a time when few knew the original languages, when there was a paucity of linguistic resources, and when translating the Bible into the vernacular was either dangerous or illegal, God raised up mighty men. Men such as Martin Luther, William Tyndale, and John Calvin. At one point I was reading about the preaching of Calvin. He spread the Hebrew and Greek texts out on the pulpit in front of him as he explained God's word to his people!

As this amazing fact sank in, I felt deeply convicted. "I have learned Greek and Hebrew without any fear of persecution or death," I thought. "I have so many amazing resources that make it much easier than these men could have ever imagined. I have been blessed with an ability that relatively few have. And yet I have not even finished reading the Scriptures in the original."

A third motivation has come from the discovery of "Daily Dose of Greek" and "Daily Dose of Hebrew." Only two to three minutes long, these online gems allow me to hear the original text spoken and explained. They review basic elements of grammar and provide more advanced observations in an understandable way. And they are so short that I sometimes find myself listening to them again or finding an older episode from the archives!

A day came when I set a goal for myself. I took stock of how much I had read in the Hebrew and Greek and decided to stretch myself. With God's help, I will have read the entire Bible in the original before my birthday in 2021.

Together, these three opportunities combined to reignite my passion to get into God's word. I get to hear from the Lord in the languages in which he spoke to the prophets and apostles of old.

So, what have been the benefits of this change in outlook and my rediscoveries of the original languages? In answering the question, let me confine myself to what I have done with Hebrew. I found that my skill with this language had deteriorated more, so the transformation has been more dramatic.

First, simply reading the Hebrew text has helped sharpen and develop my skills. I was amazed at how much I had supposedly forgotten came back when I began exercising my Hebrew muscles. Have you ever heard the comment "Use it or lose it"? From experience I can tell you that when you use it, you can regain it.

This doesn't mean that it will be easy. There were times when I simply couldn't remember what a word meant or didn't recognize what stem was being used. Yes, I was tempted to quit! But as I slogged along, a surprising thing happened: I actually got better! I surprised myself by remembering things I hadn't thought about for a long time. It started coming back, and slowly, little by little, improvement came.

A second development was unexpected. I'm a good reader and have read the English text numerous times. Apparently, familiarity breeds contempt. I simply wasn't seeing those precious new truths when I read Scripture in English because I was just sailing along. But since I don't read Hebrew as well as I do English, I am forced to go at a slower pace. All of a sudden, I see beauty where there was none the last time I passed through. Or at least I didn't notice it. Great nuggets of truth are jumping out at me just because I'm reading in Hebrew. I know it sounds crazy, but it's really happening!

Finally, there are those quirky things called "Hebraisms": the way certain ideas are emphasized because of word order, the idiomatic way of saying things that is so different from English, and the subtle nuances seen when certain stems are used. These differences in the languages intrigue me, make me smile, delight the soul. And they cause me to praise God for using the Hebrew language to express his word to us.

—Phil Neetz[a]

What should you do while reading the text? At first, we suggest parsing all verbs (and other parts of speech, if needed), paying attention to grammar. Parsing can be tricky in Hebrew with weak verbs, but don't get discouraged. As we mentioned above, have a lexicon on hand and refer to it if needed. Since we are trying to engage all the senses, write down the parsings in a journal or notebook. Once you can quickly parse, then the focus should be on reading longer portions. Of course, as we read the text, we should not merely focus on parsing and grammar, but we must remember that we are reading God's holy and inspired word. If we are not reading the Bible devotionally, but merely reading as an academic exercise, the motivation for sustained, daily reading will be difficult to maintain. Ideally, we want to get to the point where we can read the Hebrew Bible similarly to the way we can read our English Bibles.

How to Use Hebrew While Memorizing Verses in English

Many people may not find it helpful or encouraging to memorize verses in Hebrew. But memorizing Bible verses is a practice that is beneficial for all believers. We are exhorted to meditate on God's word day and night so that we will be like a tree planted by streams of water (Ps. 1:2–3). Elsewhere the psalmist speaks of storing or hiding God's word in his heart that he might not sin against God (Ps. 119:11). We are convinced that it should be the practice of every Christian to memorize God's word on a consistent basis—in your heart language. How then can Hebrew aid in this process?

The basic answer is to study Hebrew *while* you memorize verses in English. In other words, as you are considering, meditating on, repeating, and pondering the meaning of the English text (in whatever version you choose), it is also beneficial to read and analyze the Hebrew text. There are at least three main benefits to this practice.

First, it is another avenue that leads you to read the Hebrew text. In order to gain proficiency in any language, a person must repeatedly and regularly be thinking about that language.

Second, it allows you to see the translation philosophy of your preferred translation. With the English text freshly rooted into your memory, as you read over the Hebrew text, you will almost automatically compare the Hebrew original with the English translation. You will begin to see the strengths and perhaps some weaknesses of your English version. You'll be able to see addition or omission of words between the two languages, adjustments in word order, or even how consistently the committee translated the same Hebrew term in different places.

Third, you will likely be able to memorize the English faster. The reason for this goes back to some of the things we discussed in chapter 4 ("Develop a Next-Level Memory"). The key to effective memorization is association. The more items that we can associate with a word, phrase, or verse, the more likely we are to memorize it. Former US memory champion Joshua Foer notes, "People who have more associations to hang their memories on are more likely to remember new things, which in turn means they will know more, and be able to learn more."[9] In other words, the more we know, the easier it is to know more. Taking an English verse and adding to it the Hebrew original will help the new language (Hebrew) stick and will help you memorize the verse in your heart language.

By way of example, let's look at Deuteronomy 6:5. This verse is super familiar to many of us, but do we really know what it says, or *why* it says what it says? Let's look at the ESV and MT together:

"You shall love the LORD your God with all your heart and with all your soul and with all your might."

וְאָהַבְתָּ אֵת יְהוָה אֱלֹהֶיךָ בְּכָל־לְבָבְךָ וּבְכָל־נַפְשְׁךָ וּבְכָל־מְאֹדֶךָ׃

As we glance at the English of Deuteronomy 6:5, many of us have it (or at least a paraphrased form of it) memorized already. However, when you look at the Hebrew, we see that the initial verb is stated not as a command but rather as a *vav*-consecutive on a perfect (*veqatal*), changing the normal past, complete action of the perfect to an incomplete action. In other words, "you shall love the Lord your God"

9. Joshua Foer, *Moonwalking with Einstein: The Art and Science of Remembering Everything* (New York: Penguin, 2011), 209.

here is technically not a command but an expectation of ongoing love and devotion to Yahweh, the one true God (cf. Deut. 6:4). Much of the verse is similar from here on until we get to the final word. The ESV has "might," but the Hebrew is "with all your מְאֹד." For those with a basic vocabulary under your belt, you'll know that מְאֹד means "very." מְאֹד might be my favorite word in Hebrew, and this verse is one of the reasons why. I have to be honest with you that to this day, I'm not sure I can explain what it means to love the Lord your God with all your "veryness," but I absolutely love the way it is worded. "You shall love the Lord your God . . . with all your veryness." I may not be able to put that into good English, but I know even more deeply what the verse is saying.

Now, how does this help with memorizing Deuteronomy 6:5? As I mentioned before, many of us are familiar enough with this passage that we may have it memorized already. However, reading the verse in the original Hebrew brings out nuances that solidify and enhance what we already know. Now when you recite Deuteronomy 6:5, many of you may say, "You shall love the Lord your God with all your heart and with all your soul and with all your veryness." It's OK if people look at you funny. . . . They will know *exactly* what you mean!

Looking at the Hebrew text while you memorize the English provides several benefits: (1) it reinforces the Hebrew you are learning; (2) it teaches you about the translation strategy of the English version you are memorizing; and (3) it can help you to more easily memorize the Hebrew since you have another language to which you can build an association. For instance, as you seek to recall Deuteronomy 6:5, you may not have a good English word for the translation, but you remember the Hebrew and its peculiar (but glorious) nuance. This will then allow you to reconstruct the English. In the end, the more you use the Hebrew, the quicker and better you will learn it. This technique provides another method of making that happen.

──────────────── **Chapter Reflections** ────────────────

1. Can you envision yourself reading Hebrew daily? What would it take to make that happen?

2. Which Old Testament book do you think would be best for you to start reading?

3. We recommend starting with a reader's Hebrew Bible. Do you think this tool is appropriate for you?

4. What are ways in which digital tools can either help or hurt you? Write these down and reevaluate if/as you use them.

5. Can you commit to read Hebrew for at least ten minutes a day? What are ways in which using Hebrew to memorize English can be beneficial?

God's Active Memory

William R. Osborne

───────────────○───────────────

I grew up in North Carolina, and my family had a list of "hillbilly one-liners" that would knock your socks off! I can remember looking at my parents as a kid with my head cocked to the side as though asking them to translate what my grandmother was actually saying. Perhaps you, too, have sayings that you inherited from your grandparents or parents. In fact, all languages possess such phrases, and they are called *idiomatic expressions* (not to be confused with *idiotic expressions*!). These are unique, cultural expressions that capture an idea in a way that is not literal but very expressive within the given cultural context.

Hebrew is no exception when it comes to idiomatic expressions. The Hebrew Bible is filled with examples of how the Hebrew language communicates different ideas with unique, nonliteral turns of phrase. One that has always captured my attention is the way Scripture speaks about God remembering (זכר). Idioms used to describe God in human terms are often called *anthropomorphisms* (from the Greek word *anthrōpos*, meaning "human," and the Greek word *morphē*, meaning "form"), because they are describing the transcendent God of the universe with words that take on human form and perspective. Naturally, we recognize the nonliteral nature of such idioms. However, if God does not literally forget things, what does it mean to say that God remembers? Let's look at a few examples in the Old Testament where God is described as remembering.

Genesis 8:1

וַיִּזְכֹּר אֱלֹהִים אֶת־נֹחַ וְאֵת כָּל־הַחַיָּה וְאֶת־כָּל־הַבְּהֵמָה אֲשֶׁר אִתּוֹ בַּתֵּבָה וַיַּעֲבֵר אֱלֹהִים רוּחַ עַל־הָאָרֶץ וַיָּשֹׁכּוּ הַמָּיִם:

And God remembered Noah and all the beasts and all the livestock that were with him on the ark. And God caused a wind to blow upon the earth, and the waters decreased.

Exodus 2:24

וַיִּשְׁמַע אֱלֹהִים אֶת־נַאֲקָתָם וַיִּזְכֹּר אֱלֹהִים אֶת־בְּרִיתוֹ אֶת־אַבְרָהָם אֶת־יִצְחָק וְאֶת־יַעֲקֹב:

And God heard their groaning, and God remembered his covenant with Abraham, Isaac, and Jacob.

1 Samuel 1:19b–20a

וַיֵּדַע אֶלְקָנָה אֶת־חַנָּה אִשְׁתּוֹ וַיִּזְכְּרֶהָ יְהוָה: וַיְהִי לִתְקֻפוֹת הַיָּמִים וַתַּהַר חַנָּה וַתֵּלֶד בֵּן וַתִּקְרָא אֶת־שְׁמוֹ שְׁמוּאֵל

And Elkanah knew Hannah his wife, and YHWH remembered her. And in the turning of the days, Hannah conceived and bore a son and called his name Samuel.

Quickly studying these three passages, we see that God's "remembrance" of something precedes his coming action on behalf of that which he remembered. In Genesis 8:1, God remembers Noah and the animals and then acts to begin subduing the waters from the earth. In Exodus 2:24, God observes the suffering of Israel in Egypt, remembers his previous covenant with the patriarchs, and then, in the beginning of chapter 3, raises up Moses to carry out his plan of water-parting redemption! First Samuel 1:19–20 reminds us of the suffering and agony of the barren Hannah. However, God remembered Hannah, and his remembrance is portrayed in the passage as the causative force behind the miraculous birth of Samuel. The point is that God's "remembering" is actually an idiomatic way of describing how he is preparing to act. The persons remembered are then the beneficiaries of God's gracious plan playing out in their lives—whether it's Noah, Israel, or Hannah. God truly has an active memory!

Interestingly, the Bible has just as much to say about what God does *not* remember. Jeremiah 31:34 reads, "And their sin I will remember no longer" (וּלְחַטָּאתָם לֹא אֶזְכָּר־עוֹד). Just as the act of God remembering something indicates the past motivations for his present and future action, when the Hebrew reads that God "no longer remembers," it communicates that God is no longer allowing the past to dictate his posture going forward. This is incredibly good news when we consider the fact that God is "forgetting" our sin! The good news recorded in the book of Jeremiah is that God is no longer going to relate to us according to our past sins. This is not because God causes himself to literally forget our transgressions. Instead, God is covenanting that the day is coming when his relating to his people will be based no longer on judgment for past sin but on divine grace and forgiveness established by a new covenant.

The Wisdom of Resources

In a 2013 interview produced by BibleMesh, Ligon Duncan highlights that the vast number of tools we have available today in the biblical languages is both impressive and welcomed.[1] Duncan also argues, however, that these resources don't replace the hard work necessary to learn the original languages. He relays a conversation on this subject that he had with John Piper, who has a computer Bible program up from start to finish when preparing a sermon. The point that Duncan makes is that while the resources are vast, only those who know the languages will know how best to use the resources and to use resources with wisdom. In light of that, I want to encourage you to make the best use of this chapter. Don't just skip to this chapter and think this is the linchpin or magic bullet to your learning Hebrew. It will still take hours of hard work. However, as you are putting in the hard work, it is also important for you to know about the best resources.

If you're going to put this book to use and work hard to learn Hebrew, then it will be important to be able to wade through the various tools out there. We mentioned in chapter 1 that the expert

1. Ligon Duncan, "Ligon Duncan on 'Why Learn Biblical Hebrew & Greek When There Are Good Language Tools?,'" BibleMesh, YouTube, June 22, 2013, https://www.youtube.com/watch?v=nCkFnk-8NPU.

"Some translations footnote (usually one of) the grammatical options, but many do not. When, say the King James Version differs from the New International Version, how will you determine which of them gives the best sense? 'Gut feeling?' . . . Urim and Thummim? For this, readers need a knowledge of the Biblical languages and access to grammars, lexica, and scholarly commentaries that deal directly with the original text, little of which will make any sense to those unschooled in Biblical languages."
—Rob Starner[a]

with the right tools will be more effective than the novice. We are going to assume that you're reading this book because you want to move more toward the "expert" end of that spectrum, and so in this chapter we will try to help you make sense of the many resources available to study Biblical Hebrew.

My wife and I live in Louisville, Kentucky, and the restaurant choices in our city are vast. When we go on dates, one of our biggest problems is trying to decide where to eat. We begin with the choice of what kind of food we want. Barbeque? Cuban? Burgers? Tex-Mex? Let's say we choose burgers. Now we have to narrow down the burger choices. Fast food? Middle of the road? Gourmet? After choosing gourmet (of course), we now have to select which gourmet burger joint to go to in Louisville because there are so many. This may be a uniquely Louisville problem, but it illustrates the point that having so many choices can reduce us to the anxiety of indecision.

"I am thrilled that we have the tools, especially tools that work for us in the languages, but those tools aren't a replacement for the languages."
—Ligon Duncan[b]

Never before in the history of the world has there existed a language (i.e., English) with such excellent resources for reading the Hebrew Bible. Yet, if we are honest, we might cast a wistful glance at our ancestors who had only a worn Hebrew Bible and a simple lexicon by their side. Studying by lamplight has a romantic appeal, but there is no turning back the clock. And let's be honest—we really don't want to give up our antibiotics or our Bible software programs!

How is the ordinary student or pastor to make sense of this avalanche of Hebrew resources? In this chapter, we will discuss various resources to aid you in your journey of using Hebrew for life.

The Text of the Old Testament

The most essential resource to reading the Hebrew Bible *is* a Hebrew Bible. In chapter 6, we briefly discussed various print and digital formats of Hebrew Bibles. And, just to remind you, it's not wrong to use an interlinear, reader's edition, or diglot. But if you want to grow stronger in your reading, don't rely on assistance any more than is necessary. Children whose parents always cut up their food will never learn to use a knife for themselves.

Even with astounding digital tools available, students today need to rediscover the joy of reading a printed page. When we open our computers or phones to access a digital version of the Hebrew text, many of us find ourselves perusing Facebook, Instagram, or Twitter rather than actually reading the Hebrew text we intended. Maybe you're not enticed by social media, but you open your laptop and find yourself checking email, proofreading your paper or sermon, or just browsing recent news on the internet. Sometimes I even get my laptop open, get my Bible software open, and then it loads to the last project I was working on and so I pick it back up rather than simply reading like I intended to do in the first place.

It's true. While a smartphone or computer allows for immediate and helpful interaction with the Hebrew Bible, many distractions are one click away. We live in a historical moment when the enticement of what is "new" and "fresh" steals our attention away from long-term goals. People have trouble limiting their intake of new tidbits of information, simply because that information is new. Viral pet videos (or even Christian videos or blogs) can crowd out potential intake of more eternal value—namely, the actual words of Scripture. We may feel that we face worse temptations than our forefathers, but Martin Luther reminds us how frequently in church history the Bible has been shunted to the side:

> I am well aware how little the church has been profited since they have begun to collect many books and large libraries, in addition to and besides the Holy Scriptures, and especially since they have stored up, without discrimination, all sorts of writings by the church fathers, the councils, and teachers. Through this practice not only is precious time lost, which could be used for studying the Scriptures, but in the

end the pure knowledge of the divine Word is also lost, so that the Bible lies forgotten in the dust under the bench (as happened to the book of Deuteronomy, in the time of the kings of Judah).[2]

So, let us return *ad fontes* (to the sources)—to the Scriptures themselves!

Software, Websites, and Smartphone Apps

I am writing this paragraph in 2019. By the time you read these words, new technological advancements will have occurred. What will remain unchanged, however, is the availability of biblical texts, resources, and pedagogical tools in digital format. If we can exercise self-control with our technology (and not waste our time on mindless drivel or even somewhat worthwhile drivel), how valuable this technology can be! When we simply touch a word or click a mouse, full parsing and lexical information can be displayed. Multiple translations can be laid side by side for comparison. Searches of intoxicating complexity can be performed in a fraction of a second.

Given the current state of technology, let us consider the best options within various categories (Bible software, smartphone apps, etc.). In figure 7.1, we present what we believe is the best of the best.

When it comes to accessing digital texts, there are various types of reading you will do. It's good to be conscious of your style of reading and to vary your approach. Below is a brief discussion of common ways of reading the Hebrew text, with special attention to reading in digital formats:

- *Reading for Technological Competency.* Especially when you begin using a new app, website, or software, it's advisable to spend time exploring how to navigate the digital text and access resources. I recently began working with Logos Bible

2. "Preface to the Wittenberg Edition of Luther's German Writings" (1539), in *Martin Luther's Basic Theological Writings*, ed. Timothy F. Lull, 2nd ed. (Minneapolis: Fortress, 2005), 70–71.

Figure 7.1

Category	Recommendations	Comments
Bible software	Accordance Logos [BibleWorks][a]	It takes time to learn how to use any Bible software program. Such programs can also be quite expensive since you largely have to purchase modules individually. The upside of these programs is that you can tailor what you need/want.
Smartphone apps to read the Hebrew Bible	Biblearc Accordance or Logos app Olive Tree Bible Study app	Basic Biblearc is free, but the monthly subscription allows you to save your work on arcing, diagramming, or discourse analysis. The other smartphone apps provide more robust resources than Biblearc. They mirror the resources you've purchased on those platforms and thus give you mobile access to your digital libraries and resources.
Smartphone apps to learn vocab and more	Bible Vocab[b] Vocab Pro Quizlet	For Quizlet, you can search the website for vocabulary lists that have already been made and add those to your sets.
Websites to read biblical texts	www.biblearc.com www.sefaria.org	Biblearc also includes the Septuagint and Greek New Testament. Sefaria includes a massive Jewish library including Mishnah, Talmud, and other commentary in addition to the Hebrew Bible.
Websites for Hebrew instruction	www.dailydoseofhebrew.com www.introductiontohebrew.com www.animatedhebrew.com www.biblearc.com/path/hebrew/en/	For a free daily two-minute video to read and review Hebrew, sign up at the Daily Dose of Hebrew.

[a] In June 2018, BibleWorks sadly announced they were closing operation (https://www.bibleworks.com/news/nr20180601ec.html). BibleWorks affirmed, however, that they would still provide support for those who had BibleWorks 10. We are still holding out hope that someone may come along and revive BibleWorks. For now, we have left it on the list for those who purchased it before their closing and will continue to receive support and updates. As long as your computer will run it, BibleWorks is an incredibly valuable resource.

[b] For an overview video of this app, see https://www.youtube.com/watch?v=W63jhYWNNv0.

Software, and one of the big hurdles was simply learning how to use it. I watched many tutorial videos, read instructions, and clicked around on my own. In all of this exploring the new software, I was reading Hebrew texts to learn the power of the original language resources. It was a breath of fresh air when I found that I could click a word twice and bring up my *Dictionary of Classical Hebrew* or right click the word and search it in a variety of other resources. The amount of data produced without even having to leave my seat was unimaginable in an earlier era of Hebrew studies. However, to access that data in a manageable and useful way, I had to spend some time learning the technology of the software. Without some time to explore and grow more comfortable with our technological tools, we will not be able to use them effectively later. Many software programs offer blogs, podcasts, tutorial videos, and forums where you can find nearly anything you need to know about basic usage or complex searches. It's worth the time to learn how to use your software well.

- *Slow Grammatical Reading.* If you are working through a new or difficult text, it's fine to have an English translation displayed alongside. Depending on your competency level, you may need to access parsing or lexical information frequently. Even for Old Testament scholars, a foray into difficult extrabiblical texts may require such a plodding approach. The immediate goal in slow grammatical reading is to untangle and properly read the text, with the ultimate goal of coming back with greater fluency later. Bible software will allow you to search for similar grammatical constructions elsewhere in the Hebrew Bible so that you can compare how a difficult clause or phrase is translated. For those who would employ this method of reading, I would encourage you to discipline yourself to fix your eyes on the Hebrew text and only have the English text on hand in case you get stuck. As you focus on the details of grammar, use the software tools to help you discern the translation (lexica, grammars, etc.). Don't resort immediately to the English provided, and

leave the quick parsing information as a last resort. You may
even consider turning off the quick parsing information to
force yourself to look up information in the digital resources
within your software.

- *Slow Exploratory Reading.* Whether a Hebrew text is easy
or difficult, it can be beneficial to slowly meander through it,
pursuing any questions that arise. For example, you might
ask, "I wonder how many times this word occurs in the Old
Testament? (click) Hmmm. How many times does this word
occur in the Mishnah? (click) Let me skim through various
lexical entries for this word . . . (click, click, scroll, click) I
wonder how Accordance or Logos tags this grammatical
construction? (click) Does Waltke-O'Connor, Gesenius, or
Joüon-Muraoka mention this unusual use of the preposition in their grammars? (click)." Lots of learning can happen when you take time to be curious and explore. This
exploratory reading will prove to be quite helpful the more
you stick to the academic resources. In other words, it pays
off big time to click around in advanced reference grammars
or lexica like *HALOT*, BDB, or *DCH*. Diving into these
advanced resources will provide you with some higher-level
lingo even if you don't fully understand everything you're
reading in *Gesenius' Hebrew Grammar.*

- *Slow Contemplative Reading.* It's a wonderful experience
to slowly read the Hebrew Bible for spiritual nourishment.
It's not that one shuts out grammatical questions, but in
contemplative reading, the focus is on knowing God, being
nourished and challenged by his word, and responding in
faith, prayer, repentance, and obedience. If you remember the
testimony of Phil Neetz in the last chapter, his slow reading
of the Hebrew text allowed him to notice things he'd never
noticed in English. He heard the word afresh. Sometimes it
may be beneficial to pray in Hebrew or to sing Psalms in Hebrew. Have you considered memorizing Psalm 1 or other Old
Testament texts in Hebrew? If you're a cessationist, this may
be your only chance to pray in tongues.

- *Fast Reading.* When you are sufficiently familiar with a Hebrew text, you can read it very quickly. Students mistakenly
  think, "Oh, there's no reason to keep reading a text I know
  well. I already know what it means." Wrong! Imagine how
  odd it would be for young children to make this argument
  (i.e., "I'm not going to read those words anymore; I know
  what they mean"). Something amazing happens when we
  repeatedly read longer sections of Hebrew text. The Hebrew
  percolates down into our brains. Hebrew syntax begins to
  become more intuitive. It's almost like our brain suddenly
  "clicks over" to a different linguistic realm. In a conversation
  with Karl Kutz and Rebekah Josberger regarding their Hebrew grammar, *Learning Biblical Hebrew* (Lexham, 2018),
  they told me that one of their assignments each semester is to
  have students read an extended passage of the Hebrew Bible
  five days a week for the whole semester. The students read
  the Hebrew text out loud, translate more
  and more of it as the semester goes on, and
  begin to "digest" the sense of Hebrew grammar and syntax simply by becoming very
  familiar with this one passage. They learn
  to comprehend what they're reading in real
  time rather than reading phonetic values that
  mean nothing to them followed by a disjointed translation.
  This takes work, oftentimes the whole semester. However, by
  the end, most students have a solid grasp of that extended
  Hebrew passage.

> "Read biblical [Hebrew]
> text as soon and as
> much as possible."
> —Karl Kutz and Rebekah
> Josberger[c]

Lexicons and Word Study Tools

In beginning Hebrew classes, students don't really learn full definitions of words. For each Hebrew word, they usually learn a "gloss"—
a single, overly simplified rendering. All words have a range of meaning (semantic range), and part of becoming a more competent reader
of Hebrew is to nuance one's understanding of the semantic range of
Hebrew words. How do you do this? By looking up the words in a
print or digital lexicon. The best lexica for the Hebrew Bible are BDB,

> "The discovery of cognate languages affected Hebrew lexicography in a double way. It has enriched the Hebrew lexicon with many supporting statements, with a heap of parallels. On the other side what we know today of the Akkadian and Ugaritic lexicon would be impossible to a great extent without Hebrew. At the same time the consequence of those discoveries has made the Hebrew dictionary a storehouse of Semitic idioms."
>
> —Ludwig Koehler[d]

HALOT, or *DCH*.[3] After looking up a word, take some time to read through the major definitions for that word. Be selective. There is not time to do this for every word (or every time you study), but occasionally you can explore key terms in-depth. To aid in long-term retention, take some notes on what you learn.

For a broader set of theological dictionaries to aid in responsible word studies, nothing surpasses the *New International Dictionary of Old Testament Theology and Exegesis (NIDOTTE)* (Zondervan, 2012), edited by Willem A. VanGemeren. The five-volume set is organized and written in such a way that even someone with very little Hebrew can benefit. When pastors ask me what Old Testament word study tool to buy, this is my first recommendation.

For more detailed discussion of lexica, word study tools, and how to properly do word studies, the reader is referred to appendix 2 ("Noun Types and Basics for Using Your Hebrew Lexicon") of *A Modern Grammar for Biblical Hebrew*.[4]

> "The preacher who ridicules word studies merely exposes his own ignorance. The lexicon may point the way to life."
>
> —A. T. Robertson[e]

Communities of Accountability

When students think about "resources," they immediately think of books or software programs. But do not forget *human* resources. In reality, all those books and digital tools were created by people. It would be great, wouldn't it, to sit down and read through the Hebrew Bible with Bill Arnold by your side making syntactical observations?

3. See the abbreviations list for bibliographic references.
4. Duane A. Garrett and Jason S. DeRouchie, *A Modern Grammar for Biblical Hebrew* (Nashville: B&H Academic, 2009), 366–70.

Well, frankly, he doesn't have time to do that for you—but he does provide the same service in print or digital format through the publication of *A Guide to Biblical Hebrew Syntax*, 2nd ed. (Cambridge University Press, 2018).

It's also wonderful to be part of a community that enjoys reading the Hebrew Bible together and can share insights and ask questions. Face-to-face interaction is always preferred, but if you don't have any live readers of the Hebrew Bible near you, join the "Nerdy Language Majors" Facebook page, started by Will Varner of The Master's Theological Seminary. As of October 2019, the group has more than 6,100 members who ask questions related to biblical languages or sometimes share insights from their research or reading. With so many members, you can almost always get a question answered or bounce ideas off someone. Recently, I saw someone ask if the use of ברא in Genesis 1:26–27 was a dynamic verbal use. Within three comments, the question was answered quite helpfully, including someone else chiming in that he had no idea what was meant by "dynamic verbal use" (the humility was genuinely refreshing). Don't be afraid of the "scholars" groups. Jump in and enjoy the biblical text in a community that loves to discuss the intricacies of the biblical languages.

Maybe you will be motivated to start a local reading group in your town or city like the group in Sioux Falls that we read about in chapter 5. Maybe you will be that catalyst (because of your own desire to retain Hebrew) that will develop a community of people who love our Savior more because of the gems they begin to unlock in the original Hebrew.

Hebrew Guides/Handbooks

Many online students, after the initial two semesters of online Hebrew instruction, are at a loss about what to do next. If they cannot join us on campus for a one-week Hebrew exegesis course in the winter or summer, I tell them, "Never fear. You can now buy a Hebrew exegesis course in paperback." (Of course, the accountability and interaction of a real class is always preferred.) The Baylor Handbook on the Hebrew Bible series (BHHB; published by Baylor University Press) provides detailed, phrase-by-phrase grammatical analysis of Old Testament books. These volumes also sometimes include word study information or even discourse information. They provide far more than just a Hebrew text and help walk you through the grammar and syntax of the Hebrew Bible. I recommend these volumes to everyone who finishes my third undergraduate semester (equivalent to two graduate semesters) and asks, "What next?"

One of the primary benefits of the Baylor series is that it will likely take you further in your understanding of Hebrew grammar and syntax than an introductory grammar. Since Hebrew has so much to learn by way of morphology, many introductory grammars are not able to provide lengthy chapters on grammatical structures, syntactical arrangements, or discourse analysis. These are usually reserved for intermediate-level Hebrew studies. However, many of the volumes in the BHHB series address the text at the level of both microsyntax *and* macrosyntax, providing a well-rounded discussion of intermediate topics in Hebrew.

Another guide for reading the Hebrew Bible is the 2 Minutes a Day Biblical Languages series published by Hendrickson. This series currently includes two volumes for Hebrew and one for Aramaic.[5] Jonathan Kline has compiled an excellent resource here to guide readers through 365 readings from the Hebrew Bible in each volume. This series is best used as a daily format for reading but also offers a sophisticated vocabulary apparatus to help review old vocabulary and learn new vocabulary. Kline breaks each verse into simple clauses and provides English translations alongside the Hebrew clauses so that readers can see how the Hebrew should be translated. While these volumes do not provide substantial grammatical information like the BHHB series, Kline has provided Hebrew students with a simple format for reading the Hebrew Bible every day.

Commentaries

While we would love to see everyone become a Hebrew master, we also realize that not everyone will. However, I tell my students that they can become conversant enough with Hebrew at least to untangle

---

5. Jonathan Kline, *Keep Up Your Biblical Hebrew in Two Minutes a Day*, vols. 1–2 (Peabody, MA: Hendrickson, 2017), and Kline, *Keep Up Your Biblical Aramaic in Two Minutes a Day* (Peabody, MA: Hendrickson, 2017).

"It could be said that ministers who have not studied the biblical languages enslave themselves to English translations. To be sure, this need not be an absolutely fatal relationship, but it certainly puts ministers at a serious disadvantage. . . . Again, while we are blessed with a multitude of fine commentaries, they can prove to be almost useless if we cannot follow the linguistic argu-ments involved. The problem becomes critical if the pastor has a well-educated congregation—and even more so if some of the members are college students who find themselves bombarded by the arguments of unbelieving professors. Inability by the pastor to provide reasonable responses to pressing questions can prove destructive in some sensitive situations."

—Moisés Silva[f]

a poor exegetical argument that may lead to fallacious conclusions. Studying Hebrew gives students a heightened radar for flawed arguments on the text. In addition to recognizing flawed arguments, students with knowledge of Hebrew can interact with the best commentaries, which are inevitably those that engage with the meaning of the Hebrew text. To find out what are the best technical commentaries (with caveats), see Tremper Longman's recommendations in the most recent *Old Testament Commentary Survey*, 5th ed. (Baker Academic, 2013). As you read a more technical commentary, I would recommend *The Pocket Dictionary for the Study of Biblical Hebrew* (InterVarsity, 2003) to have along with you. This slim and inexpensive volume is worth its weight in gold—providing a brief definition and example of virtually any grammatical term you encounter.

Morphology Questions

Hebrew words (more than Greek words) seem to change in unpredictable ways. I use a morphology-heavy system for learning Hebrew in my classes, but inevitably I find myself explaining a complex morphology situation with the answer of my professor: "The mob rules." What he meant was that as any language is used over time, the "mob" (the crowd who uses the language in everyday speech) dictates how words are pronounced and used, and even what vocabulary is employed. As the Masoretes sought to preserve the pronunciation of the Hebrew Bible, they didn't necessarily look up all of the historical information on the words they were marking. Rather, they preserved the pronunciations as they knew them. Some of the more obscure morphological issues we encounter in Hebrew are due to this "mob rule." This happens in English too. The example I use in class is the word *police*. There are few places I've been in the United States where people pronounce the word *pōlice*. However, I usually hear *pəlice*. I use this example in classes to demonstrate a vocal *shewa* sound, but it also works here to illustrate that English doesn't have a rule or precedent for this kind of sound dissimilation, other than that this is how the "mob" pronounces the word. If we pretended to be Masoretes with an unpointed text, we would likely spell *pəlice* as פְּלִיס, just as it sounds.

As you might imagine, this is not always a satisfactory explanation for my students, but it is helpful that they see similarly difficult morphological phenomena even in English. Another example is the negation of *legitimate* (*illegitimate*), which doesn't use the prefix *in-* as other English negations do (*in*different, *in*discriminate, *in*describable). There is significant value in learning Hebrew morphology, but there are also limits. The most frustrating answer I give students to the question "Why does Hebrew do that?" is "That's just what it does." I get smirks, eye rolls, and dejected stares every . . . single . . . time.

Even though morphology can be frustrating, over time we will acclimate to certain vowel patterns, contractions, and "odd" exceptions. What we will often find is that the "exceptions" may not actually be exceptional. They may be quite normal given how the "mob" used the word. "Pak ya ca in Havad Yad" is actually quite normal to someone from Boston. My Tennessee heritage needs a translator . . . even for English! The more we encounter odd Hebrew vowel constructions, the more "normal" they will become.

We often evaluate the correctness of another language by how it compares with English or what we expect from a set of rules we've learned. In reality, language doesn't work that way. We can't force Hebrew morphology to fit into a set of rules any more than we can force the English *i* and *e* to occur in the same order every time they occur together in an English word. Regarding morphology issues, which are always related to pronunciation in Hebrew, the best rule of thumb is to realize that oddities, rarities, and "exceptions" are quite alright. In addition, it's also good to recognize that the more we read the Hebrew Bible, the more familiar these "exceptions" will become. It will take hard work to get past some of the more difficult morphological issues in Hebrew, but the payoff of enjoying the Old Testament in the original Hebrew is well worth the effort.

If you are interested in learning more about Hebrew morphology, an indispensable introductory resource is Russell Fuller and Kyoung-won Choi's *Invitation to Biblical Hebrew* (Kregel, 2006). Fuller and Choi's beginning grammar doesn't provide detailed analysis of every morphological issue in Hebrew, but their system to teach Hebrew is based strongly on morphology. You learn why vowels do what they do in certain scenarios and you learn which syllabic scenarios may produce a certain vowel change. By the end of the textbook (if you've devoted yourself to learning all the scenarios), you can easily predict what a certain vowel pattern will do, even with weak verbs! Even when you can't predict the morphological changes, you can at least recognize them and describe them when you see them in the Hebrew Bible.

Hebrew Grammars

When I began studying the original languages, one of the things that I enjoyed was the "science" of labeling syntactical relation-ships. Certainly grammar is not an exact science, but putting tags on syntactical relationships and giving them structure is enjoyable to me. For whatever reason, this was (and still is) intriguing to me. I can actually remember my eighth-grade English teacher, Mr. Pless, who taught us to label sentence parts, conjugate English verbs, and diagram sentences. I don't know if it was the teacher, the methodol-ogy, or just bizarre genetics that made me enjoy this kind of study so much. Regardless of the reason, this delight has continued into my study of Hebrew, and consequently, I love to read and incorpo-rate all sorts of information from all sorts of Hebrew grammars. From the most basic to the most complex, I simply enjoy reading Hebrew grammars. I have to admit, that's probably not normal. So, for those who *are* normal, here are some ways that you can incorporate Hebrew grammars into your study and reading of the Hebrew Bible:

- *Beginning Grammars.* Nearly all beginning Hebrew grammars cover major patterns in Hebrew nouns and verbs and present three hundred to four hundred vocabulary words. Every Hebrew student must make that initial trek through an elementary grammar (often at what they feel is a breakneck speed!). How, though, should a beginning grammar be used in later study? It's a helpful discipline to force yourself to review relevant paradigms if you find yourself struggling with basic form recognition when reading the Hebrew Bible. Small doses of review are best. If you wander too far from reading the Hebrew Bible, your passion for the language may subside. On the other hand, the more basic the fundamentals you review and practice, the more enjoyable your reading will be because you're not pausing every 17.23 seconds to look up a word or parse a form. A wonderful practice, especially for Hebrew students, is to read through an elementary grammar different from the one you initially studied. Since I first opened the cellophane wrapping to my beginning Hebrew grammar in 2005, I've read through several other Hebrew grammars and found that each of them solidified something for me about basic Hebrew.[6] While there were indeed differences in approach, I was still able to learn something from each of them.

- *Intermediate Grammars.* An intermediate grammar typically enhances a student's knowledge of syntactical categories. A beginning Hebrew student knows that a Hebrew perfect (*qatal*) translates as a simple past tense in English (e.g.,

6. A word of caution should be given here about divergent methodologies for learning Hebrew. Introductory Hebrew methodologies can be a divisive issue in higher education. There are so many grammars precisely because everyone believes their method for learning Hebrew is best. And indeed, each author should be proud of his or her work to help students learn Hebrew. However, sticking to only one methodology will restrict your ability to learn Hebrew more holistically. After you've mastered your initial grammar, I can guarantee you will benefit from reading other introductory grammars. The grammars are indeed unique. But that's the beauty of at least perusing grammars other than the one you cut your Hebrew teeth on.

כָּתַב, "he wrote"). After studying an intermediate grammar, however, the student understands that the perfect may
also be translated as a future if it has a *vav*-consecutive. Or,
depending on the stem, the perfect may not be a simple past
active verb; it may be a past tense *passive* ("it was written").
Elementary Hebrew students know to translate a construct
package with "of," whereas an intermediate Hebrew student learns that "of" may indicate the material out of which
something is made ("rod of iron") rather than merely posses-
sion. In addition, the construct chain could communicate a
subjective genitive, objective genitive, possessive genitive, and
so on. According to the late Ronald J. Williams, Hebrew can
communicate eighteen nuances with a construct phrase.[7] The
context is necessary for a student to know which to use, but
the intermediate student will be able to begin making sense
of these more advanced nuances to the language. One major
step in growing in Hebrew is learning to wrestle through
these syntactical decisions yourself. Don't just rely on the
"experts" to tell you what kind of *piel* or *hiphil* Jeremiah
is using. When you encounter an adverbial object (accusative), and you don't know how it is functioning, turn in your
intermediate grammar to the different uses of the adverbial
object. Slowly work through all the options: situation, place,
time, specification. Some resources that can be helpful here
are summary guides or laminated charts that give the major
syntactical categories.[8] It's only by wrestling for yourself that
syntactical categories become part of your own mental data-
base. Another way to make use of an intermediate grammar
is to consult the Scripture index. This is especially helpful if
you are looking at a certain passage or teaching through a
book of the Old Testament. The Scripture index will show

7. Ronald J. Williams, *Williams' Hebrew Syntax*, 3rd ed., rev. and exp. John C.
Beckman (Toronto: University of Toronto Press, 2007), §§36–49.
8. For a helpful summary guide that includes grammatical/syntactical discussion, see
Miles V. Van Pelt, *Biblical Hebrew: A Compact Guide*, 2nd ed. (Grand Rapids: Zondervan, 2019). For a laminated chart, some may find helpful the chart associated with Russell Fuller and Kyoungwon Choi, *Invitation to Biblical Hebrew Syntax* (Grand Rapids:
Kregel, 2017). This chart, published by Kregel, is forthcoming as of this publication.

you where that particular verse is referenced in the grammar, and you can then go to those places in the grammar to see the discussion on the specific passage you're laboring over. It only takes five to ten minutes, and it's a wonderful way to deepen your knowledge of Hebrew while keeping those insights tightly tied to your devotion and teaching.

- *Advanced Grammars.* Eager readers of this book may want to purchase an advanced reference grammar. A reference grammar, such as Waltke-O'Connor, van der Merwe–Naudé, Gesenius, or Joüon-Muraoka, can be used to study chosen grammatical issues in detail. As with intermediate grammars above, getting into the habit of checking the Scripture index for a reference grammar as you prepare

> "The science of theology is nothing else, but Grammar, exercised on the words of the Holy Spirit."
>
> —Johann Albrecht Bengel, attributing Martin Luther[g]

sermons or Bible lessons on an Old Testament book can be a wonderful habit that allows for the digestion of more complex grammatical knowledge in small doses.

Recommended Beginning Hebrew Grammars

- John A. Cook and Robert D. Holmstedt. *Beginning Biblical Hebrew: A Grammar and Illustrated Reader.* Grand Rapids: Baker Academic, 2013. Cook and Holmstedt have produced a grammar with elements of modern linguistics, including second language acquisition. One of the strengths of this grammar is the illustrated reader, in which Cook and Holmstedt have represented biblical stories in pictorial format (a comic book format) so that students are also seeing what they are reading. In addition, much of the vocabulary is presented with an associated picture. From a modern linguistics perspective, Cook and Holmstedt explain grammatical concepts using more updated terminology in the study of Hebrew.
- Russell T. Fuller and Kyoungwon Choi. *Invitation to Biblical Hebrew: A Beginning Grammar.* Grand Rapids: Kregel, 2006. Fuller and Choi represent an introductory grammar

that is heavy on morphology. If you want to learn the "*i* before *e* except after *c*" rules in Hebrew, this grammar provides those details. Fuller and Choi also produced a workbook and videos associated with the grammar.

- William Fullilove. *Introduction to Hebrew: A Guide for Learning and Using Biblical Hebrew*. Phillipsburg, NJ: P&R, 2018. One distinguishing mark of Fullilove's grammar is that he has the student working in the biblical text very early. The goal is to have students reading Hebrew, and so he gets them there quickly with exercises in each chapter from the Hebrew text (even in the first chapter on the alphabet). The exercises also include exegetical practices that are helpful to introduce early on. By having these exegetical practices introduced early, students can hone those skills throughout. Fullilove also includes instructional videos through the website www .introductiontohebrew.com.

- Duane Garrett and Jason S. DeRouchie. *A Modern Grammar for Biblical Hebrew*. Nashville: B&H Academic, 2009. Garrett and DeRouchie provide a thorough introduction to Hebrew. In addition to introductory Hebrew material, they provide chapters on Hebrew accents and textual structures and even an appendix on how to use the *BHS*. These additional pieces help students make the transition to exegesis rather smoothly. Garrett and DeRouchie's system also includes a workbook and videos with teaching aids and vocabulary audio files.

- Karl Kutz and Rebekah Josberger. *Learning Biblical Hebrew: Reading for Comprehension; An Introductory Grammar*. Bellingham, WA: Lexham, 2018. This might be my new favorite introductory grammar. Kutz and Josberger provide enough morphological analysis and discussion that students sufficiently learn word forms found in the Hebrew text, but their goal (like Fullilove's) is to have students reading very quickly. Kutz and Josberger offer a graded workbook with the grammar that has students beginning to read the Joseph narrative as early as week four of study.

- Gary D. Pratico and Miles V. Van Pelt. *Basics of Biblical Hebrew Grammar*. 3rd ed. Grand Rapids: Zondervan, 2019. Pratico–Van Pelt is probably the gold standard in introductory Hebrew grammars. The structure of the grammar provides the information students need in a format that allows them to enjoy the process of learning Hebrew. In addition, Zondervan has produced an entire line of products (laminated sheets, vocabulary cards, workbook, videos, etc.) related to this grammar to help students learn Hebrew.

Recommended Intermediate Hebrew Grammars

- Bill T. Arnold and John H. Choi. *A Guide to Biblical Hebrew Syntax*. 2nd ed. Cambridge: Cambridge University Press, 2018. Arnold and Choi seek to provide a classification and brief discussion of syntactical categories to help bridge the gap between merely identifying and parsing Hebrew words and understanding their roles and meanings in a Hebrew sentence. Like Williams (see below), Arnold and Choi use traditional linguistic cases (nominative, accusative, genitive, etc.) to describe Hebrew syntax even though these cases are not marked morphologically in Hebrew.
- Russell T. Fuller and Kyoungwon Choi. *Invitation to Biblical Hebrew Syntax: An Intermediate Grammar*. Grand Rapids: Kregel, 2017. This intermediate grammar largely follows a traditional Semitic approach to grammar. The primary value in this grammar is the chapter on the Hebrew accents and the compositions. Fuller and Choi provide a section on Hebrew composition akin to J. Weingreen's *Classical Hebrew Composition*.[9] The student is given an English text and asked to write the text in Hebrew. Footnotes are provided instructing the student how to construct various Hebrew idioms to communicate the English text. This exercise may feel "backward" to some, but I tell my students, "If you can write it, then you can read it." If you can get to the point of writing Hebrew

---

9. J. Weingreen, *Classical Hebrew Composition* (Oxford: Clarendon, 1957).

while looking at an English text, then odds are you know Hebrew decently well.

- Gary A. Long. *Grammatical Concepts 101 for Biblical Hebrew*. 2nd ed. Grand Rapids: Baker Academic, 2013. While this book is not technically an intermediate grammar in its scope, Long provides some helpful categorizations and grammatical tags from a linguistics perspective. Another indispensable feature of Long's book is that he associates the Hebrew concepts he discusses with English examples to show that many of these syntactical features exist in language generally, even English. When we encounter tricky Hebrew constructions, I'll tell my students, "Hebrew is not being mean to you," and then give them an example where we do the same thing in English. Long's work provides many such examples.

- Ronald J. Williams. *Williams' Hebrew Syntax*. 3rd ed. Revised and expanded by John C. Beckman. Toronto: University of Toronto Press, 2007. The primary value in this intermediate grammar is that the syntactical categories are easy to follow for those versed in syntactical discussions from Greek or Latin. Although Hebrew is not an inflected language, the discussions here follow the traditional linguistic categories of nominative, accusative, genitive, and so on. In addition, Beckman (the editor of this third edition) has added detailed footnotes to each syntactical tag, leading the reader to the major Hebrew reference grammars. These footnotes are an invaluable resource.

> "Having to establish the precise use of a case or mood or voice forces the interpreter to consider all the various possibilities of meaning inherent in the language of the text. When it comes to hermeneutics, attention to detail often brings a huge exegetical dividend from this investment."
>
> —Rob Starner[h]

Recommended Advanced Hebrew Grammars

- Wilhelm Gesenius. *Gesenius' Hebrew Grammar*. Edited and enlarged by E. Kautzsch. Translated by A. E. Cowley.

Mineola, NY: Dover, 2006. Gesenius is difficult to wade
through; technical terminology is not always clearly defined.
Sometimes *Williams' Hebrew Syntax* (see above) will direct
you to the appropriate sections in Gesenius for further study,
making it an accessible guide for navigating Gesenius.

- Paul Joüon. *A Grammar of Biblical Hebrew*. 2nd ed. Translated and revised by T. Muraoka. Rome: Biblical Institute
  Press, 2006. Like Gesenius, Joüon can be tricky to navigate.
  However, the detail of discussion in this grammar makes it
  worth getting. Even if the extent to which you use this grammar is the Scripture index or following the pathway given by
  John Beckman's expansions of *Williams' Hebrew Syntax*, it's
  worth having as a resource for higher academic discussions.

- Christo H. van der Merwe and Jacobus A. Naudé. *A Biblical Hebrew Reference Grammar*. 2nd ed. New York: T&T
  Clark, 2017. This grammar is praised by Peter Gentry on
  the back cover as "the best reference grammar of Biblical
  Hebrew bar none!" Having recently been updated, van der
  Merwe–Naudé is, along with Waltke-O'Connor, one of the
  standard contemporary reference grammars. It falls in the
  linguistics camp of Hebrew training, providing discussion on
  everything from phonetic analysis to sentence and discourse
  structures.

- Bruce K. Waltke and M. P. O'Connor. *An Introduction to
  Biblical Hebrew Syntax*. University Park, PA: Eisenbrauns,
  1990. The publication date here doesn't indicate a recent re-
  print, yet this is probably the most-used reference grammar
  in current discussions. The format is easy to navigate, and
  the authors provide examples for each syntactical tag so that
  you can see in the Hebrew text what they are discussing.

Chapter Reflections

1. When accessing the text of the Hebrew Bible, do you currently use any Bible software, smartphone apps, or web

pages? Choose one new resource, such as www.biblearc.com or the Biblearc app, to explore.

2. Skim over the different kinds of reading described earlier in the chapter (reading for technical competency, slow grammatical reading, etc.). Which types of reading have you done before? What reading approaches would be new to you? Try one today.

3. What lexicon have you used in the past? If you have not used BDB, consider trying it out at a local seminary or college library.

4. Skim back through the chapter. Make a resource "wish list" of three top items you would like to acquire for your theological library.

5. Challenge: Next time you prepare a Sunday school lesson or sermon on a text of the Old Testament, check the Scripture index of an intermediate or reference grammar for those verses. Look up all the citations. What grammatical categories were you reminded of? What new things did you learn?

Reading the Septuagint alongside the Hebrew Bible

William Ross

It might seem strange to encourage reading Greek in a book focused on practicing your Hebrew. But, historically speaking, both languages have played key roles in the creation, transmission, and interpretation of the Old Testament. So in many ways, becoming more familiar with the ancient Greek translation of the Old Testament—the Septuagint—will only encourage and facilitate greater intimacy with the Hebrew Bible.

Much could be said about reading the Septuagint and its relationship to the Hebrew Bible. But one suggestion for how to benefit from
using the former alongside the latter is to stagger your readings of
the two into textual "chunks" of different sizes. That is, sometimes
you compare little units during your study, sometimes bigger ones,
regularly switching between reading at the level of the clause, verse,
or full paragraph. Working with the Greek and Hebrew together in
this way can provide a kind of linguistic equivalent to what high-
intensity interval training accomplishes for athletes.

Comparing clauses encourages the most careful scrutiny. Is each
grammatical element of the Hebrew represented in Greek? Sometimes it takes a few words in Greek to translate just one in Hebrew
(or vice versa), such as ὁ πατήρ μου for אָבִי in Genesis 27:12. Do any
word meanings diverge significantly between Hebrew and Greek?
Some translators, reading an unpointed or unclear Hebrew text, understood their source text differently, such as καλύπτω to translate
כסה (cover) rather than כסם (shear) in Ezekiel 44:20. Does the Greek
clarify the Hebrew syntax in some way? For example, where the
Hebrew is grammatically ambiguous or underspecified—especially
in poetry—the translator sometimes appears to add elements for
clarity, as with the insertion of the explicit subject οἱ δίκαιοι in
Psalms 34:18 (33:18, Septuagint), or the addition of the connecting
words ὥσπερ and οὕτως in the parallelism of Proverbs 11:22. In
these cases, and others like them, modern English translations also
often reflect the clarification (e.g., ESV, NASB, NIV).

Looking at the Greek and Hebrew together at the verse level
highlights different but related issues. How does verbal syntax
compare between the two languages? Often the translator had to
make choices strictly from context and not linguistic form, which
affected word order, as with the Hebrew jussive verb translated
using the optative ποιήσαι μοι κύριος for יַעֲשֶׂה יְהוָה לִי in Ruth
1:17. Are there phrases present or absent in one text but not the
other? Such divergences may have arisen because of unintentional
errors like parablepsis (accidentally skipping over text), which can
happen when there are visual similarities at the point of translation
or in later transmission in either Greek or Hebrew. Other times, differences between Greek and Hebrew in a verse may have (or allow)

theological implications, as with the apparent addition of ἐπ᾽ αὐτῷ in Isaiah 28:16, later cited in 1 Peter 2:6 and Romans 9:33.

Reading entire paragraphs together facilitates broader focus on textual comprehension, especially with narrative. Minor differences can have effects at the level of textual coherence and cohesion. Are there changes in characterization? Sometimes Septuagint translators replaced proper names with alternatives, as with κύριος for יְהוָה in Genesis 39:2 and elsewhere, and ἀλλόφυλοι (foreigners) for פְּלִשְׁתִּים (Philistines). Is the discourse structured differently? Greek connectives like δέ, ὅτι, or γάρ often replace a simple Hebrew וֹ—or have no Hebrew equivalent—and thus may alter the flow of the text in subtle ways, as with the use of οὖν in Genesis 27:33 and Exodus 4:1 to mark continuity and development in the narrative.

So consider switching between these different levels of analysis during your times of language study according to your ability and the time you have available. Doing things this way will especially help those who are stronger in one language counterbalance weaknesses with the other, since it requires carefully tracking the vocabulary and syntax involved. As you increase in confidence, move up from clause-level toward comparing larger units. But even those who feel confident in both Greek and Hebrew will constantly find linguistic food for thought.

Of course, not every book in the Old Testament has a Greek version where this strategy is possible, since some books of the Septuagint differ enough that it can become very difficult (or impossible) to align them with the Hebrew text. But bear in mind that it is not always helpful to read the Septuagint with the assumption that it was meant to be a "literal" translation—even where there is word-for-word correspondence—not least since that notion is anachronistic and tends to be value-laden in the contemporary context.

The reading strategy suggested here is aimed at promoting finer analysis of the Hebrew text not only in evaluating whether and how it differs from the Septuagint but also in considering the implications. To be sure, the Septuagint is unfamiliar terrain to almost all Christians, many pastors, and even some biblical scholars. But taking a hike along new and sometimes challenging trails can, with care and perseverance, lead to some of the most stunning vistas.

Hebrew's Close
Cousin—Aramaic

Ahead of the 2011 season, the National Football League (NFL) moved the kickoff yard line from the thirty-yard line to the thirty-five-yard line, positioning the kicker closer to the opposing end zone. For NFL kickers using a tee, the sixty-five yards needed to get the ball to the opposing end zone (resulting in a touchback) isn't much of a feat. In fact, we often see NFL kickoffs sailing out of the back of the end zone, a kick pushing seventy-five to eighty yards in the air.

While the kick itself is awe-inspiring, there's one other feature of NFL kickoffs that I think illustrates a helpful mindset as we approach the Aramaic of the Old Testament. Because nearly half of NFL kickoffs result in a touchback, full-blown kick returns are rare. When the kickoff flies out of the back of the end zone, the referees blow the whistle, and the ball is placed on the twenty-five-yard line. Because a touchback is so common, some may wonder why the kicking team runs all the way down the field when they know their kicker has the ability to kick the ball out of the end zone. What's intriguing is that the kicking team will often run not only down the field but all the way to the opposing end zone, even as the return team begins to walk off the field and prepare for the ball on the twenty-five-yard line.

When I played football in college, our coaches taught the players to run all the way to the end zone on kickoffs, no matter where the ball landed. This wasn't just another opportunity for cardiovascular conditioning; rather, it instilled in our kickoff team the habit of going above and beyond the minimal call of duty so that we were prepared on every kickoff to fulfill our responsibilities exhaustively.

This is the principle that relates to Aramaic. Aramaic is the often-neglected original language of the Old Testament. However, if we are going to pursue our callings to love God and his word exhaustively, then it would only benefit us to learn Aramaic in addition to Hebrew and Greek.

Going Above and Beyond?

By way of statistics, Aramaic takes a far back seat to Hebrew and Greek as one of the original languages in the Bible. There are 269 verses in the Old Testament that are written in Aramaic or that contain Aramaic. When compared to the rest of the Old Testament text, Aramaic is just over 1 percent of the whole. That seems meager, and as a result, many students and pastors assume that pursuing Aramaic is an unnecessary project. Miles Van Pelt puts these statistics into perspective when he points out that Obadiah, Jonah, Micah, Nahum, Habakkuk, and Psalm 1 together make up about the same percentage of text as the Aramaic portions of the Hebrew Bible. In the New Testament, 1–2 Timothy, Titus, and Philemon are roughly equivalent to the same amount of text as the Aramaic in the Old Testament.[1] Surely none of us would consider disregarding these portions of God's inspired word. And yet we often neglect the Aramaic of the Old Testament and as a result call into question our own commitment to the fullness of God's word.

We have two humongous oak trees in our yard. These trees yield buckets of acorns. Buckets of acorns attract armies of squirrels. Dur-

---

1. Miles V. Van Pelt, *Basics of Biblical Aramaic: Complete Grammar, Lexicon, and Annotated Text* (Grand Rapids: Zondervan, 2011), x.

ing the late fall, we see the squirrels scurrying around our yard digging holes and burying the acorns for later use in the winter. The squirrels around our house are Eastern gray squirrels, which are scatter hoarders. They bury the acorns far and wide, and they never have just one stash. When the air temperature begins to cool, we see squirrels all over the yard burying acorns in all sorts of places.

There is way more research available than perhaps you or I want to know about how and why squirrels bury acorns in this way, but the point is that the squirrels are preparing their meals for the winter months. The squirrels busily bury acorns randomly and sometimes even pretend to bury acorns in certain locations to fool other squirrels who may try to steal the coveted nuts. Researchers at the University of Richmond point out that squirrels may actually forfeit up to 74 percent of the acorns they bury through forgetfulness, thievery, or just indifference.[2] The fascinating piece of this picture is that squirrels go above and beyond what's necessary for them to survive in the winter in order to accomplish their foundational food goals. Because of genetic and natural factors, squirrels sometimes only reap around 25 percent reward from their efforts in preparation. *But they still complete the preparation.*

Venturing back into the world of Hebrew and out of the Discovery Channel, we need more students and ministers who are willing to put in the necessary preparation and effort even if we are only reading the Aramaic portions of the Old Testament 1 percent of the time. In fact, I might even argue that this kind of preparation is *not* going above and beyond. If diving into Aramaic is fulfilling our responsibilities to know and love God through his word, then can we really "overprepare"? Is learning the original language of the last 1 percent of the Old Testament going above and beyond? Or is this how we "fulfill"

> "We must not allow either status or statistics to preclude our commitment to teach and study this biblical language in Bible colleges and seminaries as a regular part of training candidates for the ministry of God's word. Faithfulness in the littlest thing is no little thing (Luke 16:10a)."
> —Miles Van Pelt[a]

---

2. University of Richmond, "Researchers Tackle the Nutty Truth on Acorns and Squirrels," ScienceDaily, November 26, 1998, https://www.sciencedaily.com/releases/1998/11/981126102802.htm.

our ministry, as Paul's instruction to Timothy implies (2 Tim. 4:5)? From this perspective, pursuing Aramaic may be a necessary part of our work to accomplish our goal faithfully.

To be sure, it is enough labor for many of us just to learn Hebrew, and if we are going to start with one language of the Old Testament and master it, let's master the one that occurs the most. On the other hand, if we remember our primary goal of increasing our affections for God through the entirety of his word in the original languages, then Aramaic is part of that journey.

In this chapter, we will look at some ways in which the transition from Hebrew to Aramaic is actually quite simple. The goal is to give you a sense of hope that you can tackle some Aramaic in addition to your Hebrew. We will also review some resources to help with your Aramaic studies similar to the ones presented in chapter 7 for Hebrew. If you've never considered learning Aramaic, you may wonder where to start. This chapter will provide some resources to point you in the right direction.

The Ease of Transition

When I played football in college, I held a coveted position; I was a long snapper. That meant that I threw a football backward between my legs to either the punter or the holder (for field goals and extra points). The punter would stand fifteen yards away from the line of scrimmage, but the holder would stand only seven yards behind me. People would ask me all the time if it was difficult to transition between the two. The fact that I was asked this question so often suggests that people assumed the transition was difficult. I would usually answer with a shrug, a headshake, and a comment like "No, not really." In fact, I never gave much thought to the transition be-tween the two snaps, but there was indeed a transition. The transi-tion, though, was so small that in spite of the differences, I could still easily make it.

The transition from Hebrew to Aramaic is not quite that easy—or at least it wasn't for me—but the principle is the same. There are certainly differences between Hebrew and Aramaic, but the differ-ences aren't so significant that the task of learning Aramaic is completely foreign. In fact, the two languages overlap significantly in many places. We can't provide a full Aramaic grammar here, but hopefully these tidbits will convince you that you can accomplish the transition from Hebrew to Aramaic.

Areas of Significant Overlap

Some of the areas of significant overlap between Hebrew and Aramaic may seem obvious.[3] First, the alphabet is the same. In the text of the Hebrew Bible, Hebrew and Aramaic use the block script that you are accustomed to seeing in the *BHS* or whatever Hebrew Bible you use. In fact, a student once asked me if the *BHS* has the Aramaic sections of Scripture in it. I'm certain he had passed over those sections when flipping through Ezra or Daniel and didn't notice a difference because of the identical alphabet. In relation to the alphabetic similarities, we may add that final forms, BeGaD KePhaT (בגד כפת) letters, and guttural letters are all the same between the two sets of texts in the Hebrew Bible.

Second, the Aramaic vowel pointing system in the Hebrew Bible is largely the same as the system in the Hebrew sections. I say "largely the same" because Aramaic, being a distinct language, has different pronunciations, and you may see unexpected vowel patterns when compared to Hebrew. However, even though you may not recognize a vowel *pattern* in the Aramaic of the Old Testament, a *hireq* is a *hireq* in both Hebrew and Aramaic. A *qamets* is a *qamets* in both Hebrew and Aramaic. You get the picture.

Third, some Hebrew and Aramaic vocabulary overlap. In *Basics of Biblical Aramaic*, Miles Van Pelt lists fifty nouns or adjectives in chapter 1 that are identical—or nearly identical—to Hebrew words that

3. Keep in mind that we are laying out similarities between Hebrew and Aramaic as they appear in the Hebrew Bible. There are many Aramaic and Hebrew texts written in various ancient scripts, without vowels, and perhaps in mixed dialects that would not exhibit these similarities. In this section, think "similarities in the Hebrew and Aramaic texts of the Hebrew Bible," not necessarily "similarities in the languages themselves." Discussing similarities (or dissimilarities) between Hebrew and Aramaic as distinct languages is a much more complex conversation. Our goal is to help you make the shift from Hebrew to Aramaic texts in the Hebrew Bible, not necessarily for you to jump from Hebrew as a distinct language to Aramaic as a distinct language.

students should already know.[4] In chapter 12 of his grammar, Van Pelt lists twenty-five verbal roots that are identical.[5] So, of the 268 words in the Aramaic portions of Scripture that occur four or more times, seventy-five of them are identical to Hebrew words. You may already know 28 percent of the most common Aramaic words in Scripture!

A fourth area of significant overlap between the two languages is the rules of *dageshes* and *shewas*. These phonological principles, while having some differences in Aramaic, are largely the same as you've learned in Hebrew. *Dagesh lenes* occur in בגד כפת letters preceded by a silent *shewa*. *Dagesh fortes* still represent a doubled consonant and close the preceding syllable. Silent *shewas* close syllables and represent the absence of a vowel, and vocal *shewas* indicate an indistinct vowel sound, the evidence of a full vowel having "reduced." All of these phonological elements resonate between the two sets of texts in the Hebrew Bible.

Finally, the Hebrew and Aramaic texts of the Old Testament are identical regarding how to categorize syntax and grammar. Looking only at Hebrew, we must admit that scholars radically diverge at some points regarding how to categorize and tag syntactical constructions or grammatical ideas. However, no matter how you label Hebrew syntax or describe the functional grammar, your system of labeling and tagging will also work in Aramaic. If you see an infinitive absolute in Aramaic juxtaposed with its cognate verb, that is an absolute object or a cognate accusative, whichever tag you prefer. In either case, the infinitive absolute functions similarly in both languages.

Minor Differences

The next group of differences is a little more complex but still not problematic. First, there is a slight difference between the historical long vowel *holem-vav* and the Aramaic *qamets*. Hebrew often conveys the "Canaanite shift," a phenomenon where we find more "o" vowels in Hebrew than in cognate languages. The "shift" was from

4. Van Pelt, *Basics of Biblical Aramaic*, 5. Alger Johns lists forty-four identical words between Hebrew and Aramaic in his introductory chapter, but he comments that this is "besides a host of others with but minor differences." Alger F. Johns, *A Short Grammar of Biblical Aramaic* (Berrien Springs, MI: Andrews University Press, 1972), 4.

5. Van Pelt, *Basics of Biblical Aramaic*, 80–81.

"a" vowels to "o" vowels. In Aramaic, this shift is not readily appar-ent, if it's there at all. Hence, you will not find as many historic long *holem-vavs* in Aramaic; rather, the long *qamets* is a historic long vowel and will not reduce in syllables that expect a vowel to become a vocal *shewa*. This may seem like a major difference between the languages, but it's not so bad when you see something like טוֹב in He-brew become טָב in Aramaic. Yes, these words are noticeably distinct, but if you know that "o" in Hebrew is often "a" in Aramaic, you can begin to figure out vocabulary words that at first glance look new.

Second, Aramaic contractions vary slightly from their Hebrew counterparts. In Hebrew, an example of a contraction is in the 3ms pronominal suffix on a plural noun (יו֖). We also see contractions with III-ה verbs and especially with I-ו verbs. One of the most com-mon contractions is what I've learned as the "aw → o" contraction where וֹ֖ becomes וֹ֖ in I-י verbs. These contractions also occur in Aramaic and will look familiar to you. The contractions in Aramaic that are different actually are expansions of a familiar Hebrew con-traction, "ay → e" (יֹ֖ ← יֹ֖). In Aramaic, the determined gentilics—definite forms designating an ethnicity—present a complex contrac-tion that will only matter to you in a morphology-heavy system of learning Aramaic. Other than the odd determined gentilic contrac-tion, this morphological phenomenon of contractions is also similar between the two languages in the Hebrew Bible.

Third, Aramaic is the "ultimate vowel-killing language."[6] While that sounds disastrous, all it means is that you find more vocal *shewas* flying around in the Aramaic portions of the Old Testament because the vowels in both pretonic and propretonic syllables have reduced. This leads to more "*shewa* fights" than in Hebrew, but again, these are not new phenomena.[7] Once you know they exist in Aramaic, the transition becomes quite simple.

---

6. This quote is attributed to Russell Fuller in his Aramaic classroom notes. These are unpublished notes that I used when taking Aramaic in seminary. Lord willing, he will publish these materials in the future. His Aramaic materials build largely from his morphology-heavy system in Hebrew, so those who have used *Invitation to Biblical Hebrew: A Beginning Grammar* (Grand Rapids: Kregel, 2006) would be able to more easily transition to Aramaic.

7. A "*shewa* fight" is when, upon constructing a noun form, you get two vocal *shewas* side by side at the beginning of a word. Neither Hebrew nor Aramaic will

Fourth, Aramaic exhibits consonant interchanges in some words. Some consonants in Hebrew words will be different consonants in the Aramaic words with the same meaning. For example, זָהָב (gold) in Hebrew is דְהַב in Aramaic, and the ז to ד interchange occurs quite consistently. Similarly, שׁ and ת often interchange in Aramaic, so the Hebrew root ישׁב (to sit/dwell) is in Old Testament Aramaic יתב. Like many of these areas of minor differences, this may seem daunting at first. However, once you know the differences exist, you can begin to make the adjustments in your linguistic neurons easily.

Significant Differences

Even the significant differences are not that bad. We've already seen how many similarities there are between the two languages, and so these "significant differences" constitute a minority in the transition from Hebrew texts to Aramaic texts in the Old Testament.

The first significant difference is in the masculine/feminine plural and the determined state (corresponding to the Hebrew definite article). In Hebrew the masculine plural absolute is ◌ִים, but in Aramaic it is ◌ִין. For the feminine plural, the Hebrew is ◌וֹת, whereas the Aramaic is ◌ָן. Hopefully, you're thinking, "That's not too bad." And you'd be right. In the determined state, Aramaic can get complicated morphologically. The major change here is that in Hebrew the definite article occurs on the front of the word, whereas in Aramaic the definite article is suffixed to the end (◌ָא). Since it is suffixed to the end along with the masculine and feminine plural distinctives (◌ָן/◌ִין), the determined state can begin to look a little odd. You don't need to know the details of morphology now, but below is a chart of the Aramaic determined state:

Masculine Singular	Masculine Plural	Feminine Singular	Feminine Plural
◌ָא(ה)	◌ַיָּא	◌ְתָא	◌ָתָא

The other significant difference is the verbal system. Rather than the familiar *qal*, *niphal*, *piel*, *pual*, *hiphil*, *hophal*, and *hithpael*, Biblical

---

allow this, and so the resulting vowel pattern we see in the Hebrew Bible is usually a *hireq/shewa* combination (◌ְ◌ִ◌◌ ← ◌◌◌ְ◌). I learned this concept as a "*shewa* fight," and I can't break the habit of calling it that.

Aramaic has *peal, pael, peil, haphel, hithpeel, hithpaal,* and other variations of these (*aphel, saphel, shaphel, hithaphal, histaphal*). Now, this can look overwhelming. However, once you learn how these stems relate to the Hebrew stems you already know, you will discover that the syntax and usage are very similar. *Peal* is the base stem like the *qal,* and it functions like the Hebrew *qal. Pael* is the Aramaic intensive/extensive stem like the *piel,* and so it functions syntactically like the *piel.* The ת stems (*ithpeel, ithpaal, ithaphal, hithpeel, hithpaal, hithaphal, histaphal*) are variations of the passive/reflexive similar to the *hithpael* in Hebrew. *Haphel* is the Aramaic causative like *hiphil* in Hebrew. There are so many similarities of usage that this "significant difference" could be considered an area of significant overlap. At the end of the day, don't be alarmed by what appears to be a complex verbal system. You already know a good deal about how the verbal system works, so you'll just need to take some time to identify the distinctives of these stems for parsing purposes and learn how they relate to their close cousins in Hebrew.

> "If our common endeavor helps breathe new life into the consonantal sequence of any Aramaic text, transforming it into a course of pleasurable reading, we shall feel amply rewarded."
> —Isaac Jerusalmi[b]

I hope that you've seen in this section that you already know a good deal of Biblical Aramaic. Of course, with these few areas of convergence, you won't be able to pick up the Targums or Aramaic Qumran documents and breeze through them. But with your knowledge of Hebrew, an awareness of these differences, and a few good resources, you will be able to maneuver your way around the transition to Biblical Aramaic.

How to Get Started: Aramaic Resources

Perhaps at this point you're motivated to begin your pilgrimage into Aramaic, but where do you start? What resources are available, and which are the best ones? In this section, we will list a sampling of the resources available and comment on each. At the end of the day, the best resources are the ones that work for your learning style. Some of these resources are highly academic, while others help bridge the gap between your knowledge of Hebrew and your Aramaic aspirations.

To find the best resource for you, read the reviews and summaries online, check out the book at a nearby college or seminary library, and flip through it before deciding. The best resources are the ones you'll actually use, so take the evaluations here at face value and decide for yourself which ones you prefer.

Grammars

Arguably, the most recognized and accessible Aramaic beginning grammar is Miles V. Van Pelt, *Basics of Biblical Aramaic* (Zondervan, 2011). This introductory Aramaic grammar builds on the same system as the popular Hebrew grammar that Van Pelt wrote with Gary Pratico. In addition to the concepts of Aramaic language, the grammar also includes a robust vocabulary (268 words; 91 percent of the Aramaic vocabulary in the *BHS*), practice exercises, and annotated readings from the Hebrew Bible. The annotated readings include all of the Aramaic in the Hebrew Bible from Genesis, Jeremiah, Ezra, and Daniel. Van Pelt often refers the reader to *Basics of Biblical Hebrew*, 3rd ed. (Zondervan, 2019), so that students can see the many connections between what they already know in Hebrew and what they're learning in Aramaic. Van Pelt's Aramaic grammar is one of the best places to start, especially if you have used *Basics of Biblical Hebrew* previously.

A second introductory grammar that provides a systematic and pedagogically beneficial approach is Frederick E. Greenspahn, *An Introduction to Aramaic*, 2nd ed. (Society of Biblical Literature, 2003). Greenspahn acknowledges in the preface to the first edition that those approaching Aramaic should have at least a rudimentary knowledge of Hebrew, and so he approaches "Aramaic as if it were a dialect of Hebrew, without trying to cover all of the language's depth and richness." His justification of this approach is "pedagogical utility," and so the grammar "has been kept as non-technical as possible."[8] As with any language, some technicalities are imperative, but the overall goal of the grammar to accommodate students with a rudimentary knowledge of Hebrew makes for a successful introductory Aramaic grammar. Each chapter includes exercises for both the material in that chapter

---

8. Frederick E. Greenspahn, *Introduction to Aramaic*, 2nd ed. (Atlanta: Society of Biblical Literature, 2003), xi.

and translations from Aramaic to English. This is an excellent way to expose students to Aramaic texts very early in their Aramaic ventures.

Two grammars that may prove to be helpful to have on the shelf are Alger F. Johns, *A Short Grammar of Biblical Aramaic* (Andrews University Press, 1972), and Franz Rosenthal, *A Grammar of Biblical Aramaic*, 7th ed. (Harrassowitz, 2006). These two grammars are significantly shorter than the others already listed. Johns, like the others, presupposes a knowledge of Hebrew, but Rosenthal does not. Johns offers very few exercises but at least gives some Aramaic translations at the end of each section to allow the student to review key concepts in actual Aramaic sentences. Rosenthal does not provide any exercises. Even though the size of these volumes is minimal and the additional exercises within are scarce, these two grammars provide concise discussions of morphological and syntactical aspects of Aramaic. Perhaps you want an Aramaic grammar you can carry around in your book bag easily. One of these two would be a good choice for reference.

The last grammar to mention is Andreas Schuele, *Introduction to Biblical Aramaic* (Westminster John Knox, 2012). Schuele has produced an extremely concise grammar based on years of teaching Aramaic in the classroom using Rosenthal's grammar. Since Rosenthal's grammar does not contain exercises, Schuele has included some of those in his grammar, though they are not as extensive as Van Pelt's or Greenspahn's. Schuele presumes that you have a knowledge of Hebrew and shows clearly the areas of similarity in helpful charts and diagrams throughout his grammar. One exciting feature of Schuele's grammar is the appendixes where he provides some Aramaic texts outside the biblical corpus (Zakkur Inscription, three texts from Qumran, and two short selections from the *Wisdom of Ahiqar*). These appendixes help the student see how wide the world of primary texts opens after only an introductory study of Aramaic.

Lexica

In keeping with the thrust of this chapter devoted to Aramaic, I want to begin with a lexicon that is devoted completely to Biblical Aramaic: Ernst Vogt, *Lexicon of Biblical Aramaic*: *Clarified by*

Ancient Documents (Gregorian and Biblical Press, 2011). This work is an English translation by Joseph A. Fitzmyer of Vogt's Aramaic lexicon, which was originally written in Latin. It is a tidy lexicon: Biblical Aramaic words are listed in alphabetical order with extensive definitions based on evidence from the Aramaic Qumran documents that were available when Vogt finished the original work. Fitzmyer, in addition to translating the work, also updated some entries. This lexicon provides definitions only for the words that occur in the Hebrew Bible, but it also gives definitions of those words from other texts. This provides a fuller meaning—contextual meaning—to the words we find in the Hebrew Bible. Because this lexicon is limited to Biblical Aramaic vocabulary, every form in the Hebrew Bible is listed in the lexicon, even conjugated forms. In those cases, the lexicon points the reader to the cognate roots for definitions. All in all, this is a simple and highly usable lexicon that you can easily carry with you.

The next two lexica to mention are probably familiar to you already: *Hebrew and Aramaic Lexicon of the Old Testament* (*HALOT*) and *The Brown-Driver-Briggs Hebrew and English Lexicon* (BDB). Both of these lexica are used primarily for the study of Hebrew, but as the title of *HALOT* reflects, it also includes Aramaic words. Likewise, some editions of BDB include the subtitle *With an Appendix Containing Biblical Aramaic*. Both of these trusted lexica can be useful for your studies of Aramaic. If you already own *HALOT* or BDB, you're good to go and can use them for Aramaic word studies too.

The final Aramaic lexicon to mention is Marcus Jastrow, *Dictionary of the Targumim, the Talmud Babli, and Yerushalmi, and the Midrashic Literature* (Hendrickson, 2005). This behemoth volume, as the title conveys, provides lexical information for a much wider camp of Aramaic documents. This may not seem immediately helpful to the beginning Aramaic student, but the Aramaic words that occur in the Scriptures are also here. Therefore, this lexicon would not only help you with reading Biblical Aramaic but would also help you when your enthusiasm for Semitic languages leads you to read the broader corpora of Aramaic documents.

Readers

Assuming that you're not using Van Pelt's introductory grammar with its annotated reader, where else might you turn to find the Biblical Aramaic texts with annotated parsings and grammatical notes? My first recommendation would be *Biblical Aramaic: A Reader and Handbook* by Donald R. Vance, George Athas, and Yael Avrahami (Hendrickson, 2016). This Aramaic reader provides a clear and readable text of the Aramaic portions of Scripture along with footnoted parsing information, grammatical discussion, and direction to other resources for further study. The footnoted handbook information is not overly burdensome with additional comments and thoughts about what might be going on in the text. Rather, the handbook apparatus gets to the point with a system of abbreviations that provide the reader with the necessary information to keep reading the text and reinforcing his or her Aramaic knowledge. Another feature of this resource is the extensive word lists compiled by Jonathan G. Kline that organize Biblical Aramaic word forms into what seem to be endless (and helpful!) categories. These lists help the student to see patterns of certain types of verbs, to see connections between certain vocabulary roots, and to access lists of vocabulary by frequency so that you learn the most common words first. Apart from a combined resource like Van Pelt, I would recommend starting with *Biblical Aramaic: A Reader and Handbook*.

The next Aramaic reader I would recommend is Takamitsu Muraoka, *A Biblical Aramaic Reader: With an Outline Grammar* (Peeters, 2015). Without all of the vocabulary lists, Muraoka's volume is much smaller than the previously discussed reader. However, Muraoka includes in his volume an outline grammar. By "outline" he means a simplified and succinct grammar. The entire outline covers thirty-eight pages, but this gives the student the opportunity to review key paradigms, review key grammatical features, and refer back to grammatical discussions using the keyed notes from the reader. Muraoka references his outline grammar in the reader, so students can read the Aramaic text, study Muraoka's notes on the text, and then review the grammatical concepts all in the same volume. Coming in at a total of eighty-two pages, you could literally slide this reader into your

BHS and take it with you. (I'm assuming you already take your *BHS* with you wherever you go!)

Vocabulary Guides

To the best of my knowledge, there are no hard-copy vocabulary guides that exclusively have Biblical Aramaic vocabulary.[9] However, there are two Hebrew and Aramaic vocabulary guides that I think are helpful. I tell my students all the time that you may be able to parse every detail of a verb and give me every exception for an expected vowel point, but if you don't know the definition of the root word, then you can't translate. Therefore, vocabulary is essential, especially in Aramaic when we move beyond those words that we know from Hebrew.

The first recommended guide is Larry A. Mitchel, *A Student's Vocabulary for Biblical Hebrew and Aramaic* (Zondervan, 2017). Mitchel's vocabulary guide displays a simple layout. The Aramaic section lists all words that occur in the Aramaic portions of Scripture in groups based on frequency (50+, 20–50, 13–19, etc.). Within each frequency section, the words are listed alphabetically. Each entry also includes a transliteration for pronunciation purposes, which can be helpful if you use mnemonic devices for memorization that are associated with the sounds of the words. As most any vocabulary guide would do, Mitchel provides only gloss definitions for each word, but it is a concise and easy place to begin.

The second vocabulary guide I would recommend is Gary D. Pratico and Miles V. Van Pelt, *The Vocabulary Guide to Biblical Hebrew and Aramaic* (Zondervan, 2019). This guide is an updated edition of the 2003 guide that Pratico and Van Pelt published, and one of the delightful updates is the inclusion of Aramaic vocabulary. The Aramaic portion of this guide contains all Aramaic words in the Scriptures (705) listed by frequency only. This format can be helpful because you learn the most common words first. Each entry has the word number (in sequential order), the Aramaic word or root, a couple of gloss definitions, and the number of times that word occurs in

---

9. For an online set of Aramaic vocabulary flash cards, see https://decks.memrise .com/course/5585010. Thanks to Greg Wolff for directing us to this resource.

the Aramaic portions of Scripture. Like Mitchel's vocabulary guide, Pratico and Van Pelt's guide also includes Hebrew words, so either of these guides would be a handy resource to have on hand to continue building your Old Testament language vocabulary.

Many biblical language students are familiar with Jerome and the important work he did on the Latin translation of the Bible. What many of us don't hear about is his wrestling with the languages. This quote from Jerome's preface to Daniel is particularly apropos to our discussion of Aramaic:

> When I was a young man, after working my way through the flowers of eloquence to be plucked from the books of Quintilian and Cicero, I opened myself up to the hard labor of learning this language [Chaldean, i.e., Aramaic], and only after a great deal of time and toil was I able (just barely) to begin to utter the raspy and hissing words. It was like walking through a dark crypt, glimpsing only the occasional ray of light shining down from above. When I finally threw myself against Daniel, so great a weariness came over me that, in sudden despair, I almost wanted to cast aside all my previous work. But there was a certain Hebrew who encouraged me and often admonished me with the old Latin proverb, in his own language: "Dogged effort overcomes every obstacle"; and so, though I knew that among the Hebrews I was only a rank amateur, I once more became a student of Chaldean. And to tell the truth, to this day, I am still better able to read and understand the Chaldean language than to pronounce it.[10]

Even though Jerome's commission was to translate the Bible—demonstrating that someone was confident that Jerome had this language skill set—he still wrestled not only with learning Aramaic but also with enjoying it. He was honest about his abilities and honest about his feelings for the language. Even after much labor, he could still translate better than he could pronounce. But he kept at it with the encouragement of—you guessed it—a Hebrew brother,

10. I'm grateful to Dr. Tyler Flatt, my colleague and Latin scholar, for directing me to this preface to Daniel in the Vulgate and for his delightful translation conveying the honest struggles Jerome had with Aramaic. See Bonifatius Fischer, Robert Weber, and Roger Gryson, *Biblia Sacra: Iuxta Vulgatam Versionem* (Stuttgart: Deutsche Bibelgesellschaft, 2007), 1341.

and he persevered so that he could provide numerous people with the word of God in translation. Our purposes are much the same as Jerome—namely, to translate the Aramaic portions of Scripture for understanding rather than to phonetically read them aloud in liturgy. Therefore, let us never forget the value of the hard labor that goes into learning the biblical languages no matter how difficult the process may be. Perhaps you've already devoted a significant amount of time to learning Hebrew. It's not a big step to finish the task and dive into Aramaic as well. Let us not just rake for leaves in Ezra and Daniel; let us dig for gold even there.

Chapter Reflections
---

1. Honestly assess your current level of Hebrew study. Can you see yourself studying Aramaic too? Are you perhaps more fearful of the transition than you should be? If the task of learning Aramaic seems too daunting, what incentives could you put in place to motivate you to pick up Aramaic as well?

2. Identify the two or three primary things that might be keeping you from diving into Biblical Aramaic. What are some specific steps you can write down and execute to overcome these hurdles?

3. Consider whether learning Aramaic would legitimately be "going above and beyond" or whether it would be "finishing the task" of knowing God's word in the original languages. In either case, write down what you think would be your response to having either finished the task or gone above and beyond. Both can be rewarding.

4. Write down some things that were particularly challenging to you in Hebrew, and then look those same things up in one of the recommended Aramaic grammars. See if the transition from Hebrew to Aramaic in that particular area is as difficult as you may have initially thought.

5. Look back over the recommended grammars. Since we all have different learning styles, which one do you think would serve you best in learning Aramaic?

Jeremiah 10:11

Steven Hallam

———————◯———————

"Speak now to your servants in Aramaic, for we understand it; and do not speak with us in Judean [Hebrew]."

—2 Kings 18:26 NASB

One of the many fascinating passages in Biblical Aramaic lies outside the larger Aramaic corpora—an Aramaic island within a sea of Hebrew—just fifteen words nestled in the midst of the book of Jeremiah (10:11).[11] Many readers simply glance over this small passage without a second thought, or with nothing more than a quick glance at the footnote. There is no warning of the switch and no mention in the text to alert the reader of the change. It almost reads like an afterthought—as if it were no big deal that the language of the text just switched, and then switches back. Parsed out, it looks as follows:

Jeremiah 10:11

דִּי־שְׁמַיָּא	אֱלָהַיָּא	לְהֹום	תֵּאמְרוּן	כִּדְנָה
di + noun: determined masculine plural	noun: determined masculine plural	lamed + 3mp	verb: peal imperfect 2mp	kaph + demonstrative pronoun (ms)
whom the heavens	gods	to them	you will say	according to this

11. It is interesting to note here that Jeremiah contains more Hebrew words than any other book in the Bible.

מֵאַרְעָא	יֵאבַדוּ	עֲבַדוּ	לָא	וְאַרְקָא
preposition + noun: determined masculine singular	verb: *peal* imperfect 3mp	verb: *peal* perfect 3mp	negative particle	*vav* + noun: determined masculine singular
from the earth	they will perish	they made	not	and the earth
		אֵלֶּה	שְׁמַיָּא	וּמִן־תְּחוֹת
		demonstrative pronoun (pl)	noun: determined masculine plural	*vav* + preposition + preposition
		these	the heavens	and from under

Translation: *Therefore, you will say to them, "These[12] gods that did not make the heaven and the earth will perish from under the earth and under the heavens."*

This passage has captivated and puzzled the imaginations of many biblical students and scholars. Many cautiously explain it as a comment that was written in the margin (called a marginal gloss) that had mistakenly made its way into the text.[13] This sort of explanation is very popular within the Greek New Testament, where the scribes were known to be a little "freer" in their copy habits, but would be uncharacteristic of the early Hebrew scribes, who were

12. Note that the demonstrative pronoun "these" could either be in relation to the noun "gods" or "heavens." Therefore, an alternate translation could be ". . . from under the earth and under these heavens."
13. A typical example: "Verse 11, to begin with, is an obvious gloss: it is a sentence in prose which both interrupts the thought and is written in Aramaic." John Bright, *Jeremiah*, Anchor Bible (Garden City, NY: Doubleday, 1965), 79. See also J. A. Thompson, *The Book of Jeremiah*, NICOT (Grand Rapids: Eerdmans, 1980), 330; Douglas R. Jones, *Jeremiah*, NCBC (Cambridge: Cambridge University Press, 1973), 172; J. Gerald Janzen, *Studies in the Text of Jeremiah*, Harvard Semitic Monographs 6 (Cambridge, MA: Harvard University Press, 1973), 132; E. W. Nicholson, *The Book of the Prophet Jeremiah: Chapters 1–25* (Cambridge: Cambridge University Press, 1973), 102; B. Duhm, *Das Buch Jeremiah*, Kurzer Hand-Commentar zum Alten Testament (Tübingen: Mohr Siebeck, 1901), 101.

scrupulous copyists.[14] Additionally, it has been shown that the major themes in the verse do fit within the overall idea of the passage— which discusses the nations (Jer. 10:2), who create idols for themselves out of material things created by human hands (10:3, 8–9).[15]

However, one feature that does not receive emphasis in the many treatments of the passage is this: Could the Aramaic language be a key piece in the prophetic foreshadowing of the events to come? After all, the language was that of the Babylonians, who would soon take Judah captive. So apart from only a rhetorical emphasis on the difference between God and the gods of the nations, the Aramaic here could be a way for God to communicate a deeper message to those listening.

Later in the book, Jeremiah is very specific regarding the coming captivity in Babylon (Jer. 25:8–9 and 27:5–7). It appears that the use of Aramaic here could be another case of this. Jeremiah was one of the last prophets to Judah before the Babylonian captivity, and a major theme in the book is a prophetic warning to Judah of judgment (see the temple sermon in 7:1–13 for a good example). Aramaic was the language spoken in Babylon and was soon to become the first language of the Judean captives and their families. Since Aramaic was the language of the coming exile, a day was approaching when the Israelites would have limited familiarity with Hebrew. This transition from Hebrew to Aramaic was so pronounced that, upon returning to Jerusalem only seventy years later, many Israelites were not familiar with Hebrew at all. For example, Nehemiah 8:8 records that they needed the law of God translated, presumably into Aramaic, so the people could understand it.[16] A

14. To the early Hebrew scribes, the text itself was sacred, a view that was not shared by the Greeks and Romans, who viewed the message as sacred.

15. Garnett Reid, "'Thus You Will Say to Them': A Cross-Cultural Confessional Polemic in Jeremiah 10.11," *JSOT* 31, no. 2 (2006): 221–38.

16. Also note: "At this time, an interesting development in the Hebrew language occurred. Until this point, Hebrew writing had made use of its own particular script, based on the Phoenician alphabet. However, when the Babylonians exiled Hebrew-speaking Jews to Babylon in the sixth century BCE, it seems those Hebrew speakers began to adopt the Aramaic alphabetic script for writing Hebrew. The original Hebrew script did not die out completely, the Aramaic script became the default script of the Hebrew language—a practice that was taken back to Jerusalem by those who eventually returned there. . . . Thus many students are often surprised

prophetic language change like this is unique to the entire Old Testament, as God would be using the language itself as a means to communicate his message.[17]

One additional feature of this text attests to this particular time from which it was written. Within this verse is a puzzling and wonderfully subtle small spelling change. The verse has two ways of spelling "earth":

אֲרַק   אֲרַע

ara'   *araq*

Why would the original include different spellings in such close proximity? In 539 BCE the dominance of the Achaemenid (Persian) Empire was established through the defeat of the Babylonians—the same Babylonians who took Israel captive in Jeremiah's day. This is what also led to the emancipation of the Jews from Babylon and their return to Jerusalem under Cyrus the Great (see the books of Ezra and Nehemiah). This established a vast empire, which adopted Aramaic as their language. This standardized the language throughout the kingdom, with Old Aramaic giving way to what is known as Imperial Aramaic.

The first form of the word "earth" to appear (אַרְקָא) is the Old Aramaic form, and the second (אַרְעָא) is the Imperial Aramaic form. These two spellings represent distinct markers between the two forms of the language—and they appear in the same verse![18] There are many theories as to why this might be the case, and there are no clear answers here.[19] But what can be appreciated is the evidence

---

to discover that the Hebrew Bible is, perhaps ironically, written in the script of its 'one percent' Aramaic (compare, for instance, English, which is written in the Latin script)." Donald R. Vance, George Athas, Yael Avrahami, and Jonathan G. Kline, *Biblical Aramaic: A Reader and Handbook* (Peabody, MA: Hendrickson, 2016), x.

17. See Reid, "'Thus You Will Say to Them,'" esp. 231–37.

18. Vance et al., *Biblical Aramaic*, xi. Here it is identified as an isogloss. The book goes on to summarize: "It is difficult to know whether the preservation of the two forms is deliberate or inadvertent, but it is nonetheless indicative of the linguistic transitions that occurred during the sixth century BCE."

19. Perhaps it was a set phrase or word that was known to many of the audience at the time. Set phrases in language tend to preserve older language features, especially in religious language. For a modern example, when most people quote John

of the shift that was taking place in the language within this single Aramaic verse. Represented here is the language in transition, from forms before the captivity (the Old Aramaic of Babylon, the nation that would conquer Judah) to emerging forms that would dominate after the captivity (the Imperial Aramaic of the Persians, who let the Israelites settle back in Jerusalem). This linguistic shift is preserved here in the text, captured by the eyes of the reader who understands the Aramaic.[20]

In this one passage there is an abrupt language change, Old Aramaic mixed with Imperial Aramaic, and a slew of additional unanswered questions that can send the imagination running in several directions at once—and this is just one verse! In fact, many more questions about the Aramaic in the Bible linger, awaiting study from capable students of the Bible. The doorway through which one enters Aramaic is one that leads to many other passages and, like most good endeavors, begins with more questions than answers. And the questions go on and on, through passageways and back alleys of scholarship. These paths are often intimidating from their lack of travel but are nonetheless intriguing and fascinating. Yet they are accessible only by entering through the first door—that of developing a working knowledge of Aramaic.

3:16, they quote the King James Version. It is not as if they, in everyday language, use words like "begotten" and "whosoever believeth"; it is just the manner in which they know the verse. This is an even more interesting phenomenon considering that many people do not know what "begotten" means anymore. This view of the Aramaic words could be supported somewhat, though not completely, by the fact that the introductory material of the phrase ("Therefore, you will say to them") is in Aramaic and not Hebrew.

20. Note that the spelling change is not carried through into the early cognate languages. For example, the Septuagint uses the same word in both occurrences for "earth" (γῆ), as does the *Peshitta* (ܐܪܥܐ).

9

Getting Back in Shape

Most of us are familiar with muscle atrophy. When you don't exercise for a few weeks, muscle tone and mass decline. According to Dylan Holly in an article at the Huffines Institute for Sports Medicine and Human Performance website, part of the reason for muscle atrophy is that muscle tissue is itself "energetically costly."[1] What he means is that it takes a lot of energy for your body to just maintain muscle tissue, and so when you don't use it, your body doesn't leverage other energy resources to maintain it. Instead, your body simply gets rid of the costly muscle tissue.

For those with eyes to see and ears to hear, you're probably tracking the analogy. Maintaining your Hebrew is "energetically costly." Holly gives three passing scenarios that cause atrophy: bed rest, immobilization, or microgravity (outer space). Is your Hebrew on bed rest? How long has your Hebrew been immobilized? Ten days? Ten years? Has your Hebrew perhaps been jettisoned to outer space? Maybe you feel like Ezekiel, looking out over a valley of dry bones.

1. Dylan Holly, "Muscle Atrophy Cures Found at the Supermarket," Huffines Institute, May 28, 2018, https://www.huffinesinstitute.org/Resources/Articles/Article ID/1696/Muscle-Atrophy-Cures-Found-At-The-Supermarket.

"I was discouraged about needing to start reminded myself that I went to seminary from the beginning to regain what I had for the opportunity to better understand lost. My pastor introduced me to the the hard questions (like the Trinity) so Daily Dose of Greek and the Daily Dose I could better explain them to children. of Hebrew. For a long time, I watched That continued to be my motivation as the videos without understanding much I began working through my old biblical of the original text. Still, I was pleasantly languages textbooks." surprised at how much I did remember. I

—Nancy Ruth[a]

"Can this Hebrew live?" Within the analogy, Hebrew is akin to biological muscle tissue—if we don't use it, we lose it.

Let me encourage you from my decade of teaching experience. I assure you that there is more Hebrew in the deep recesses of your brain than you realize. You can get it back. When our physical muscles atrophy, we still have the building blocks of muscle tissue in our bodies. We have the amino acids and protein enzymes necessary to produce more muscle tissue. Similarly, the building blocks of your Hebrew are still there. You may have to dig them out of the far corners of your cerebral cortex, but the information is there. You might be shocked at how quickly you can get it back. Not only can you get it back, but you can progress in the language and become a skilled reader and exegete of the Hebrew Bible.

In this chapter, we provide you with both guidelines and inspiration for getting back your Hebrew. You will find a few more testimonials in this chapter than in previous chapters. Why? Because former students like you are both comforted and motivated to hear stories of "Hebrew loss" followed by "Hebrew recovery." Your story of recovery can soon be added to the testimonials in this chapter.

Rediscover Your Why

Have you ever been part of a church or organization where a leader clearly and repeatedly articulated a vision of where the group was headed and why? When that sort of vision casting is done well, you don't even notice it. Going in any other direction doesn't seem reasonable.

To regain your Hebrew, you need to reignite your vision for why the language is worth it. What value have you placed on a deep knowledge of God's word, and what value do you want to put on a deep knowledge of God's word? If your actions don't reflect your desire, then you have a resource of potential energy (stored energy) that can become kinetic energy (energy in action). You have a goal and desire; all you need is to jump-start your action to match that desire. Maybe you'll go back and read (or reread) chapter 1, in which we articulate the reasons that Hebrew study is worth the struggle. Skim through this book and read the many quotes and devotional asides. Be infected with a burning passion to be as close as possible to the Spirit-inspired words of the prophets. Don't be content to minister as a "second-hander," sharing others' insights from Scripture. Who wants to kiss "through the veil" (of translation) when "kissing on the lips" (Hebrew, Greek) is so much better?

Shame and regret do not provide lasting motivation, so take those emotions to the Lord in prayer. Be assured that the Lord has taken away your shame. Spend time in God's presence, basking in his full acceptance of you in Christ. Ask for empowerment to regain your Hebrew skills and employ the language for the edification of the church and the glory of God. "Commit to the Lord whatever you do, and he will establish your plans" (Prov. 16:3 NIV).

Be Honest about the Facts

Alongside regaining vision, it's important to face the dual realities of your Hebrew skills and your schedule. Can you still read Hebrew words? Or do you need to relearn the alphabet and how to pronounce Hebrew? Have you forgotten all your verb and noun morphology or just the rarer forms? Before you start to exercise these muscles again, take some time to evaluate your current ability *honestly*. Don't let this initial inventory destroy your motivation. Being honest now will save potential frustration down the road.

Also, honestly evaluate your time. Where are you really spending your time? Realistically, where will you be able to insert Hebrew into an already busy schedule? Chapter 2 of this book contains much information on time management, especially with regard to taming the distractions of technology.

Actively Leverage Your Time

After you assess where your time is going, you're ready to make changes. Just one or two strategic changes in the way you spend your time will give you the minutes you need to regain Hebrew. A few possible ideas are listed below:

- Set specific limits for TV and movies—only on weekends, for example.
- Install a Hebrew flashcard app on your phone (e.g., Bible Vocab, Quizlet). Or, better, find a set of hard-copy vocab cards like the ones associated with Pratico–Van Pelt. Keep a Hebrew grammar in your car. When you are waiting to pick up your kids from school or for your spouse to come out of a store, seize those five minutes to study Hebrew. Let Hebrew be your default activity when waiting in the car. This may not end up being your lifelong method to pick up your Hebrew pieces off the floor, but while you're getting jump-started again, it will be helpful to have as many outlets to engage with Hebrew as possible.
- On the flip side of installing a flashcard app, remove time-wasting apps from your phone (e.g., Facebook or Instagram). Looking back on your life, do you really want to say, "You know what characterized my life on a daily basis—a

constant willingness to look at the latest distraction, shiny thing, or viral video that entered my field of vision." I (Rob) once heard someone say, "If I printed out all the stuff I read on the internet and bound it together as a book, I would never buy that book. It would be a terrible book. Why, then, do I waste my time looking at that stuff?"

- Plan a "phone fast" one day per week. It sounds radical, but you can experience what life was like for most Americans before 1997. Although a phone fast may not be a spiritual discipline, I like the analogy of a fast, because usually the hunger pangs during a food fast remind you to seek the Lord in prayer. When the "phone pangs" come, go to your Hebrew Bible. Use the extra time you find to reconnect with Hebrew—and to connect with the local community you have set up, with whom you enjoy this language journey.

- Hang up a laminated list of Hebrew paradigms and vocabulary words in your shower or next to the bathroom mirror. Make a habit of reviewing Hebrew while showering, shaving, or brushing your teeth. I reproduce for my classes a page of review paradigms that are affectionately known as "Shower Sheets" for this very purpose.

No matter your schedule, there is time in your day that can be redeemed for Hebrew. Find those few moments and start to form the habit of using them well. Remember that consistency will bring a far greater return than intensity. Ten minutes every day will pay off more than four hours once a week.

Be Inspired by Others

When I was a teaching assistant while earning my MDiv, my professor taught me a helpful learning strategy for students who were doing Hebrew drills in class. The students would partner up and work drills on the board together. When my professor had me organize the pairs, he would ask me to intentionally pair a stronger student with a weaker student. This naturally helped both partners. The stronger student was able to "teach" the weaker student, thus solidifying the material in his or her mind. Additionally, the weaker student was able to see someone who understood the material in action and could seek to emulate that person. Organizing the pairs like this gave the weaker students someone to look up to.

However, this structure could potentially lead to discouragement for the weaker student. If you feel like a "weaker student," you can combat the discouragement by recognizing that everyone could use some help. Your Hebrew studies will benefit when you surrender your pride and look to others for help. Most of the time, they will inspire you to press on.

Here are some suggestions for how to be the best "weak" student you possibly can be:

- Acknowledge your struggles with the language unashamedly.
- Rejoice in the gifts and abilities God has given to others to learn Hebrew and be encouraged by their progress rather than being jealous of it.
- Be humble enough to accept help from others.
- Develop a work ethic that will push you to learn even if you don't feel hardwired to learn languages.

Perhaps for some of you, the challenge is not admitting that your language abilities are weak but admitting that you've let your knowledge of Hebrew wane. You need examples of others who have fought to get it back. Nancy Ruth is one of those examples. Nancy studied Hebrew and Greek in college and seminary, but life and ministry crowded out her upkeep of the languages. See her testimony below.

Nancy's story is not overly complicated. She had the desire and motivation to rekindle her language skills, she developed a plan, and then she executed that plan. As I hope you've gathered so far in this book, you *can* resurrect your Hebrew skills. Some of you just need the motivation of having seen others do it to know it's possible.

Nancy Ruth's Testimony

[My] next step was to pick up the Hebrew. I could not find my old Hebrew textbook. It was in one of the many boxes that fill the shed. Instead, I bought a new one, complete with the companion workbook. I began working through it but quickly got discouraged. . . . Then I found the app Ginoskos. I began working through the exercises, which more rapidly brought back the morphologies. I also started working on my Hebrew vocabulary. I found the key was knowing the vocabulary. The more words I could define, the better I could translate the Daily Dose of Hebrew verses before the instructor. Then it was time to transition into translating larger passages of Scripture. I was in a time crunch since I hoped to begin PhD studies soon. So I registered for a week-long intensive Hebrew review course from Southern Baptist Theological Seminary. As part of this class, we would be translating the book of Ruth.

The other important element to my renewed biblical languages study was a commitment not to let them lapse again. I have been experimenting with ways to incorporate it into my daily routine. The first step was the Daily Dose videos. I then added time (even five minutes) each day on the Ginoskos app. I also began listening to the Scriptures in Hebrew and Greek while following along. Following the review course, I plan to translate for ten minutes a day in each language, using a biblical language-based commentary to supplement my studies.

—Nancy Ruth[c]

We can also be inspired by historical figures as we find their stories of learning Hebrew. William Bradford was born in March 1590 in Austerfield, Yorkshire, England, and became the governor of Plymouth Colony for thirty years. Bradford recorded the difficulties of the sea voyage on the *Mayflower* in addition to details of life in Plymouth in his work *A History of Plimoth Plantation, 1620–47*. In the beginning pages of this work, Bradford wrote a brief description of his

desire to learn Hebrew, which he began in his old age (see fig. 9.1).
Here are Bradford's words (with original spelling and formatting):

> Though I am growne aged, yet I have had a longing
> desire, to see with my owne eyes, something of that most
> ancient language, and holy tongue, in which the Law,
> and oracles of God were write; and in which God,
> and angels spake to the holy patriarks, of old
> time; and what names were given to things,
> from the creation. And though I cañot
> attaine to much herein, yet I am refresh-
> ed, to have seen some glimpse hereof;
> (as Moses saw the Land of ca-
> nan afarr of) my aime and
> desire is, to see how the words,
> and phrases lye in the
> holy texte; and to
> dicerne somewhat
> of the same,
> for my owne
> contente.[2]

In addition to Bradford's spoken desire to learn Hebrew late in life,
he also documented some of his study exercises. These included some
short sentences that he would translate, as well as lists of vocabulary
words in his own handwriting (of course). Bradford also has a couple
pages of Hebrew vocabulary transliterated into English, suggesting
that he relied on pronunciation to learn his vocabulary. One of the

2. William Bradford, *A History of Plimoth Plantation*. We discovered this text in a
blog post by Phillip Marshall at Houston Baptist University (HBU), "It's Never Too Late
to Learn Hebrew . . . ," *Biblical Languages* (blog), October 25, 2018, https://biblical
languages.net/2018/10/25/its-never-too-late-to-learn-hebrew/. Marshall comments
that Diana Severance, the director of HBU's Dunham Bible Museum, sent him this
text with the image of the page in Bradford's manuscript. The digital manuscripts
of Bradford's work can be found on the website of the State Library of Massachusetts, https://archives.lib.state.ma.us/handle/2452/208249. A special thanks to Diana
Severance for her help in locating these resources and to Phillip Marshall for drawing
our attention to them.

Figure 9.1

> Though y am growne aged, yet y haue had a longing
> desire, to see with my owne eyes, somthing of that most
> ancient Language, and holy tongue, in which tho Law
> and oracles of god were write; and in which god,
> and angels spake to the holy patriarks of old
> time; and what names were giuen to things,
> from the creation. And though y cañote
> attaine to much herein, yet y am refresh-
> ed, to haue seen some glimpse hereof;
> (as moyses saw tho Land of ca-
> nan a farr of) my aime and
> desire is to see how the words,
> and phrases lye in the
> holy texte; and to
> discerne somewhat
> of the same,
> for my owne
> Contente.

חֶסֶד יהוה מָלְאָה הָאָרֶץ	The earth is full of y mercie of yehouah
שָׁם פָּחֲדוּ פָחַד לֹא הָיָה פָּחַד	Ther they feared a fear, wher no fear was
וַיַּרְא אֱלֹהִים כִּי טוֹב	And god saw that it was good
הוֹן יוֹסִיף רֵעִים רַבִּים	Riches gather many friends
לֹא טוֹב הֱיוֹת הָאָדָם לְבַדּוֹ	Yt is not good that man should be alone
רַע רַע יֹאמַר הַקֹּנֶה	Yt is naught, it is naught, saith the buyer
כַּבֵּד אֶת־אָבִיךָ וְאֶת אִמֶּךָ	honour thy father, and thy mother
מָצָא אִשָּׁה מָצָא טוֹב	he that findeth a wife findeth good
וּשְׂמַח מֵאֵשֶׁת נְעוּרֶיךָ	And rejoyce with the wife of thy youth
וַאֲנִי בְּרֹב חַסְדְּךָ אָבוֹא בֵיתֶךָ	But y in multitude of thy mercies, will come into thy house
זְנוּת וְיַיִן וְתִירוֹשׁ יִקַּח־לֵב	whordome, and wine, a new wine take away the harte
וְהָיָה כְּעֵץ שָׁתוּל עַל־פַּלְגֵי מָיִם	And he shall be as a tree planted by the brooks of waters
קוֹל דְּמֵי אָחִיךָ צֹעֲקִים אֵלַי	The voyce of thy brothers blood crieth unto me
חַכְמוֹת נָשִׁים בָּנְתָה בֵיתָהּ	A wise woman buildeth her house
lying y judge the דָּן בִּין צֶרֶי	נְקִי כַפַּיִם וּבַר לֵבָב Ynnocente in hands, & pure in harte

joys of finding manuscripts like this is that we see a busy man later in his life desiring to learn Hebrew. No matter your age, you can look to William Bradford for motivation to pick up Hebrew and enjoy God's revelation of himself in the Old Testament.

When my wife and I adopted our son from the Democratic Republic of the Congo, we were encouraged by so many others around us who had adopted or who were in the process. We looked to their examples for guidance and motivation. Some people talk about the "adoption bug," or the notion that once a family adopts, they can't help but adopt again. I would argue there isn't a bug per se, but people who have adopted tend to do it again *because they learn it is doable*. Something that may seem so monumental—raising funds, mountains of paperwork, international details—turns out to be doable. People who have adopted don't get a bug for the process; they get a bug for the outcome of adoption. Similarly, regaining your Hebrew competence is doable. You won't catch a bug for the difficult process to get it back, but you may catch the bug for the outcome of knowing God through the Hebrew of the Old Testament. Like my family, you may just need some encouragement from others who have gone before you and have come out on the other side with a deep joy in the Hebrew Bible.

Aim Low

The value of a practice is not found in our ability to do it perfectly. I don't often—who am I kidding, I never—recommend Urban Dictionary. However, in preparing this section I learned a new word: flawsome. Urban Dictionary defines this word as "something that is totally awesome, but not without its flaws."[3] It seems that the most common use of this word is in relation to an experience, which doesn't actually fit our context here. Also, I don't want to imply that "flawsome" communicates something about the value of Hebrew— "Hebrew is great and all, but I'd call it flawsome"—implying that

3. https://www.urbandictionary.com/define.php?term=Flawsome. This is not to be confused with "flawesome," which Urban Dictionary defines as an under-the-breath, sarcastic way of making someone think you actually said "awesome."

the study of Hebrew has its flaws. Rather, I would argue that *we* are "not without flaws" in our pursuit of learning and retaining Hebrew. And that's OK.

In an MIT article by Winslow Burleson and Rosalind Picard, the authors investigate the cognitive "affects" of those who learn through failure.[4] One of the detriments to our learning is our inability to properly deal with the negative affections of failure. In the article, Burleson and Picard define a state of "Stuck" in which there is a sense of being out of control, lack of concentration, mental fatigue, the feeling that this task will take forever, and a perceived mismatch between the challenge and one's skill. If we are honest, many of us live in this state of "Stuck" regarding our Hebrew study, and it cripples us rather than motivates us.

The reality is that we learn more through failure and our inabilities than we do through our perceived perfection. We need to learn to embrace our cognitive weaknesses and continue the valuable pursuit of learning Hebrew. The perfect can be the enemy of the good. If the activity we are doing is worthwhile, we should not be paralyzed by our inability to do it perfectly. We should strive to do our work as well as we can with our imperfect abilities and limited time. If we end up doing it minimally, it was still worth doing.

> "And whatever you do, whether in word or deed, do it all in the name of the Lord Jesus, giving thanks to God the Father through him."
> —Colossians 3:17 NIV

As you come back to Hebrew, it's OK to read it poorly. It's OK to take two years to relearn what you learned in one semester initially. It's OK to use an interlinear. It's OK to have forgotten morphological patterns. It's OK to not even remember what a root is!

One way to embrace our inabilities and continue learning is by setting attainable goals. By doing so, you are positively reinforcing the experience of successfully learning Hebrew. Shoot for reading one verse per day. After you've done that for a while, you can gradually increase your commitment.

4. Winslow Burleson and Rosalind Picard, "Affective Agents: Sustaining Motivation to Learn through Failure and a State of 'Stuck,'" (paper, MIT Media Lab, Cambridge, MA), https://affect.media.mit.edu/pdfs/04.burleson-picard.pdf.

Maybe your attainable goal is to start with a book intended to expose readers more broadly to the Hebrew language (rather than expecting readers to master paradigms and vocabulary). One book for this is Lee M. Fields, *Hebrew for the Rest of Us: Using Hebrew Tools without Mastering Biblical Hebrew* (Zondervan, 2008). If you struggled with English grammatical concepts in the past, you might consider starting with the slim paperback by Miles Van Pelt, *English Grammar to Ace Biblical Hebrew* (Zondervan, 2010). What if you committed to read one of these texts for just five minutes per day? Over the course of the year, you would spend more than thirty hours relearning Hebrew. You don't have to do everything. Just choose one small and achievable goal within your limitations. Write it down. Commit to it. Share that commitment with someone who will keep you accountable. Now, in the midst of all your flaws, do it.

> "The characterization of pastoral ministry as somehow incompatible with the languages (due to busyness, or other causes), is an unfortunate misunderstanding of what a pastorate is all about. No doubt, pastors should be busy shepherding their flock, meeting with ministry leaders, and running the church. But, the core of the calling is to be a 'minister of the word.'"
>
> —Michael Kruger[d]

Harness the Power of Ritual

Most of us naturally fall into various routines or rituals. We sit in the same place at church or in classrooms, we park in the same parking spaces at work, or we begin our days with coffee or tea. Humans are really good at developing habits or rituals and often do so without knowing it. If we can put a little thought and effort into our ability to develop habits, we can leverage those automated behaviors for learning Hebrew. By consciously embracing nonsacred rituals, we attach the totality of ourselves to a habit, directing our lives toward things we choose to value.

In a blog post titled "How to Turn an Ordinary Routine into a Spirit-Renewing Ritual," Brett and Kate McKay list the essential elements of a ritual as (1) location and atmosphere, (2) objects,

(3) timing, and (4) mindset.[5] A ritual is a habit performed in self-reflection and style—a method of consciously imprinting a behavior onto *all* of one's senses and thus making the habit stick more easily while increasing one's joy in practicing it.

What would it look like for you to turn your reading of the Hebrew Bible into a ritual? It might mean you buy that expensive calf-leather Hebrew Bible that feels so supple and smells like a new belt. And you might read it in the same favorite place every day. Maybe you read by a fire to remind you of Mount Sinai burning as God revealed the law to Moses. You might enjoy a cup of coffee as part of this daily ritual. The feel of leather. The smell of coffee. A familiar seat. The crackle of a nearby fire. A warm and familiar mug in your hand. A consciousness of being part of the body of Christ to whom this inspired text was written long ago. An expectation of hearing the Spirit speak through the word. By involving your various senses, you create an expectancy in your total person for this daily ritual.

Recruit a Team

I (Rob) recently appeared on a panel that was being asked questions by young men entering the ministry. One questioner asked, "If you could go back twenty years and tell yourself one thing, what would you say?"

"Buy Apple stock," I answered.

"And," I added more seriously, "I would tell myself to be sure to have faithful Christian brothers to walk side by side with me in my life and ministry—men to whom I could confess my sin and who would pray for me and hold me accountable" (James 5:16).

God created us to live in community. How foolish we are to attempt life or ministry alone—or to think we can persevere in a biblical language by ourselves. As you reboot your Hebrew, prayerfully seek other Christians who can join you in that commitment. Better yet, find someone who is faithful in reading the Hebrew Bible and ask

5. Brett McKay and Kate McKay, "How to Turn an Ordinary Routine into a Spirit-Renewing Ritual," *The Art of Manliness*, December 7, 2015, http://www.artofmanliness.com/2015/12/07/how-to-turn-an-ordinary-routine-into-a-spirit-renewing-ritual/.

that person to pull you along. With social media, it should be easy to reconnect with an old friend from college or seminary. If there is someone in your city with whom you can read the Hebrew Bible

Testimonial from a Children's Minister

Have you ever hit your alarm's snooze button because when you saw the time you thought, "No! It is too early"? That feeling became familiar to me during my three semesters of early morning Hebrew classes. The challenge of vocab cards and parsing often kept me up late the previous night. However, getting out of bed was worth every wink of lost sleep. Why? Learning Hebrew taught me more about God's word than I knew it would before I started class. Not only does each verse of Scripture come alive with deeper meaning, but learning Hebrew also taught me how to read my Bible more faithfully. Hebrew takes me into the deepest parts of the text. Here I can hear the Holy Spirit with more clarity, and see how the whole Bible is a unified, redemptive story that leads to Jesus. As a children's minister, I am equipped to dig deep into the truths of God's word so that my kids know why God is the only one worthy of worship. Hebrew studies go beyond flashcards. Hebrew has helped me teach little Johnny about faith in Jesus. Nothing could be more worth our time than Hebrew because nothing is more life changing than God's word.

My friend Jonathan and I both love to study. Despite living in different states, we are able to study together once a week via FaceTime. To keep our Hebrew fresh, we bought the Baylor handbook on Deuteronomy. Each week we translate a few verses before getting together. During our call, we read the text aloud, discuss grammatical issues, and iron out the best translation. A few minutes each day combined with an hour a week on the phone helps us grow together in our knowledge of Hebrew. We find that together we sharpen one another's understanding, and we give necessary accountability when one of us is tempted to hit the snooze button. Hebrew is worth it, so keep up the diligent work and remember that vocab covers a multitude of translation sins.

—Ethan Graves[e]

(another pastor, perhaps), how wonderful to enjoy face-to-face fellowship over the word of God!

Become a Hebrew Scribe

At this point in the book, you have no shortage of time-management and study methods from which to choose. So, what's one more? Maybe you need one final audible or trick play in order to gain an advantage over the Hebrew defenses. Here's my suggestion: write down at least one Hebrew verse in longhand every day, saying it aloud, reading it, and writing it. If you want to make writing Hebrew more of a ritual (see above), perhaps use a leather journal and fountain pen and write by candlelight.

My wife does this in English with a resource called Journibles.[6] These are premade books that have blank lines for you to write the verses and jot down some thoughts from the passage. Perhaps you purchase one of these but write the text in Hebrew. Recent studies show that information that is written by hand is retained better than typed information or information that one simply reads or hears. Researchers do not fully understand why, but various studies reach the same undeniable conclusion—handwriting one's notes results in better learning.[7]

Seek Professional Intervention

Another desperation call from the line of scrimmage: seek the help of a professional. We all seek professional intervention at times. When your health fails, you go to a doctor. When your car breaks, you go to the mechanic. When your marriage is struggling, you go to a counselor.

If you have employed tactics mentioned above and you are still struggling, why not seek out professional help to resurrect your

6. Reformation Heritage Books currently has Old Testament volumes for Genesis, Exodus, Leviticus, Deuteronomy, Proverbs, and Psalms; see https://www.heritage books.org/categories/Journibles/.

7. See the various studies summarized in Robert Lee Hotz, "The Power of Handwriting," *Wall Street Journal*, Tuesday, April 5, 2016, D1–D2.

Hebrew? Be willing to spend a little money for the professional help too. I've found that people take more seriously the things that they are actually paying for—note, for example, the amazingly high attrition rates of students in free online courses.[8]

What would seeking professional help look like? Here are some possible avenues:

- Take an online or on-campus Hebrew course at a college or seminary.

- Contact a Hebrew professor and ask for recommendations in hiring a graduate student to tutor you. Skype or Google Hangouts makes remote tutoring available in almost any location.

- Do you have a vacation home in Hawaii? Contact a Hebrew professor (e.g., the one helping with this textbook) and trade a few days of full-fledged Hebrew intervention for a week's use of your vacation home. ☺

Spare the Next Generation

In Deuteronomy 6:6–7, Moses encourages Israel to diligently teach (שׁנן) "these words" (הַדְּבָרִים הָאֵלֶּה) to their children. Deuteronomy 6 continues by saying that these words will be integral to Israel's existence as a people and that they will be a teaching tool when future generations ask about the Lord's mighty acts. I'll grant you that the illustration breaks down. If we pass on to our children the original biblical languages, there is something fundamentally different from that than passing on to them the mighty acts of God in their heart language. Even so, think of the joy it could bring to pass on those mighty acts of God in the original languages.

It is pretty well established that children learn new languages faster than adults. How we all wish we could go back and study Hebrew and Greek in our childhood! We cannot. But we can give the next generation what we failed to receive. You can teach Hebrew to children in

---

8. Jonathan Haber, "MOOC Attrition Rates—Running the Numbers," *HuffPost*, November 25, 2013, http://www.huffingtonpost.com/jonathan-haber/mooc-attrition -rates-runn_b_4325299.html.

your home, in a local Christian middle school, or in a homeschooling cooperative. And if you do this, you will experience a wonderful truth: there's nothing like teaching something to really make you learn it—or relearn it. In addition to teaching them the original biblical languages, you will also help establish in your children or students skills and accountability so they don't share your story of regret (assuming you have spent time wandering from the Hebrew fold).

I realize how radical this suggestion sounds. Some of you may be just trying to learn basic vocabulary again, yet I'm suggesting that you teach Hebrew to the next generation! But what if this vision of seeing others delight in Hebrew to the same degree you will is what motivates you to jump in with both feet? What if the drive to teach others the original language of the Old Testament motivates you not only to learn a few additional vocabulary words but also to develop your own memory devices for the *qal* paradigm?

When I was in high school, I spent three years studying Spanish. I never really felt like I knew Spanish super well while studying it, but to this day I can remember more than I thought I learned at the time. While working at the gym during seminary, I learned to interact with the Spanish-speaking community in our town (at least insofar as I could make sure they understood the terms of the gym contract). It was so rewarding to be using information I learned years ago, information I honestly didn't know I had retained. In my current position, I practice speaking Hebrew with a colleague, and he is the director of the Hispanic programs at our institution. I sometimes find myself speaking to him in Hebrew and then randomly throwing in a Spanish word. I'm not consciously thinking to switch to Spanish. But when my brain switches out of English, I'm not yet good enough at modern, spoken Hebrew to keep out the Spanish influences. The point is that I learned far more Spanish as a youngster than I thought.

There's something about the young human brain that absorbs knowledge like a sponge. The church father Irenaeus (ca. 130–202), reflecting on the strength of his childhood recollections of Polycarp, poignantly captures this reality:

> I remember the events of those times [my childhood] much better than those of more recent occurrence. As the studies of our youth

growing with our minds, unite with it so firmly that I can tell also
the very place where the blessed Polycarp was accustomed to sit and
discourse; and also his entrances, his walks, the complexion of his life
and the form of his body, and his conversations with the people, and
his familiar [discussions] with John, as he was accustomed to tell, as
also his familiarity with those who had seen the Lord.[9]

Let us labor to imprint the words of Scripture on the next generation's minds—even the Hebrew words of the inspired authors. What
a joyful and momentous task! If we teach others (or even if we teach
ourselves), let us whisper under our breaths this prayer/poem of the
Greek grammarian James Hope Moulton:

At the Classroom Door

Lord, at Thy word opens yon door, inviting
Teacher and taught to feast this hour with Thee;
Opens a Book where God in human writing
Thinks His deep thoughts, and dead tongues live for me.

Too dread the task, too great the duty calling,
Too heavy far the weight is laid on me!
O if mine own thought should on Thy words falling
Mar the great message, and men hear not Thee!

Give me Thy voice to speak, Thine ear to listen,
Give me Thy mind to grasp Thy mystery;
So shall my heart throb, and my glad eyes glisten,
Rapt with the wonders Thou dost show to me.[10]

---

9. Eusebius, *Ecclesiastical History* 5.20.5–6, trans. C. F. Cruse (Peabody, MA:
Hendrickson, 1998), 178.
10. Poem printed on unnumbered front page of the first separately published
fascicle of James Hope Moulton, *A Grammar of New Testament Greek: Accidence
and Word-Formation*, vol. 2, part 1, *General Introduction: Sounds and Writing*, ed.
Wilbert Francis Howard (Edinburgh: T&T Clark, 1919). The poem, written in Banga-
lore, India (where Moulton was serving as a missionary), is dated February 21, 1917.

Chapter Reflections

1. Name one adjustment in your daily schedule that would allow for five minutes of Hebrew study or reading of the Hebrew Bible. Can you make that adjustment right now?

2. List elements of a morning or evening ritual that you can combine with the study of Hebrew or the reading of the Hebrew Bible. Try rebooting a Hebrew habit through your new ritual.

3. Do you need professional intervention? Contact a local Bible college or seminary about an on-campus or online class. Or look into hiring a skilled graduate student to tutor you.

4. Who could walk together with you as you reconnect with Hebrew? If you can't think of someone, prayerfully ask the Lord to direct your path to a Hebrew co-laborer.

5. Is there someone to whom you can teach Hebrew? Your children? Perhaps you can teach at a local Christian school or homeschool co-op? Start your own YouTube channel? There's nothing like teaching Hebrew to really learn it!

After you finish reading this book, consider signing the pledge below. Make a copy of your signed pledge and display it somewhere to remind you of your commitment.

The Hebrew Bible

READER'S PLEDGE

*With the help of God,
and as long as he gives me
strength to do so,
I will read and study
the Hebrew Bible.*

_____
Signature

_____
Date

The Exegetical Value of the Masoretic Accents in 1 Kings 18:29

Adam J. Howell

———————————————○———————————————

"And it came about at the passing of the midday, that they prophesied intensely until the offering of the oblation; but there was no voice, and there was no answer, and there was no attentiveness."

וַיְהִי כַּעֲבֹר הַצָּהֳרַיִם וַיִּתְנַבְּאוּ עַד לַעֲלוֹת הַמִּנְחָה וְאֵין־קוֹל
וְאֵין־עֹנֶה וְאֵין קָשֶׁב:

—1 Kings 18:29

The interpretive benefit of the Masoretic accents is a debatable topic.[11] However, since these were originally cantillation marks (for singing and memorization), they at least play a minimal role in where the emphasis of the verse may lie. The accents do not always point to an important interpretive key to a verse, but they can provide insight into an interpretation or nuance of the text that may not be apparent in an English translation.

In 1 Kings 18:29, the Masoretic accents provide direction on where to break the translation in order to emphasize that no one heard the prophets of Baal crying out. The ESV translates 1 Kings 18:29 as, "And as midday passed, they raved on until the time of the offering of the oblation, but there was no voice. No one answered; no one paid attention." This translation captures the general idea of the verse and can be trusted. However, notice the difference between my translation above and the English translation represented here. The ESV puts a period after "voice," suggesting that there is a major thought break in the sentence. In this sense, the main point is "there was no voice," and "no one answered; no one paid attention" is a further clarification of "there was no voice." The Hebrew,

---

11. This devotional originally appeared at https://adamjhowell.wordpress.com on October 29, 2016.

however, places all the negative particles together and by repetition emphasizes the idea that no deity in the entire cosmos heard the outcry of Baal's prophets.

The *athnah* is the key accent in 1 Kings 18:29. In the translation above, the *athnah* would be represented by the semicolon after "oblation." It represents a minor but significant pause in the verse. Following the *athnah*, the Hebrew Bible gives a threefold negation, all with the negative particle אֵין: "There was no voice, there was no answer, and there was no attentiveness." This threefold negation provides an emphasis similar to the "holy, holy, holy" of Isaiah 6, and the *athnah* sets these phrases off grammatically. This minor change in the punctuation of 1 Kings 18:29 emphasizes the lack of response from anyone in the cosmos. Absolutely no one, neither in the created world nor in the spiritual world, heard the cry of the prophets of Baal.

The deafness of false deities reminds us of the folly of turning to anything or anyone besides the Lord God. The Lord God has provided every good and perfect gift to his people in Christ. As Peter says in John 6:68, "To whom would we go?" The deafness of false deities helps us realize how ridiculous we are to call on any "god" besides the Lord (cf. Isa. 44:9–20). There will be no voice; there will be no answer; there will be no attentiveness. The Lord God is the only God (2 Kings 19:19; Ps. 86:10; Isa. 37:16; John 1:18; 1 Tim. 1:17; Jude 25).

SOURCES OF FEATURED QUOTATIONS

Chapter 1: The Goal of the Harvest

a. As quoted in Daniel Jang, "Kissing through a Veil Is Not Intimate Enough," *Christianity Today*, July 19, 2019, https://www.christiantoday.co.nz/news/kissing-through-a-veil-is-not-intimate-enough.html.

b. Bruce K. Waltke, "How I Changed My Mind about Teaching Hebrew (or Retained It)," *Crux* 29, no. 4 (1993): 14.

c. Martin Luther, "To the Councilmen of All Cities in Germany That They Establish and Maintain Christian Schools," in *The Christian in Society II*, ed. Walther I. Brandt, trans. Albert T. W. Steinhaeuser and Walther I. Brandt, Luther's Works 45 (Philadelphia: Muhlenberg, 1962), 359.

d. John Piper, *Brothers, We Are Not Professionals: A Plea to Pastors for Radical Ministry*, updated and expanded ed. (Nashville: B&H, 2013), 100.

e. Waltke, "How I Changed My Mind," 11.

f. Scott Hafemann, as part of "The *SBJT* Forum: Profiles of Expository Preaching," *SBJT* 3, no. 2 (1999): 88.

g. Bruce Steventon, email to Adam J. Howell, August 9, 2018. Cited with permission.

h. Waltke, "How I Changed My Mind," 14.

i. Stephen J. Andrews, "Some Knowledge of Hebrew Possible to All: Old Testament Exposition and the *Hebraica Veritas*," *Faith and Mission* 13, no. 1 (1995): 107; italics added.

j. Enoch Okode, "A Case for Biblical Languages: Are Hebrew and Greek Optional or Indispensable?," *African Journal of Theology* 29, no. 2 (2010): 96.

k. Rob Starner, "7 Reasons to Study Biblical Hebrew and Biblical Greek," ThoughtHub, September 24, 2015, https://www.sagu.edu/thoughthub/study-biblical-hebrew-and-greek; italics original.

l. Waltke, "How I Changed My Mind," 10.

m. Piper, *Brothers, We Are Not Professionals*, 102.

n. Jason S. DeRouchie, "The Profit of Employing the Biblical Languages: Scriptural and Historical Reflections," *Themelios* 37, no. 1 (2012): 46.

o. DeRouchie, "Profit of Employing the Biblical Languages," 46.

p. Waltke, "How I Changed My Mind," 12.

q. Andrews, "Some Knowledge of Hebrew," 107.

r. Jeremy Bouma, "Why Study Biblical Hebrew? Neglect the Languages, Lose the Gospel, Says Luther!," *Zondervan Academic Blog*, August 19, 2014, https://zonder vanacademic.com/blog/why-study-biblical-hebrew-neglect-the-languages-lose-the -gospel-says-luther/.

Chapter 2: Weighed in the Balances and Found Wanting

a. Will Durant, *The Story of Philosophy: The Lives and Opinions of the Great Philosophers of the Western World* (New York: Simon & Schuster, 1961), 61.

b. Jerome, "Letter 125, 'To Rusticus,'" in *Select Letters of St. Jerome*, trans F. A. Wright (Cambridge, MA: Harvard University Press, 1933), 419–20.

c. Jodi Hiser, email to Adam J. Howell, August 17, 2018. Jodi's testimony regarding learning Hebrew is reproduced here with permission.

d. Jim Elliot, *The Journals of Jim Elliot*, ed. Elisabeth Elliot (Grand Rapids: Revell, 1989), 103–4.

e. Phillip Dormer Stanhope, *Dear Boy: Lord Chesterfield's Letters to His Son*, ed. Piers Dudgeon and Jonathan Jones (London: Bantam, 1989), 140.

f. Alan Jacobs, "I'm Thinking It Over," *American Conservative*, January 4, 2016, http://www.theamericanconservative.com/jacobs/im-thinking-it-over/. Justin Taylor's blog, *Between Two Worlds*, first pointed us to this article.

g. Cary Stothart, Ainsley Mitchum, and Courtney Yehnert, "The Attentional Cost of Receiving a Cell Phone Notification," *Journal of Experimental Psychology: Human Perception and Performance* 14, no. 4 (2015): 893–97. The quotation is from the article abstract found at http://psycnet.apa.org/buy/2015-28923-001.

h. "3 Questions with Tim Challies," *Towers* [newspaper of Southern Seminary], April 2016.

Chapter 3: Review the Fundamentals Often

a. S. M. Baugh, *A New Testament Greek Primer*, 3rd ed. (Phillipsburg, NJ: P&R, 2012), vii.

b. Joshua Foer, *Moonwalking with Einstein: The Art and Science of Remembering Everything* (New York: Penguin, 2011), 65.

c. Foer, *Moonwalking with Einstein*, 128.

d. Foer, *Moonwalking with Einstein*, 128.

Chapter 4: Develop a Next-Level Memory

a. "He Took Me Overseas to Break Me: A Conversation with Dr. William Barrick," The Master's Seminary, May 22, 2018, https://www.tms.edu/tyndale/articles /he-took-me-overseas-to-break-me/.

b. Harry Lorayne, *How to Develop a Super-Power Memory* (Hollywood, FL: Frederick Fell, 2000), 9.

c. Joshua Foer, *Moonwalking with Einstein: The Art and Science of Remembering Everything* (New York: Penguin, 2011), 53.

d. Dominic O'Brien, *You Can Have an Amazing Memory* (London: Watkins, 2011), 180, 187.

e. O'Brien, *You Can Have an Amazing Memory*, 21.

f. Harry Lorayne and Jerry Lucas, *Memory Book: The Classic Guide to Improving Your Memory at Work, at School, and at Play* (New York: Ballentine, 1974), 21.

g. George M. Landes, *Building Your Biblical Hebrew Vocabulary: Learning Words by Frequency and Cognate* (Atlanta: Society of Biblical Literature, 2001), ix.

h. Foer, *Moonwalking with Einstein*, 203, quoting Tony Buzan.

i. Foer, *Moonwalking with Einstein*, 100.

Chapter 5: Strategically Leverage Your Breaks

a. John Piper, *Brothers, We Are Not Professionals: A Plea to Pastors for Radical Ministry*, updated and expanded ed. (Nashville: B&H, 2013), 100.

b. Piper, *Brothers, We Are Not Professionals*, 99–100.

c. John Owen, *Biblical Theology, or the Nature, Origin, Development, and Study of Theological Truth in Six Books*, trans. Stephen P. Westcott (Morgan, PA: Soli Deo Gloria, 1994), 701. The Goold edition in Latin: *The Works of John Owen*, edited by William H. Goold (Edinburgh: T&T Clark, 1862), 479.

d. Bernard Ramm, *Protestant Biblical Interpretation: A Textbook of Hermeneutics*, 3rd rev. ed. (Grand Rapids: Baker, 1970), 117.

Chapter 6: Read, Read, Read

a. Phil Neetz, personal correspondence, January 2019.

Chapter 7: The Wisdom of Resources

a. Rob Starner, "7 Reasons to Study Biblical Hebrew and Biblical Greek," ThoughtHub, September 24, 2015, https://www.sagu.edu/thoughthub/study-biblical-hebrew-and-greek.

b. Ligon Duncan, "Ligon Duncan on 'Why Learn Biblical Hebrew & Greek When There Are Good Language Tools?,'" BibleMesh, YouTube, June 22, 2013, https://www.youtube.com/watch?v=nCkFnk-8NPU.

c. Karl Kutz and Rebekah Josberger, *Learning Biblical Hebrew: Reading for Comprehension; An Introductory Grammar* (Bellingham, WA: Lexham, 2018), xxiii.

d. Ludwig Koehler, from the preface to the Hebrew part of the first edition of *Lexicon in Veteris Testamenti Libros*, which later became in English *Hebrew and Aramaic Lexicon of the Old Testament*. This quotation is from the English edition: Ludwig Koehler, Walter Baumgartner, M. E. J. Richardson, and Johann Jakob Stamm, *The Hebrew and Aramaic Lexicon of the Old Testament* (Leiden: Brill, 1994–2000), 1:lxx.

e. A. T. Robertson, *The Minister and His Greek New Testament* (1923; repr., Birmingham, AL: Solid Ground Christian Books, 2008), 22. Originally published in 1923.

f. Moisés Silva, *God, Language, and Scripture: Reading the Bible in the Light of General Linguistics* (1990), in *Foundations of Contemporary Interpretation: Six Volumes in One*, ed. Moisés Silva (Grand Rapids: Zondervan, 1996), 278.

g. John Albert Bengel, *Gnomon of the New Testament*, vol. 1, trans. James Bandinel, rev. and ed. Andrew R. Fausset (Edinburgh: T&T Clark, 1858), 44. The Latin original of Bengel's quote (given in the translator's footnote) is "Nil aliud esse Theologiam atque Grammaticam, in Spiritus Sancti verbis occupatam." I (Rob) have been unable to locate the original quote in Luther's writings. Perhaps Bengel is para-phrasing these words of Luther: "Spiritus sanctus habet suam grammaticam" (The Holy Spirit has his own grammar). See Martin Luther, *D. Martin Luthers Werke, Weimarer Ausgabe* [Weimar: Böhlau, 1883–1993], 39/2:104.24.

h. Starner, "7 Reasons."

Chapter 8: Hebrew's Close Cousin—Aramaic

a. Miles V. Van Pelt, *Basics of Biblical Aramaic: Complete Grammar, Lexicon, and Annotated Text* (Grand Rapids: Zondervan, 2011), x.

b. Isaac Jerusalmi, *The Aramaic Sections of Ezra and Daniel: A Philological Commentary with Frequent References to Talmudic Aramaic Parallels and a Synopsis of the Regular Verb* (Cincinnati: Hebrew Union College–Jewish Institute of Religion, 1982), vi.

Chapter 9: Getting Back in Shape

a. Nancy Ruth, email message to Adam J. Howell, January 2, 2019. Nancy was a student in my week-long Hebrew Review course on our campus. Used with permission.

b. From the blog post "Three Investments with an Instant Guaranteed Return," *Mr. Money Mustache* (blog), November 15, 2015, https://www.mrmoneymustache .com/2015/11/15/three-investments/.

c. Nancy Ruth, email message to Adam J. Howell, January 2, 2019. Nancy was a student in my week-long Hebrew Review course on our campus. Used with permission.

d. Michael Kruger, "You Don't Think Learning the Biblical Languages Is Worth It? Think Again," *Canon Fodder* (blog), August 18, 2014, https://www.michaelj kruger.com/you-dont-think-learning-the-biblical-languages-is-worth-it-think-again/. Kruger is the president and professor of New Testament and early Christianity at Reformed Theological Seminary in Charlotte, North Carolina.

e. Ethan Graves, email message to Adam J. Howell, December 10, 2018. Ethan was a student in my Hebrew classes during his time at Boyce College. He is currently a chil-dren's minister at Hays Hills Baptist Church in Austin, Texas. Used with permission.

DEVOTIONAL CONTRIBUTOR BIOGRAPHIES

Tom Blanchard

Tom Blanchard and his wife, Lucy, served for thirty-three years in France with The Evangelical Alliance Mission (TEAM) in both church-based leadership training and as professors of Old Testament at Bible institutes in Paris and Geneva. Tom has published numerous study guides and edited two books in French on the Old Testament. He and Lucy are enjoying retirement and are actively involved at Camelback Bible Church in Phoenix, Arizona.

William Fullilove

William Fullilove is associate professor of Old Testament and dean of students at Reformed Theological Seminary in New York City. He earned his PhD in Semitic and Egyptian languages and literatures from the Catholic University of America, focusing his research on the Dead Sea Scrolls. Bill and his wife, Jill, have two children.

Peter Gentry

Peter Gentry is the Donald J. Williams Professor of Old Testament Interpretation at the Southern Baptist Theological Seminary. He has served on the faculty at Toronto Baptist Seminary and Bible College, in addition to teaching assignments at University of Toronto, Heritage Theological Seminary, and Tyndale Theological Seminary. Peter is currently involved in editing *Ecclesiastes* and *Proverbs* for the Göttingen Septuagint series and leads the Hexapla Institute.

Steven Hallam

Steven Hallam is associate professor and chair of the General Studies department of Alaska Christian College in Soldotna, Alaska. He earned his PhD from Gateway Seminary. His research focuses on biblical languages and early biblical translations, as well as statistical linguistics and analytics.

Dominick Hernández

Dominick Hernández is assistant professor of Old Testament interpretation at the Southern Baptist Theological Seminary and serves as the director of the seminary's online Hispanic program. Dominick holds degrees from Columbia University and Princeton Theological Seminary and completed his PhD at Bar-Ilan University in Israel.

Adam J. Howell

Adam J. Howell is assistant professor of Old Testament interpretation at Boyce College and Southern Seminary in Louisville, Kentucky. He earned his MDiv and PhD from Southern Seminary, with special attention given to Old Testament languages. Adam and his wife, Liz, live in the Louisville area and have four children: Noah, Tovah, Judah, and Norah.

William R. (Rusty) Osborne

William R. Osborne serves as associate professor of biblical and theological studies at College of the Ozarks in Point Lookout, Missouri.

He has written, coauthored, and edited several books and articles on the Old Testament.

William Ross

William Ross is assistant professor of Old Testament interpretation at Reformed Theological Seminary in Charlotte, North Carolina. He earned his MDiv at Westminster Theological Seminary in Philadelphia and his PhD at the University of Cambridge. William and his wife, Kelli, live in the Charlotte area and have three boys.

NAME INDEX

SCRIPTURE INDEX

SUBJECT INDEX